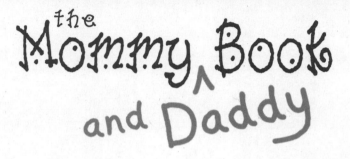

the Mommy ∧ Book
and Daddy

KAREN HULL

the Mommy and Daddy Book

PRACTICAL TIPS FOR NEW PARENTS
FROM PARENTS WHO'VE BEEN THERE

ZondervanPublishingHouse
Grand Rapids, Michigan

A Division of HarperCollinsPublishers

The Mommy and Daddy Book
Copyright © 2000 by Karen H. Hull

This is an updated and expanded edition of *The Mommy Book.*

Requests for information should be addressed to:

ZondervanPublishingHouse
Grand Rapids, Michigan 49530

Library of Congress Cataloging-in-Publication Data
Hull, Karen H.
    The mommy and daddy book : practical tips for new parents from parents who've been there
/ Karen Hull.
      p.   cm.
    Rev. ed. of: The mommy book. ©1986.
    ISBN 0-310-22814-X
    1. Child rearing.   2. Parent and child.   3. Child rearing—Religious aspects—Christianity.
I. Hull, Karen H. Mommy book.   II. Title.
HQ769 .H83 2000
649'.1—dc21   00-043773

All Scripture quotations, unless otherwise indicated, are taken from the *Holy Bible: New International Version*®. NIV®. Copyright © 1973, 1978, 1984 by International Bible Society. Used by permission of Zondervan Publishing House. All rights reserved.

The poem "I Want You to Know" by Katherine Tracy on pages 220–21 is used by permission of Katherine Tracy.

Interior design by Melissa Elenbaas
Printed in the United States of America

00 01 02 03 04 05 06 /❖ DC/ 10 9 8 7 6 5 4 3 2 1

To Jon, Megan, and Anna

Contents

Acknowledgments 9

Introduction 11

One   Surviving Mommyhood:
Things They Never Told You in Childbirth Class . . .13

Two   We're in This Together 43

Three   Diaper Duty—and Beyond 75

Four   Breast and Bottle .87

Five   Solid Food: The Adventure Begins 103

Six   Crying, Teething, and Other Fun Things 113

Seven   A Busy Baby Is a Happy Baby 137

Eight   Never Too Little for Jesus 147

Nine   Who's in Charge Here, Anyway?
A Loving Foundation for Discipline 169

Ten	Still in Charge? Loving Discipline for Toddlers	.187
Eleven	Someone Special, That's Me!	.211
Twelve	The Working Mommy	.229
Thirteen	Making Memories	.249
	Index	.275

Acknowledgments

Special thanks to Christine Thomas for giving me the idea for this project (and to her sister, Debby Clack, for giving *her* the idea) as well as for her encouragement and organizational help on the original edition.

Special thanks also to Jan Strader for allowing me to use her handwritten book of friends' advice as a starting point; to Dr. Daniel Leviten for donating his time and knowledge; and to the many parents who read and gave their approval of the finished manuscript.

Thanks also to Cindy Hays, my editor on the revised edition of *The Mommy Book*, for her wisdom and encouragement, and to the staff at Zondervan for their talent and support.

To my family and my church family: You'll never know how grateful I am for your constant love and encouragement.

Most of all, very special thanks to the ninety-four parents who ultimately became involved in this book. With last names omitted to protect their privacy, they are:

Stella and Tim, Dana, Kim, Carol, Lynne, Ruth, Brynn and Tom, Linda, Rita, Wanda and Dennis, Kim and Chris, Jennifer and Scott, Stephanie, Carol and Chris, Michele, Cheryl and Phil, Julie and Doug, Patti, Karen, Lois, Glenda, Julie, Connie and Shelby, Luellen, Helen, Lisa, Trudy and Tim, LeEtta, Christin, Shannon and Loren, Cheryl and Rodger, Marilee and Jeff, Karin and Wayne, Nancy and David, Adrienne and Dick, Kristin, Cil and Marty, Jan, Joyce, Jennifer, Shelley and Glenn, Chris and David, Jackie and Dan, Kathy and Hugh, Pene and Tom, Patty, Elizabeth and Mike, Shari and

Jeff, Cindy, Dawn, Debby and Joe, Donna, Janet, Janice, Kristy, Lynda, Mary Ann, Nancy, Pat, Patty, Rosemary, Sofie and Paul, Sonja, Sylvia, Terri, Trina, Vicky, and Virginia.

May the advice they've shared in these pages help others to become as good at parenting as they are.

Introduction

This book was (ahem) conceived when my neighbor Jan had her baby three months after my own little girl, Megan, was born. A group of mothers from our church put together a small book of advice for Jan, each writing several pages of practical tips that had helped with her own children.

When Jan's gift was complete and we all took a look inside, we were amazed at the creativity, common sense, and wisdom that had come from our group effort. Tips that seemed obvious to the mother who had written them often astounded the rest of us with their practical simplicity.

The book that resulted, *The Mommy Book: Advice for New Mothers from Women Who've Been There*, took the best advice from that project and widened the contributing circle of mothers to include other creative Christian women committed to raising secure, happy, healthy children. Today, fourteen years after its original publication in 1986, *The Mommy Book* has reached into more than one hundred thousand homes.

The continuing success of *The Mommy Book* has convinced me of two things: First, parents have a lot to offer each other. Second, new parents are especially hungry for contact with other people who've walked the same road and who can tell them, "You're not alone. I know exactly how you feel. Here's what worked for me."

In this revised and expanded edition, we've included more helpful and encouraging advice from a new crop of mothers, and we've widened the circle of contributors even further to include more input from their husbands. The "Daddy to Daddy" chapter that was tacked on at the end of the original *Mommy Book* has been expanded, renamed "We're in This Together," and moved to the front of the book. You'll also find more input from fathers throughout the book, especially in the character-building chapters (8–11).

The reason for these changes in a book originally written by and for mothers? After more than twenty-two years of marriage and more than seventeen years of parenting, and after many interviews with young parents of both the thriving and the struggling varieties, I've come to this conclusion: Any book on parenting that doesn't contain advice on building the husband-wife partnership is shortchanging its readers. To reflect the revised book's emphasis on parenting as a partnership, we've retitled it *The Mommy and Daddy Book: Practical Tips for New Parents from Parents Who've Been There.*

From my experience with young parents, I feel sure that only the most heroic and involved young fathers will read through this entire book with their wives. On nuts and bolts issues — such as breast- and bottle-feeding, diapering, crying, and bathing — Mom usually ends up as the house expert, offering tips as needed to Dad. Because of that, I've addressed those chapters to her.

Some chapters, though, you really do need to read and discuss together. Chapter 1 will help both of you understand the changes, both physical and emotional, a new mother goes through. Chapter 2 will help you understand how a new father's life changes when his baby is born and will point the way to help you build a thriving family. Chapter 7 is full of play ideas to help you spend time with your little one, and chapters 8–11 and 13 will teach you how to mold your child's character and build a rich, rewarding relationship, as well as how to create lifelong memories.

In the years since *The Mommy Book* was published, I've gone from being the mother of one toddler (Megan was three) to being the mother of a college-bound teenager and of a second daughter, Anna, who is teetering on the brink of adolescence. And I've discovered during those years that parenthood is more than I ever thought it would be — more love, more joy, more excitement about the future, more fatigue, more frustration, more heartache. Most of all, more growth — and more awareness of my need to depend on God.

Is it worth it? You bet! I'm more proud than I can say of the young women my daughters are becoming, and I am blessed to count them — even during these transitional, push-for-independence years — among my closest friends.

I wish the same for you.

Chapter 1

Surviving Mommyhood

Things They Never Told You in Childbirth Class

Now, don't let the title of this chapter give you the wrong idea. We, the mothers in this book, love our children and happen to believe that motherhood is the single most fulfilling profession around when it's handled the right way. It's just that life with a newborn baby, especially when it's your first, takes a little adjustment.

Well, no, not really. It takes a *lot* of adjustment.

In this chapter, we'll try to give you an idea of the changes a new mother can expect and of ways we dealt with them in our own lives. Think of it as your briefing session just before you leave the carefree land of Independence, where you've spent your life up till now, to live in Parenthood, a country shrouded in weird superstitions, where the inhabitants practice all sorts of odd customs.

The analogy is more accurate than you might think. You really can fall victim to culture shock during your first weeks in Parenthood, especially if you're unaware of the ways people must conduct themselves there to thrive. The most fascinating thing about Parenthood is that the little person who ushers you into it and takes up residence with you is constantly changing and demanding that you change too. But once you adapt to the necessary changes, you'll find that Parenthood is a great place to be and you wouldn't go back to Independence for the world.

And it's a good thing.

Great Expectations

There are two basic types of expectant mothers: the Nervous Expectant Mother and the Smug Expectant Mother. The NEM has no idea what motherhood will be like, and she fears the worst. The SEM, on the other hand, tells everyone how long she plans to be in labor and insists to all who will listen, "There's no need for the baby to disrupt our lifestyle. He'll just have to fit into our schedule."

Although the SEM is undoubtedly more at ease during her pregnancy, on the whole the NEM is the better off of the two. When her baby is born, she usually discovers that things aren't as hard as she expected them to be, and she relaxes as she gets to know her baby. On the other hand, there's nothing like the devastation experienced by the SEM who has just had the rug pulled out from under her and all her grand expectations.

Believe me, I know.

If you've already made it through your baby's first few months, you probably won't find too much new material in this chapter. (You'll want to read it anyway, though, just to see how far you've come.) If you're pregnant with your first child, you're about to have some of your fondest fantasies of motherhood blown to smithereens. That isn't meant to scare you — it's meant to give you the comfort of knowing, during the first weeks and months after your baby arrives, that yours isn't the only one who turned out to be a real-life, squalling human infant instead of a china doll.

You're not alone if you expect your baby to be a model child. The moms in this book did too. "I thought it was going to be easy, like all the commercials and TV programs showed," says Adrienne. "I just knew I'd have a rosy-cheeked baby who went to bed when I wanted him to and was always good and sweet, and who ate without spitting everything out."

Christine adds, "I thought I might have to get up maybe once or twice a night, and I thought there'd be a few dirty diapers, and that's about the extent of the badness I expected. I expected the baby to sleep maybe eight hours a day, and I'd be working around the house all the time and would hardly even know it was there except when it was time to nurse. The reality was that the very first day we brought Ashley home from the hospital, she would not stop screaming long enough for us to sit down and eat. Some friends had brought lunch over for us, and my parents met us at the house, and my mom and dad had to stay in the living room and hold Ashley the whole time we were eating so David and I could sit down with our friends. From that moment on, she cried constantly."

Ashley's crying was due to a severe case of colic (usually assumed nowadays to be abdominal pains, although the medical community still isn't sure). Most of our babies had little trouble with colic. But if your baby is a member of the very vocal minority, life can be rough for the first three months or so until she's over it. Chapter 6 gives advice on helping your baby with this problem, although time will be the most effective healer.

For Cheryl, even her baby's appearance was a shock: "When Emily came out, she didn't look like the pictures of cute, pudgy babies on TV. She looked more like a baby lizard."

Brynn says, "I have nieces and nephews; I taught children. I thought, *I have an Early Childhood Education degree, I've been around kids. I know exactly what to do.* My son Cole arrived and rocked my world. Everything I'd ever learned, everything I had ever done — I had to rethink it all. He didn't follow the book."

Few of these moms said that motherhood turned out to be what they thought it would be. Expectations are tricky things, mainly because they're almost never fulfilled. What you expect to be the most wonderful experience of your life — say, senior prom or your wedding day — will probably disappoint you; whereas something you expect to be the most awful ordeal you'll ever go through will pleasantly surprise you.

Your baby may be easygoing and predictable like Stella's two little girls, or she may have horrendous bouts with colic and cry for hours on end like Christine's daughter Ashley and Trina's little girl Audrey. In reality, though, your little one will probably be somewhere in between. If it comforts you, feel free to expect your baby to be an adorable little angel whose diapers never leak, who cries only when she's hungry and drifts off to sleep in her bassinet without requiring hours of being nursed or rocked. It may happen. But feel free also to turn back to these pages for a little commiseration and advice if it doesn't.

And take comfort in this: Many of the surprises the parents in this book encountered were pleasant ones. Just about all of them said they discovered emotions and capacities in themselves they never dreamed possible. "I was surprised by the overwhelming love I had for Nathaniel," says Shannon. "I never dreamed I could feel that way." Not all of the parents I interviewed fell in love with their children right away. (We'll discuss those feelings later.) But once they did, they discovered to their astonishment that they really did have the capacity to love another person enough to be willing to die for him without thinking twice about it.

Another surprise was how natural it felt to put their babies' needs ahead of their own — to give up hours of sleep, to adapt to their children's feeding schedules, to do whatever needed to be done — without seeing it as a sacrifice. "I wouldn't get up to feed my husband, Tom, in the middle of the night," laughs Brynn, "because I know he could get whatever he needs himself. But your motivation as a mother is totally different. I didn't look at it as how many hours of sleep I was losing."

A friend once told me, tongue in cheek, "God gives us children to help *us* grow up." While I know that's not the real reason, it can certainly be one very positive result. In the school of life, parenthood is a long-term course in unconditional love.

The First Few Weeks

The moms in this book agree that life as a new mother is much easier if, right from the start, you do as any other sensible person would do upon entering an important profession: Establish priorities and stick to them. Luckily, priorities for the first few weeks of motherhood are simple: (1) Get to know your baby and (2) rest. If you want to be really efficient, do both at once. That's why the Lord invented nursing.

> Luckily, priorities for the first few weeks of motherhood are simple: (1) Get to know your baby and (2) rest. If you want to be really efficient, do both at once. That's why the Lord invented nursing.

Not long ago a national magazine for new parents did a survey of their subscribers. To the question, "What surprised you most about having your baby?" the most popular answer was not how hard labor was or how messy their baby looked when he or she popped out. The answer thousands of new parents gave was, "We never expected to be this tired!"

Fatigue is the natural result of going through a long pregnancy, enduring a workout in the hospital that would put Arnold Schwarzenegger to shame, and being routed out of bed by cries from the nursery several times a night immediately upon arriving home. Even so, it came as a shock to these moms. "Audrey was up every two hours," says Trina. "I was exhausted. Sleep became so precious to me that I would rather have had it than a million dollars. If it hadn't been for my mother's help, I would never have made it."

The maxim "Sleep when the baby sleeps" has been handed down from experienced mothers to inexperienced ones ever since Eve started giving advice to her daughters. But it can be hard counsel to take unless you have help with the housework, and these mothers generally found that even the most helpful husband was no match for a mother or mother-in-law when it came to keeping the house in order.

Stella says, "My mother-in-law did laundry, she cooked, she cleaned house for me, and you'd better believe it was a blessing! All I had to do was take care of the baby. But you've got to have someone who's not going to take over the baby — you have to be allowed to be a mother."

Most of the grandmas who came to help out behaved themselves admirably, but a couple of mothers did have trouble with their supposed-to-be-live-in helpers. And since your first weeks after childbirth are hardly the time for you to be waiting on houseguests, it's a good idea to spell out what's expected before your help arrives. Have your husband talk to his mother, and you make your needs known to yours. "And make sure that whoever's coming is someone you get along with," says Adrienne.

If you don't have a mother or mother-in-law handy, and if you can afford it, hire someone to come in once a week to help clean the house. (Ways to find household help are covered in chapter 12.) Or if you have a friend who keeps saying, "Let me know if you need anything," take her up on it. Tell her, "Well, my house really needs to be vacuumed . . ." or, "I have this pile of laundry . . ." Sometimes the best baby gift a friend can give is to help with the housework or just come and watch the baby while you take a nap. Don't be afraid to ask. You can always return the favor later, and if your friend has children of her own, she'll understand.

Lisa says, "Learning to take people up on their offers of help was difficult for me. I tend to be very self-sufficient, which is both a blessing and a curse. But accepting them helped me get back into the swing of things more quickly." She recommends, though, "If you have too many offers, it might be wise to ask a few potential helpers if you can call them back in four weeks or so, when a nap or a shower is even more needed. I found that the worst fatigue usually set in about the time all the help left and I'd had little sleep for four weeks."

Shari says, "I welcomed the meals our church friends brought over, but as far as accepting help with the house, I was too embarrassed. It was definitely a pride issue. The ladies in my church were sincere about wanting to help, but it was too hard for me to pick up the phone and call them. As I've matured, I really wish I had. It would have kept me from being as stressed-out as I was making myself."

Nancy says, "It helped that David and I had made a concerted effort to be generous with friends before and during my pregnancy. That's just Christian kindness, but it also kept me from feeling guilty about calling on friends to help after Hannah was born. Our church friends were great about providing evening meals for us after we brought her home." Over and over during our interviews, I heard praise for the tremendous support small groups at church offer new parents. Not only can they provide meals and other practical help, they can also be sources of information, role models, and emotional support. (Some of the most common small groups include Sunday school classes, cell groups, home Bible studies, women's ministries, and parenting classes.)

Even if grandmas, housekeepers, and friends are all out of the question, there are still things you can do to keep the house from falling apart while you convalesce. Try to put things away as soon as you use them, and ask your husband to do the same. And if you possibly can, make several weeks' worth of casseroles before the baby comes and put them in the freezer along with some frozen breads and vegetables. Just doing these two things will keep you from having to worry about making dinner and will at least put your housework on hold until you feel well enough to get to it. Pene used paper plates during her first few weeks as a mother, and she adopted a relaxed attitude about dishes even after that. "I told my husband the dishes were very happy just sitting there in the sink," she says. "I just walked by every now and then and waved at them."

Adding to your fatigue, in the hospital and at home, will be all the well-wishers who want to see the baby. "I was glad they cared, but I was so exhausted," says Pat. "For the first month or two people just kept dropping by." Visitors are a fact of life when you have a new baby, and according to Patti it's best to adopt an "Oh well" attitude about them: "When friends come to visit, don't feel bad if your house is a mess. Especially if they have kids themselves, they expect it and they don't care." If you get caught in your robe with no makeup on, look at the bright side: Your visitors are less likely to expect you to run around offering refreshments if you look as if you're really convalescing. Learn to rise with a smile and say, "Thanks so much for coming. Please visit us again," when you become tired.

No matter how much you enjoy showing off your new baby, drop-in visitors at naptime are no joke, especially if you don't have someone who can help screen them. Joyce's four children are all grown, and most of them are married and gone, but she still remembers how she handled a sticky situation when her first son was a baby: "One of the men in our church who had a large family informed my preacher husband that they would be visiting us on Sunday afternoon. My husband passed the information along to me with the added message, 'You'll have to entertain them, because I have to rest after preaching to prepare for the night service.'

"I won't tell you my first reaction! I asked my heavenly Father for wisdom, then made a poster with a picture of a sleeping baby and drew a clock underneath with the hands pointing to four o'clock. The message on the poster read, 'Baby and mother nap until . . .' I secured it to the front door.

"Sure enough, up drove the big station wagon on Sunday afternoon and out piled all the kids, with Mother following Dad and his guitar. I watched from my vantage point behind the curtain. The parade halted at the front door; the lead child turned back to the car; and all the rest followed. Needless to say, our Sunday afternoon rest time was respected from then on. I later invited them over at my convenience, and everyone was happy." If you have a chronic problem with drop-in nap interrupters, make your clock with movable hands and put it up whenever you and your baby go to bed.

"I screened calls through my answering machine during the first few months," says Lisa. "Many times I'd get the baby down for a nap and be on the way to a nap myself when the phone would start ringing. It's amazing how fast two or three 'quick chats' can turn into an hour and a half. I even turned off all the ringers, except on one phone farthest from the bedrooms. As often as I could during the first few months, I let the answering machine pick up. Then I could return the calls when I had more time and energy." If you don't have an answering machine, unplug the phone at naptime. (Just remember to plug it back in when you get up!)

An understanding, knowledgeable doctor is another great asset for new parents. My pediatrician gave me permission to blame things on him during Megan's first few months. He had told me to keep her away from other children until she was at least a month old, so when friends wanted to bring their children over, it was fairly easy to say, "We'd love to have you, but Megan's doctor said . . ." It's a real blessing to be able to blame the doctor when people ask why you haven't started feeding the baby solid food yet, or why you didn't bring the baby to church until he was six weeks old, or why you're still breastfeeding.

It may be difficult, but try to remember that the advice and interference you find offensive is usually offered with the best of intentions, and it's probably just what another mother is longing for. Patty was upset to the point of tears when people constantly wanted to take her baby at church, whereas Pene would have loved to have someone else hold Aaron while she listened to the sermon. Because of this difference between new mothers, it's essential to your peace of mind that you learn the simple art of refusing graciously. It will stand you in good stead a few years from now when you're asked to come up with forty dozen cookies for the PTA bake sale.

Getting Back in Gear

It's possible — if you have a lot of household help during the first couple of weeks after your baby is born and especially if you have help with the nightly feedings — that the real fatigue stemming from the daily routine of new motherhood won't hit until after your help leaves. That can be depressing, because just when your mind decides it's time to get the household organized, your body decides it wants to go back to bed and stay there for a few years. We'll talk about depression in the next section. This section is about how to gradually get yourself organized without wearing yourself out.

"The thing that went down the most with me was my appearance," says Karin. "Having Matthew was such a change in my life. I had worked as a legal secretary in an office where everyone dressed to the T, and I didn't quit work until the week I had him. I had always been so chic, then suddenly I was wearing nothing but my robe, and there was always some kind of mess on my lap or my shoulder. Wayne would come home from work at the end of the day and my hair would be sticking out all over and my makeup hadn't even been washed off from the day before. He would ask, 'What have you been doing all day?'

"I was used to working in an office and feeling productive, so that question broke me down to tears. And it wasn't as if I had just been lying around. The TV hadn't been on; the radio hadn't been on. I'd spent all day feeding the baby, dressing the baby, changing the baby, holding the baby. I just couldn't get into the swing of taking care of another person besides myself. Wayne finally had to help me set some basic goals, because I was walking around like a zombie."

> Being a new mother takes time. One reason for this is that most babies like to be held. A lot.

The daily goals Wayne and Karin agreed on for her first six weeks as a mother were as follows: "Getting dressed, making the bed, and cleaning up the breakfast dishes. That doesn't sound like much, but it's a lot when you're a new mother," she says. "It was my goal to get those things done, even if it was five-thirty and Wayne was pulling up in the driveway!"

Being a new mother takes time. One reason for this is that most babies like to be held. A lot. "And don't think that holding your baby is going to spoil her!" says Stella. "I don't think you can hold an infant enough. It puts a security into your relationship."

In the last generation, new mothers were cautioned against holding their babies when they cried, for fear of spoiling them. Heaven only knows what damage that well-meant advice caused. Today, however, most experts espouse holding and cuddling your baby as much as he seems to want it, until he's at least six months old and can be encouraged to play with his toys while you get some housework done. "Besides," says Christine, "when he's two or three years old you'll have a hard time getting him to sit still long enough to hug him, so enjoy it while you can!"

Patti has three children and one on the way, so she's had lots of experience with the first few weeks of motherhood. She says, "I tell all my friends who've just had a baby not to have high expectations of what they're going to accomplish during the first six weeks. I got so depressed after my first baby came because I didn't even have time to wash the dishes and fix dinner. So I learned to set one goal for the day—say, to get the dishes washed. Not make the beds, not cook, because maybe dinner was in the freezer. Anything I did above that one goal made me feel good."

"I consider myself an organized person," says Nancy. "I owned and managed my own clothing store for seven years. But having a baby threw me for a loop! I couldn't get a handle on organizing my day. Finally, I remembered the saying 'This too shall pass.' I realized it wouldn't always be this way and that I should just enjoy every moment with Hannah. My husband, David, encouraged me that I was doing the most important job in the world. That helped me decide that there would be many opportunities in the future to wash dishes and vacuum. It was three months before I felt like I really had it all together again."

She adds, "Since David and I knew I might need help with dinner or housework, we saved up money beforehand. That way, when it got to be 4:30 P.M., and I hadn't been to the grocery store in a week and a half and was too exhausted to think about cooking, I didn't feel guilty about calling for pizza—again!"

After your baby's first six weeks or so, gradually add chores to your daily schedule as your baby's temperament and your own energy permit, until you finally feel everything is accounted for. This process will take longer for some moms than for others. Stella was fortunate. Her two little girls each took long naps from the very beginning and slept through the night after only a few weeks. "With that kind of situation," she says, "it's easy to get back into a regular schedule right away." My daughter Megan, on the other hand, had an erratic nap schedule and the strange idea that the way to have a good time was to see how often she could get Mommy up at night, so it was months before life became normal around the Hull house. Marilee agrees: "It depends a lot on what your baby allows you to do. David would sleep for two hours, then be up for two hours all day long, and I could do all the housework I wanted to. But then Althea woke up and wanted to nurse every hour and a half, day and night, and it just wiped me out. I didn't get anything done."

"I think it's great to have a written list of goals for the day," says Cheryl, "because as you check them off you can actually see what's getting done. And of course, you set priorities in case you don't make it to the bottom of the list — that's just good time management." Several mothers warn against setting your goals too high, though. Lisa says, "I've always been a huge fan of 'to do' lists. But in the first few months after having my baby, I found I had to be very careful what I put on the list. A long, ambitious list that doesn't get done can be depressing." Lisa eventually learned to change her list to reflect her real priorities as a new mother: "I listed even the most basic things — make the bed, do the dishes, brush my teeth, feed the baby, play with the baby. Seeing it on paper helped me realize I *was* getting things done — maybe just not the same things I *used* to get done. It gives me an immense sense of satisfaction to cross each accomplishment off with a red marker. At the end of the day, I've even been known to add things to my list that I unexpectedly did, just so I can cross them off too! Making a long-term list, as well as my daily list, helped me realize I could put some things off for a while and it wasn't the end of the world."

The idea of having your housework all done at once is a fantasy for a new mom. When I worked fulltime before Megan was born, I became accustomed to doing most of my housework on weekends. During the week I didn't have to worry about much besides the dishes and the laundry. After Megan came, I kept trying to get it all done in a day. When she was six months old, I finally gave up and developed a more practical system.

Like many of our other moms, I learned to divide my housework into manageable segments. I found I was much more likely to get my work done if it was broken into little chunks, and if I missed a given day's work it was no great disaster — I just made sure I got to it on the proper day the following week. Big jobs, such as cleaning out closets or washing windows, were worked on whenever convenient, and daily jobs, such as dishes, laundry, and picking up clutter, got done daily — usually. The house was never spotless, but at least this way I was a little more in control.

Several moms point out that the new mother who wants a spotless house — unless she can afford a maid — not only is dreaming the impossible dream but also has a bad case of misplaced priorities. "Realize that your baby will be little for only a short time," says Terri. "Spend as much time as you can with him. If someone drops in, just say, 'Excuse my house, but I've been playing with my baby.' Maybe she'll be inspired to go home and spend some extra time with *her* children."

Even though it'll probably be a while before your house is spotless again, constant clutter is another animal altogether. Cluttered surroundings are depressing, whether they're an office or a home. And the state of your home affects your husband as well. "Keep your house picked up on a continual basis," says Patty. "Train yourself to put things away as soon as they're no longer needed."

A few additional words on keeping up appearances: If you're like these mothers, the days when you drag around in your pajamas with unwashed hair and no makeup are the days when you feel homely and stupid, even if you're really a raving beauty with a Ph.D. But it's possible that, like Karin, you'll have trouble figuring out how to take care of another person without neglecting yourself. "You have to work your schedule around the baby," says Stella, "and it's hard to fit yourself in. I used to think, *How can I take a shower? What if the baby wakes up?*"

Most of these mothers worked before their babies were born, and were accustomed to taking an hour or so to dress in the morning. That became impossible after their little ones arrived. After feeling ugly for a while and deciding they didn't like it, they learned to condense their morning ritual. "What took a half hour before," says Stella, "I learned to do in five minutes." Instead of slathering your face with foundation, blemish cover, blush, powder, and shadow, learn to get a simpler effect with a little blush, eyeliner, brow pencil, and mascara. Home lighting is much kinder than the fluorescent lighting used in offices, so all that extra goop really isn't needed anyway.

> "If someone drops in, just say, 'Excuse my house, but I've been playing with my baby.' Maybe she'll be inspired to go home and spend some extra time with *her* children."

Several mothers also suggest a change of hairstyle — a cut that can be blown quickly into place or a perm that can be just dampened and combed out. "But do it before you have the baby," says Christine. "If you wait until afterward, you'll be trying to get used to a new hairstyle while coping with a newborn. You'll go nuts." And make sure it's a style that flatters you; quick and easy doesn't count if it makes you feel like a gargoyle.

It will probably come as a rude awakening that all the weight you gained while you were pregnant doesn't fall off while you're in the hospital. But cheer up — about half of the mothers in this book lost most of their weight during the first three months after their babies were born.

At any rate, the clothes you wear during your first few months postpartum will need to have forgiving waistlines — in other words, elastic. If it's summer, and if you can afford it, invest in some bright, inexpensive sundresses. Or if it's winter, maybe a couple of bright warm-up suits or pants in a size larger than your goal and some flattering but inexpensive sweaters. You'd be amazed at what looking nice will do for your energy level and your general outlook on life. Dawn says, "When I feel sick or tired, getting dressed and putting on makeup makes me feel better. And if when I pass myself in the mirror I know I look good, it makes me feel good about everything else too."

Cheryl saw a movie that really hit home for her: "In *Mr. Mom*, where the husband stays home and takes care of the kids while his wife goes to work, he did everything the typical new mother does. He let everything go, and he looked awful for a couple of weeks until his wife finally told him, 'You're not taking any pride in yourself. You used to take pride in your work at the office, but you're not taking pride in your work here.'

"That's the way I felt. Just because we're Christians doesn't mean that we can take no pride in our homes or in our appearance and everything will just flow right along. There were times when my self-esteem was low, but I tried to fight it because I felt that if I wasn't the best person I could be, I'd be putting temptation in front of my husband to look elsewhere. My attitude would tell him, 'I don't care about you *or* myself.' That's why I made sure I had five minutes to put on a little makeup before Rodger came home for lunch, even if Jason had to cry for a few minutes. I decided, 'I'm going to do this, because it's important to my self-esteem and my marriage.'"

Probably the single most encouraging bit of advice in this chapter is this: *It gets easier as your baby grows older.* Memorize it. If possible, engrave it on a locket and wear it against your heart. It will help get you through the months ahead as you and your baby adjust to each other.

Christian Mommies and the Baby Blues

Before their babies were born, many of the mothers in this book regarded "Christian" and "postpartum depression" as a contradiction in terms. "I thought postpartum blues were not something a Christian would have," says Cheryl, "but I had a lot of blue days for a while."

Actually, baby blues can hit Christian mothers even harder than the rest of the populace, because on top of the emotional ups and downs is the guilty notion that you wouldn't be feeling this way if you were really trusting the Lord. That assumption might have some merit if the baby blues had their roots in your spiritual life, but they don't. They hit or don't hit depending on your hormonal balance and the fatigue induced first by your pregnancy and then by a radically changed lifestyle.

The best advice these mothers have for a new mom afflicted with the baby blues is this: Hold on. You will not feel this way forever. We've been through it too, and life is great on the other side. Tell yourself, "I will get through this, and I will not allow it to affect my behavior toward my child and my husband. With God's help, I will emerge from this victorious." If you find yourself completely unable to function, or are still having problems after several months — most of these mothers weren't — have your obstetrician check you to see whether you need medical treatment. If not, seek out a qualified Christian counselor who is familiar with postpartum depression and its ramifications.

Below are some of the emotions the mothers in this book experienced either before or shortly after the births of their babies. Don't let the long list frighten you — some moms went through just about all of these emotions, but many had just one or two, and a few blessed women had none at all.

Resentment because of a surprise pregnancy and then guilt for feeling the resentment. One excellent, dedicated mother says, "When I found out I was pregnant, it really hit hard. I never expected it to happen immediately after we were married! And then came the guilt for feeling so negatively about this gift from God. I honestly expected God to punish me because of the feelings I had."

> Actually, baby blues can hit Christian mothers even harder than the rest of the populace, because on top of the emotional ups and downs is the guilty notion that you wouldn't be feeling this way if you were really trusting the Lord.

"I had a terribly negative reaction to my pregnancy," says Christine. "David and I had been married for only five months, and I knew we weren't being too careful, but somehow I just didn't expect to get pregnant. David was thrilled. He knew I had some ambivalence about it, but to this day he doesn't know how badly I *didn't* want to be pregnant. I really had to pray. I went into my room and said, 'Okay, Lord, I know I can't keep feeling this way because it will affect my baby, and I know you have a reason for this or it wouldn't have happened.' I just kept praying until I finally prayed myself through, I guess. By the time I was three months along, I had become adjusted to it, and by about six months I was really looking forward to the baby and starting to get the nursery fixed up."

Nowhere is a person's maturity more clearly displayed than by the way she deals with life's unavoidable inconveniences, and it's sad that our generation has learned to deal with its unavoidable inconveniences by figuring out ways to avoid them. But even though they struggled for a while, these mothers showed their maturity by accepting their situation and making the best of it. They acknowledged that, planned or not, the baby was coming, and they determined with God's help to make their child's life something wonderful.

Christine still has a soft spot in her heart for other women struggling with surprise pregnancies. "Those are strong feelings," she says, "and you can't change yourself when you feel that way. The Lord has to change those feelings."

An overwhelming feeling of responsibility — also known as "the mommy jitters." With Pat, this feeling hit as she was on her way to the labor room: "Tears just started running down my face. The nurse looked at me and said, 'Your contractions must be pretty hard now.' I nodded, but that wasn't really what it was. I just got so scared — I thought, *I'm having a baby!* I had waited so long and wanted it so badly, but all of a sudden the responsibility just overwhelmed me."

The jitters hit Adrienne as she and her husband were bringing Jennifer home from the hospital. "I had never babysat before or anything, and on the drive home I looked at my beautiful little baby, then at my husband, and said, 'Dick, what am I going to do with her?' I started crying — I still get teary-eyed just thinking about it."

Cheryl, an experienced mother with three young children, says, "I was afraid even to change Emily's diaper for the first time — I made my husband do it." She laughs about it now: "As time went on, I learned to change a diaper in the dark, half asleep at three in the morning."

Even Stella, who adopted her first little girl, had a brief bout with the mommy jitters. "We'd been waiting and praying for nine years for this baby. But the first night, I was weak from the excitement of the day, and I looked at her and asked myself, *Am I going to be able to handle this?* The next morning the Lord gave me my answer — it was as if I'd had a baby all my life."

Mommy jitters can be compared to the wedding jitters a bride and groom feel just before their marriage — except they're worse. For years, our society has been trying to convince us that if a person isn't happy with her spouse, it's perfectly acceptable to take him back and exchange him for a new one, but even the most liberal society doesn't condone doing that with children. When you have a baby, you're making a drastic change in your life that can't be undone.

And if you haven't had experience with babies, you're stepping into unknown territory — no matter how much material you've read on motherhood. The best thing that can be said about the mommy jitters is that they usually don't last long. They vanish as soon as you get your little one home and discover that, strange and intimidating as your new job is, you *can* do it.

🌙 *Confusion and guilt for not immediately falling in love with the baby.* With the mothers I interviewed, the division was almost right down the middle between those who fell in love with their babies right away and those who didn't, with the ones who didn't predominating slightly. Christine says, "I had a friend who told me before I had Ashley, 'Now, Chris, when you have that baby in the hospital, don't panic if you don't have an immediate gush of love for that child, and don't think you're a terrible mother. You have to get to know the baby, and you'll learn to love it.' If she hadn't told me that, I would have thought I was losing my mind, because when I first saw Ashley I thought she looked about as messy as most babies do, and I wasn't filled with love and awe. I was thinking, *What am I going to do with it?* She had to grow on me."

Kathy adds, "My sister just had her baby, and she expected this flood of emotion to hit her when he came out. She had been so excited all nine months, but when he finally came, she was just numb. I was with her when she had him, and I kept telling her, 'Oh, Nancy, a boy! Look, blond hair! Look at his little fingers! Aren't you excited?' She told me later that she wasn't; the emotions she had expected didn't come. She looked at him, and yet he didn't seem part of her. Not until they brought him to the room and she began to nurse him did that bond start."

Lisa now has three children. She says, "Each time I went through childbirth, I thought, *Surely with this one I'll have a terrific birth experience and feel that rush of love so many of my friends talk about.* But with all three births — and none of them was especially traumatic — all I ever felt in the first few hours was relief that it was finally over! Bonding and love came as I cared for them."

With these mothers, there was a big difference between the protective maternal bond and the eagerly expected rush of love — the "whatever did we do without this little darling" feeling. The first happened right away and made sure they would protect and care for their babies, but the second sometimes took a while.

Cheryl says, "I found out how quickly the maternal bond takes hold after one full day of being in the hospital. They had done my C-section so quickly that I developed an infection from an unsterile environment. I had a high fever, so there were about thirty-six hours when I could not nurse or see or hold Jason after he was born. I have never been as emotional as the day I found out I couldn't hold my baby." (That's saying a lot — Cheryl is the epitome of the cool, unruffled businesswoman.)

For some people, simply knowing that a baby is "theirs" is enough to inspire warm, loving feelings. For others, those feelings require knowledge and time.

Marilee and Pene had similar experiences. Pene's first son, Aaron, had to be in an incubator for his first couple of days, and she found herself going down to the nursery and just looking into the incubator, crying. "I thought, *This is stupid. Why am I standing here crying and looking at this little baby?*"

For many of the parents in this book, both mothers and fathers, feelings of love developed over time as they grew to know their children. Perhaps this has something to do with the personality of the parent. For some people, simply knowing that a baby is "theirs" is enough to inspire warm, loving feelings. For others, those feelings require knowledge and time. But here's an interesting footnote: Two of our mothers who adopted their little girls fell in love with their babies immediately. That makes our other moms suspect that a big reason for the numbness we felt was fatigue — something adoptive mothers don't have to contend with, at least not to the degree that a new mother recuperating from childbirth does.

Ambivalent feelings about motherhood during the first few weeks. The mothers in this book who had fairy-tale expectations of mommyhood took a little while to adjust to the hard reality of 2 A.M. feedings, spit-up, leaky diapers, and gas pains. "I was so tired," says Adrienne. "I started to resent everybody — my husband, the baby, myself."

One of the rudest surprises awaiting these mothers was that their babies weren't completely under their control. Shock of shocks — they were little people with real minds of their own, even from the very beginning. They tended to wake when they were expected to sleep, sleep when they were expected to be awake, and cry when they were expected to be quiet. Patti says, "I remember a feeling of helplessness with my first baby. I felt so helpless at not being able to control this child and not always being able to satisfy her."

Christine adds, "When a baby has colic, it seems as if there's nothing positive to make you love her. All there is, is constant crying. But you can't take care of someone day after day without starting to love her, even if she's not the most pleasant person in the world. When Ashley was about three months old, she started getting cute. She'd go for longer periods without crying, and I started really being able to respond to her. I no longer had to will myself to love her; I couldn't *help* loving her."

I had a similar experience with Megan, even though she had little trouble with colic. Jon and I had carefully planned her arrival, but after she was born, the rush of "mother-love" I expected was several weeks in coming. A friend who is also a young mother called me when Megan was about two weeks old and exclaimed, "I'm so happy for you! Don't you love being a mother? I just knew you would!"

My answer was guarded: "Yes, I do, and I'll love it even more when she starts sleeping through the night." My love for Megan during those first few weeks was more an act of mind and will than an effortless flood of emotion. But the effortless flood did come, and it wasn't long before I could shamelessly tell all inquirers that I was madly in love with my little girl.

After having had six children, Adrienne has developed a stock answer for well-wishers who gush about how wonderful new motherhood is: "I always tell people, 'Yes, it's wonderful, but the first three months are the hardest. I love my baby, and I'll be glad when she's three months old.'" And so, once again, the encouraging note here is: *It gets easier.* As your baby grows older, he'll be less and less fussy and will settle down to a reasonably predictable sleeping schedule.

One of the rudest surprises awaiting these mothers was that their babies weren't completely under their control.

The main thing that helped these mothers overcome their feelings of ambivalence during those first few weeks was feeding time. A new mother can't expect much from her baby in the way of love and gratitude, since his first social smile won't make its appearance until he's at least three or four weeks old, but a feeding baby will give his mommy some adorable sleepy smiles. (People will tell you they're caused by gas, but Karin's answer to that is, "I don't smile when I have gas, so why do people say babies do?") The closeness of those moments with a contented baby is very special.

🐤 *Shock at the total change of lifestyle.* For some women, motherhood comes as naturally as taking the next step on a well-marked path. For others, it's like going to live on another planet. Shari says, "When we walked into the house and I put Hannah in the bassinet, I felt as if I were in another world. It was as if she was abstract, almost. It felt surreal, like my world was spinning. I just kept looking at her, thinking, *What do I do now?* It took some time to get used to my new reality."

"I wasn't prepared for the dramatic effect my baby's little life would have on me," says Patty. "I was consumed by her arrival. Everything changed; there was not one thing in my life left unchanged."

Brynn says, "The hardest thing for me was giving up control. I'm a big checklist person, and I'd make a plan of what I wanted to get done, and Cole would decide he needed to spit up or mess up his diaper right before we needed to leave the house to be somewhere at a certain time. There were so many things I couldn't control. I was happy just to get a shower some days. I was a very structured person — and that went out the window."

"I'd say the same thing," says Jennifer. "I'm very much a 'list' person, and I used to know exactly how much I could accomplish in a given amount of time. Now I have to realize that the most important thing in my day is spending time with Wes. If I can get a few other things done, that's okay, but I don't have to do it all. It was a big adjustment to accept that the house can't be clean all the time or that I can't run all my errands in one day."

Many of the parents I interviewed mentioned their surprise at how much time parenthood takes. Shelley says, "It made me wonder, *What did I used to do all day?*"

In the midst of all the changes, it helps to know you're not alone. Kim and her husband, Chris, agree that their church Bible study group of young parents has been "the best thing ever." Kim says, "It's so comforting to go to someone and have her say, 'Oh, yeah! I remember that,' or, 'This is what we did.' It's great to have women I trust that I can call."

Spiritual dryness. "My spiritual life went down the tubes," says Adrienne, "only because I didn't have the time I'd had before. It was so frustrating to get everything together and go to church prepared for a good sermon, wanting to drink it in because I needed it so badly, then have to get up and go outside because the baby was crying."

Even if you're a vibrant, spiritual Christian, the fatigue and hormonal changes of new motherhood — as well as a radically changed schedule — will probably make God seem far away at times. "At first I was really discouraged because I wasn't able to spend the amount of time studying the Bible and in prayer that I used to," says Kim. "Life had changed drastically. Then a friend told me I was right in feeling that it was important to continue my time with the Lord, but I needed to give myself grace. My quiet time might take a different form now. Since then, I've found that often my prayer time has been dispersed throughout the day, often while I'm feeding Mollie. I may not get to read my Bible first thing every morning, but it helps to turn on some praise music to bring my heart into worship." Christian music can be a wonderful tool for helping you keep your spiritual focus. If you're blessed to have a good Christian radio station in your city, take advantage of it! And your local Christian bookstore is sure to have dozens of CDs and cassettes by artists in all musical styles.

"You may think you're losing out because you're not hearing the Word as much," says Stella, "but there's a spiritual relationship that develops between you and your child too at that time. You just have to relax and say, 'It's okay. The Lord understands, and he will give me strength.'" Several mothers mentioned that becoming parents gave them insight into God's love they'd never had before. Lisa says, "I know how much I've come to cherish my children, how I would do anything for them. How much more must our heavenly Father love us?"

She goes on, "Prayer was my lifeline during the first few months. Even if I couldn't sit in a quiet place and study God's Word in depth, I could always pray. The Lord has always honored my cries for help. It's hard to believe, but he even cares about me finding time to do laundry and brush my teeth. He cares that I'm exhausted and tired of dirty diapers. Keeping his boundless love for me in mind helps me bring everything to him, however small it may seem. Sharing my daily, even hourly, struggles with God helps me know I'm not alone. He gives me just enough strength for one chore or responsibility at a time. Prayer was my primary — and sometimes my only — spiritual stimulation during the first few months before I could get back into the swing of things at church."

> Several mothers mentioned that becoming parents gave them insight into God's love they'd never had before. Lisa says, "I know how much I've come to cherish my children, how I would do anything for them. How much more must our heavenly Father love us?"

It's important, though, to get back into a regular devotional time and to resume worshiping at church as soon as you're able. (Chapter 8 covers ways to keep up your relationship with God.) Motherhood takes a lot out of you physically, emotionally, and spiritually. "And you've got to be filled up sometime," says Adrienne. "That's why your spiritual life is so important."

🚼 *Disappointment if the delivery didn't go as planned.* Karin had been all geared up for a natural delivery, but she developed toxemia and had to have an emergency cesarean section. She says, "I sat there waiting in the hospital while all the other women went home with their babies, and I kept thinking, *This isn't fair!* You expect the birth of your first baby to be a wonderful experience, but it's not wonderful when everything goes wrong." Karin felt a sense of failure at not being able to go through with the natural delivery—a feeling that Cheryl, who also had an emergency C-section, relates to.

What finally got Karin through it was realizing that if she had been pregnant in the days before C-sections were possible, both she and her baby would probably have died in childbirth. "I thought, *Well, the baby's healthy, and we're both alive.* I kept thanking God that at least everyone was alive." Even a Christian who's trusting the Lord will go through some rough emotional waters when her baby's birth doesn't turn out as expected. It's true that God will be faithful to bring good from even our most difficult experiences, but that can be hard to remember while you're staring down at the ashes of your dream.

Lisa points out, "Often the people who tell you how wonderful their childbirth experiences were have had some time to forget the pain and glorify the good. Childbirth is not a blessing, even at its best. It's the child who is the blessing."

I was a confirmed SEM and just knew I was going to have an easy time of it in the labor room. My doctor inadvertently supported that attitude by telling me that my above-average height boded well for a fast delivery, and I blew her encouraging words way out of proportion. But evidently my insides were smaller than my outsides, and I ended up pushing for five times longer than the average thirty minutes. The experience shocked me so badly that for several weeks I was unsure whether I ever wanted to go through it again, and I was bitterly disappointed that Megan's birth wasn't the beautiful memory I had wanted it to be. It helped when I finally realized that the big events in my life, such as my wedding and the birth of my first baby, didn't happen in order to give me beautiful memories; their purposes were to get me married and to give me a child. The memories are being built as Jon, Megan, Anna, and I live and love together day by day.

A quick footnote regarding my fears of ever going through childbirth again: When Anna was born, my obstetrician introduced me to a wonderful device called a "squat bar"—a metal bar that stretches above the delivery bed. The mother reaches up and grabs the bar, pulls herself to a squatting position, then pushes. After one push, my doctor yelled, "Hey, wait a minute! I'm not ready yet!" A few more pushes, and Anna was out.

🐤 *Unexplained emotional outbursts.* "There were times right after the baby came," says Kathy, "and even while I was still pregnant, when I would think, *Why did I just get so upset about that? It never used to bother me before.* It was almost as if I didn't understand myself."

Sonja's hormonal imbalance after the birth of her first child was bigger than most, and it caused some real emotional upsets: "I look back in amazement at some of the decisions I made and the ridiculous hard feelings I caused with my husband and other people I care about. I warned my husband about it the second time around, and he reassured me that he would try to be understanding. I agreed to trust his judgment as the better of the two, even concerning decisions I normally made alone, and it went much better the second time."

🐦 *Oversized fears — also known as "mommy paranoia."* This malady goes beyond just checking on your baby at naptime to make sure he's still breathing, and seems to be more connected with the personality of the mother than with hormones. With me, it took the form of making me reluctant to leave Megan with anyone, no matter how trustworthy. I finally forced myself to start leaving her periodically to spend an evening out with Jon. I consoled myself by screening my babysitters extra carefully. It became easier as time went by, and I was eventually able to leave only one page of instructions for the sitter instead of the usual five.

Sonja had her bout with mommy paranoia before her baby came: "I was afraid I would have the baby, go home, and then wake up one morning having forgotten all about it, get dressed, and run out the door as usual. I actually had nightmares about it. But when the time came, there was no chance of its really happening — I was so exhausted, sore, and heavy-breasted with milk that I needed no reminders of my responsibility."

Cheryl says, "I remember waking up in the middle of the night, screaming, 'Where's Emily?' I woke Phil as I frantically searched the bedsheets. I had forgotten that I'd put her back in the cradle after I nursed her in bed. Phil and I both lay there for a long time afterwards with our hearts in our throats, shaken by the thought of her smothered in our bed. We laugh about it now, but it wasn't funny then."

Dawn's fears took a different twist because her baby was adopted: "Every time the phone rang, I thought it was a social worker or someone who was going to say, 'I want my baby back.' I knew that the Lord had performed miracles to bring Melody into our lives, but for months I was afraid someone was going to come and take her away."

Often mommy paranoia involves taking a real but unlikely danger and magnifying it out of proportion. Sometimes, though, as in Nancy's case, the danger doesn't need magnifying: "Hannah's conception and birth were such miracles," she says. "We had been trying to conceive for four years and had almost given up hope. She was born prematurely and had to stay in ICU for two weeks, then had to be hooked up to a heart monitor every night for her first three months at home. The monitor went off the first night, scaring everyone in the house and sending us into a panicked rehearsal of infant CPR. Her heart rate recovered on its own, but we didn't sleep well for a number of nights.

"I was afraid to have anyone else care for Hannah. When she was four months old, my husband surprised me by arranging for a weekend away for our anniversary. I was really nervous about leaving her — I almost canceled the trip."

When we step across the threshold into motherhood, we find ourselves emotionally vulnerable in ways we've never been, to degrees we never thought possible. Even if you're fairly comfortable with the idea of your own mortality, having a tiny, helpless child come to live in your home and cuddle up to your heart can make life suddenly seem desperately fragile.

Kim says, "I was not prepared for the first time Natalie got sick. All my logic went out the window. That's scary — you feel like you have no control, and you don't know what to do, but you think you should because you're the parent."

There's a big difference between having a healthy concern for your child's safety and becoming obsessively worried about it. Healthy concern motivates you to do what you can to protect your child; worry paralyzes you with thoughts of what might happen. Several mothers said they were better able to put their fears into perspective when they kept in mind to Whom their children really belonged. As she struggled with her decision regarding whether to leave Hannah behind for a weekend with her husband, Nancy says, "Finally, I realized that Hannah is God's little girl. He has given me the joy of her presence for the time being, and he loves her more than I ever could. If he wants her back, it's in her best interest."

> When we step across the threshold into motherhood, we find ourselves emotionally vulnerable in ways we've never been, to degrees we never thought possible.

> Healthy concern motivates you to do what you can to protect your child; worry paralyzes you with thoughts of what might happen.

Lisa adds, "They are first and foremost God's kids! We are blessed to have and raise them for however long he allows us to. Easy to say, difficult to take to heart — but nonetheless true."

Our last emotional issue is big enough to have a section of its own:

Self-Esteem: Avoiding the Pits (or Climbing out of Them)

Several factors combine to fill the path through new motherhood with self-esteem pitfalls. We'll tackle them one at a time, but first let's talk about the number one preventive measure for the self-esteem pits: Have an encouraging husband.

Maybe that sounds ridiculous — after all, you can't make your husband encourage you. You can, however, help him see how important that role is for him. I've hung a poster of H. Jackson Brown's "Twenty-one Suggestions for Success" in both of my daughters' rooms. At the top of the list is this bit of advice: "Marry the right person. From that one decision will come 90 percent of your happiness or misery." (Of course, husbands need encouragement too, and in the best marriages each partner serves as the wind beneath the other's wings. We'll talk more about that in chapter 2.)

Your husband can't single-handedly keep you out of the self-esteem pits. There are steps you must take on your own. But if he's not encouraging you, or if he's actively tearing you down, it will be extremely difficult to stay out of them.

Read this chapter and chapter 2 together, to help you both understand what to expect during the first few months of parenthood and to introduce you to the principles involved in building a strong, positive partnership. And if you find yourself struggling in your marriage relationship, ask your church for the name of a good Christian family counselor. It's crucial to nip marriage problems in the bud. A strong marriage is the foundation on which a thriving family is built.

That said, let's take a look at some self-esteem pitfalls.

Fluctuating hormones. If you normally feel emotionally vulnerable just before your period, don't be surprised if you feel the same way during at least part of your pregnancy and immediately after giving birth. Again, check with your doctor if your mood swings seem unusually serious.

Physical appearance. "I didn't believe Tom when he said he still thought I was beautiful," says Brynn. "He was going to the office every day, where the women were wearing makeup and nice clothes and had their hair done. You don't feel beautiful when you're a new mother — your body's all different. Things don't go back the way they were!" The tips on pages 23–24 can help in this area, and healthy eating and regular exercise can go a long way toward both improving your mood and getting your body back in shape. Among the mothers in this book, the two most popular forms of exercise are walking (with the baby in a stroller or baby backpack) and working out to aerobics videos, which can be done during the baby's nap. (A quick caution: If you use a treadmill, exercise bike, or other exercise equipment at home, please use extreme caution when your children are near and make sure the equipment can be locked in place when you're not using it. Every year many children are injured by home exercise equipment.)

Loss of status as an income producer, combined with difficult-to-measure progress in their new position as mothers. For several mothers, this threw their self-confidence for a loop. (And it's important to note that often the loss of status was strictly in their own eyes.) Shari was sure of herself as a computer operator and supervisor, but it took her a while to find herself as a mother. She says, "I was floundering, trying to find out who I was really supposed to be. I'd think, *Am I supposed to be like that mother? Dress like that, look like that, act like that?* I kept comparing myself with other people. I wasn't trying to be myself; I was trying to be someone else. And I wasn't allowing myself to be who God wanted me to be. It took me a while to do that."

Kim says, "So often when the day is done and Rob and I are crawling into bed, I think, *What have I done all day?* It's hard sometimes to keep the big picture in mind." (She says keeping a daily list of her new priorities, as Lisa describes on page 22, helps.)

"I felt bad about Wayne's money," says Karin. "I knew it wasn't *his* money, but when we were both working, we earned about equal salaries. I was accustomed to being able to spend money and not think anything of it. Then, after I quit work, I felt guilty if I wrote a ten-dollar check at a discount store." There's a postscript to Karin's story, though: "When I quit work, the country was in the middle of a recession, and Wayne had just opened a business. Times were rough, but it's been only two years since then, and Wayne makes more money now than we made together back then. I really believe God honored my desire to stay home and take care of my baby."

Stella agrees: "We pulled our belts in and did it. And now, eight years later, I would do it all over again. Our budget was tight, but it was worth it. We gave up things we thought were necessities, but they weren't — they were luxuries. My baby was far more important than having all the material things I wanted."

If you're feeling guilty because you no longer contribute to the family coffers, it can be like rubbing salt into a wound every time you write a check and the clerk asks, "Are you employed?" A couple of mothers developed stock answers. Christine's was, "Not me, honey! I stay home with my baby, and I love it!" When Karin is asked about her line of work, she answers, "I develop personalities and build morals."

It's easy to feel unproductive when you're a new mother, especially before you develop a reliable daily schedule and get a handle on your housework. There's not much said these days about taking pride in our work as homemakers; our society seems to think that fulfillment and challenge come only from work outside the home. But the at-home mothers in this book have grown past that point, and you will too if you keep in mind that you've just done something incredibly productive: You've produced a human being. And you're in the process of rearing him to be a responsible person who is sensitive to his Creator and to the needs of the people around him. It's hard to see all that at first, before your baby's understanding starts to peek through, but every time you show love, every time you come when he's hurting or hungry or just needs to be held, every time you read a book or play a game with your baby, and every time you enforce an established "no-no," you're shaping the person your child will become. What job could possibly be more important — or more challenging and fulfilling?

Isolation. This can be a huge issue for at-home mothers. Kathy says, "I look forward so much to getting out. I look forward to Sunday school and church because I want to see the people and hear the message. I go into stores sometimes and don't know how to put the outfits together. I'll ask the salesgirl, 'What is everybody wearing nowadays?' I'll be all right for a while, and then it'll hit me again. I talk to my husband about it, but of course, he doesn't quite understand because he's out around people all day."

Christine puts the feeling of being housebound high on her list of big adjustments. "Since Ashley was my first baby, I was afraid to take her anywhere for fear she'd catch cold. And because she had colic, I hesitated to take her visiting or shopping for fear she'd cry the whole time."

It's easy to fall into the habit of staying in the house around the clock, emerging only to check the mailbox. But if you're not careful, you can develop a bad case of cabin fever and start resenting your little one for keeping you penned in. God created us as social creatures — it was "not good" for man to be alone, and it's not good for new mothers either! "It helps just to find a friend in the neighborhood," says Pene.

Isolation can contribute to depression and low self-esteem, and can create a downward spiral: The more depressed you are and the lower your self-esteem, the less likely you are to feel like getting out, and the more isolated you become.

Julie went through serious depression after her first baby was born: "We were so young. We had Stephanie the month after our first anniversary, and I was terrified. I had taken a leap of faith by quitting my job, but then my self-worth plummeted because I was no longer bringing in any income. Here I was with this baby, and I didn't know what to do. I was depressed for about three months."

The answer to Julie's problem was the same answer I heard from many other women: namely, *other women*. She said, "Two women in my church reached out to me. I got into a Bible study class, got involved with Mothers of Preschoolers (MOPS), just really surrounded myself with other women. I grew so much during Stephanie's first year of life. And God just kept telling me, 'Trust me. It'll get better.' And it did."

If you find yourself in the pit of isolation, you'll need to do some climbing. Check with your church about support groups, Bible studies, and classes for young parents; call other churches if necessary. But I guarantee you this: Once you begin climbing, you'll look up to see other women at the top with their hands extended to help pull you out. And before long, you'll be one of those women yourself, helping others out of the pit.

Isolation can contribute to depression and low self-esteem, and can create a downward spiral: The more depressed you are and the lower your self-esteem, the less likely you are to feel like getting out, and the more isolated you become.

Sometimes new mothers just need to get out of the house. Cheryl says, "It's easy to get out when your family has two cars, because you can either take the baby with you or find a good Christian day care center or Mother's Day Out. But if you don't, the only thing to do is sit down with your husband and explain to him that you need to have time away from the house. Work out a way to have the car one day a week."

Patty agrees: "Treat yourself and the baby to a special outing at least once a week — go to a park, out for ice cream, whatever. And just go out and get some fresh air whenever the weather permits. It renews both of you."

Unless your baby has severe colic, it's no big deal to take him with you, especially if you're nursing and don't have to pack bottles. An excursion every now and then will expose him to all kinds of new sights and sounds and will keep you from getting into a rut. Babies are very portable little creatures if you're equipped with a good stroller or baby backpack. But as nice as it is to get out with the baby, it's even better to go out without him every once in a while. Kim says, "It wasn't until I left Mollie for the first time that I realized how emotionally draining it is to be so depended on. It was a great feeling to walk out of the house without a diaper bag and be free from being needed for a couple of hours. I love Mollie so much, but sometimes I just need to spend some time away from her even when I don't feel I need it."

"The solution for me was Grandma," says Stella. "Even though my babies were very good and took long naps, I was housebound because they did sleep so much. Grandparents are a real blessing, and if you have one who will come over and sit with the baby while he's sleeping, it's tremendous. Just go to the store for an hour. Or go for a walk or visit a neighbor or do anything just to get out for a little while." Some grandparents adore getting a chance to babysit, but others come to resent it. Have a frank discussion with both sets of your baby's grandparents to find out where they stand. They'll appreciate knowing that you honestly don't want to impose on them.

When her daughter was a year old, Cil joined a babysitting co-op that worked on a ticket system. "We had thirty-minute tickets. For instance, say I needed to go to the doctor. I'd call a friend in the co-op and ask if she could sit. She could say no if she needed to, in which case I'd call someone else in the co-op. If I thought I'd be gone about two hours, I'd give my friend four tickets. Then I'd return the favor later, at my convenience." The mothers in the co-op organized play outings and socials too, so the group became a major source of support for Cil. She says, "I developed some really close relationships with people who are still good friends today."

Nancy adds, "Before we had Hannah, I wanted to spend any extra time I had with my husband, David, because he's my best friend. He's still my best friend, but I find that now I need some time alone, without him or the baby, so I can recharge and appreciate what I have."

I have a helpful husband, and when Megan was little I sometimes told him when he came home from work, "Okay, you keep Megan for a little while. I'm going down to the library (or shopping, or for a walk)." I nursed her right before I left and made sure I was home in time for her next feeding. "David helped me a lot that way, too," says Christine. "He would watch Ashley right when he came home in the evening, and it was so wonderful just to know that even if she cried I didn't have to do anything." Rehearsing with the church choir while your husband watches the baby can give you a ministry outlet as well as an evening out.

At the same time, it's important to use discretion in this area. Brynn's husband, Tom, says, "There was a period of time when I'd come in the door, put my stuff down, change clothes, she'd hand Cole to me, and then she would leave. Finally, after it happened — I don't know if it was truly a lot of times, but it felt like it — I got upset. We talked about it." Mike adds, "We've almost got to fight to keep from being a tag team. Elizabeth takes the kids during the day, and when I get home it's my turn. Sometimes it seems like when we're horizontal and sleeping is the only time we have together." It may take a while, but you and your husband will learn to balance your need for time together with your need for time alone. (Again, we'll talk more about your relationship with your husband in chapter 2.)

Also, Stephanie says, "Sometimes daddies need a break too, and moms need to remember that. Because they're as busy as we are. Maybe more, because sometimes we get a nap and they don't."

🐘 *The need for intellectual and creative challenge.* Your baby will probably take most of your attention during his first few weeks, but the mothers in this book feel it's important to develop some kind of additional creative pastime as soon as you can. You may feel guilty about taking the time for it at first, especially if the house isn't completely in order, but it's important to keep yourself growing as a person. I found that unless I made continual efforts to stretch myself, I became very boring; when Jon came home, my big, exciting news for the day was, "Megan spat up all over the couch."

"Be sure to take time for yourself," says Connie. "Find something you love to do, and do it often." Trina draws and paints, and several of our other moms do counted cross-stitch — all hobbies with the added advantage of helping them come up with inexpensive Christmas presents for their families and friends. Other moms have discovered a love for gardening, which gives them a chance to get out of the house as well as to enjoy seeing things grow. Christine bought a baby monitor and kept it in Ashley's room at naptime. She kept the receiver with her and could hear right away when Ashley woke up, even if Christine was outside pulling weeds. Still other moms have developed a love of reading or of good music, both of which relax them and improve their minds at the same time.

Christine gave up on her garden: "It was all I could do to keep it alive until I got four okras out of it! But I love to cook. So when Ashley was little, David would take over with her in the evenings while I went into the kitchen." Other hobbies, such as crafts and dressmaking, can even be the start of a home-based business. (We discuss home-based businesses in chapter 12.)

Much of the work involved in motherhood is repetitive. Diapers aren't forever — although sometimes it may feel that way — but laundry, dishes, meal preparation, and picking up clutter are. No matter how clean your kitchen is today, it will be dirty again tomorrow. Or tonight. Whoever wrote "Woman's work is never done" wasn't kidding. I have an Erma Bombeck quote taped to my refrigerator: "Housework, if you do it right, will kill you."

Repetition can become drudgery and burnout if you're not careful. So even though I could easily fill my days working around my house and spending time with my children, I've found I'm a much better and more cheerful mother if I'm also working on some kind of challenging project — whether it's taking or teaching a class, involvement in a ministry, gardening, working on crafts, writing, or decorating my house. When I have a project I'm excited about, I can let my mind work through various aspects of it while I do the laundry or the dusting or the vacuuming. I develop a "just do it" approach to daily chores that would otherwise make me groan, "Not again! I'll do it later."

> Whoever wrote "Woman's work is never done" wasn't kidding. I have an Erma Bombeck quote taped to my refrigerator: "Housework, if you do it right, will kill you."

Only you can decide the best way for you to stretch. There are just two requirements: It has to be a challenge, and you have to enjoy it. No — make that three requirements. You also have to keep in mind why you're doing it: To help you fill your primary role of wife and mother more effectively and in a better frame of mind. When you find something you love to do and begin to see progress in it — especially if it's a project that helps others — you'll be tempted to move it to the head of your priority list, but that spot is already filled. Be sensitive to signs that you need to pull back: stress, fatigue, infringements on family time. Someone once said, "Eternal vigilance is the price of freedom." It's also the price of a thriving family.

Chapter 2

We're in This Together

We've been talking a lot about the changes a new mother goes through, but your new baby has two parents, and Dad's life has changed too.

It needs to be said up front that, just as not all women go through the upheaval of postpartum depression, not all men are thrown by the adjustments involved in new fatherhood. Some of the men I interviewed made the transition smoothly and welcomed the change to a new season of life. (This was especially true for dads blessed with compliant, noncolicky babies.) At the same time, if you're a new father who is experiencing culture shock, you're definitely not alone.

"I was shocked by the time involved," says Chris. "I had so many things planned; I was working and going to college, and I remember thinking, *I don't have time for this.* Parenthood is great, but you don't realize how much of a commitment it is."

Scott says, "I was really surprised at how high-maintenance and dependent Wes was. Cleaning the umbilical cord was like, 'What is *this?*'" He laughs. "It was hard initially not to be frustrated by it sometimes — 'Gosh, I have to change his diaper, clean his umbilical cord, do all this stuff, and make sure I'm careful because he's so small.' It felt like a big responsibility."

Responsibility. Commitment. With the fathers I interviewed, those words came up often. But before their children came, it was typical for them to underestimate the impact the new baby would have on their lives. Tim says, "Before

Darcy was born, my expectation was, 'No big deal.' I didn't realize how being a dad would change me. It wasn't until after she was born that I realized, *I'm a dad now. I have to be more careful how I drive, how I live my life.* The reality of being a provider, of my need to give stability to my family, really changed me inside. But I didn't feel the weight of parenthood until after she was born."

Another word that came up often was *fear.* Fear that they would accidentally hurt their tiny, delicate babies. Fear that they wouldn't be able to protect their children from everything life would throw at them. Fear that they weren't up to the task of being a good father. Financial fears too, since most of these families gave up the wife's income to allow her to stay home with the baby.

Hmmmm . . . less time, less money, more responsibility, feelings of fear and insecurity. Why would any sane guy want to get himself into such a situation? I asked several young fathers that question. Funny thing was, many of them had never thought it through. Scott says, "When you first asked that, I thought, *Because Jennifer wanted to have kids.*" He laughs. "I always wanted kids — she just wanted them sooner." As these fathers thought through their reasons for wanting children, the most common answers were to leave a legacy behind them in the world and to experience what it would be like to be a father.

> One of the biggest benefits these young fathers see in parenthood is their own growth. Fatherhood is helping them develop spiritual and emotional muscles they never knew they had.

When I asked them, "Is it worth it?" their answers were quick and enthusiastic. Jeff says, "Yes. Exclamation point. Shari and I were close before, but we've been closer since our kids came. Having kids forces you to be a team." Tim adds, "There's a real joy that kids bring — how special and original they are, how much fun it is to teach them things, to pour your love into them, passing on who you are to your children. It's worth it!"

One of the biggest benefits these young fathers see in parenthood is their own growth. Fatherhood is helping them develop spiritual and emotional muscles they never knew they had. "I learn things from each of my kids every day," says Doug. "I learn things from my wife. It's been a process. I'm not there yet, but I'm a lot more effective as a dad, ten years into marriage, than I ever thought I'd be. If you'd dropped the news on me back in 1988 that I was going to be a father of four before the year 2000, that would have terrified me. But God teaches you."

"Having kids teaches you not to be selfish," says Marty. "You have to become a very giving person if you're going to be a good parent." Glenn, a highly motivated engineer, says parenthood has helped him redefine his priorities: "I'd rather have a degree from the University of Fatherhood, for being a good parent, than a CEO title. I have a bigger chance of making an impact on my child's life than I do in my company. When I die, the company will go on and forget about me. My child's not going to do that."

The most enjoyable aspect of parenthood, according to these young fathers, is the relationship they're developing with their children. "It's a totally different relationship than I've ever had before," says Scott. "My wife relies on me, and I rely on her, but we could survive physically without each other. Wes is completely dependent on us." At the beginning of this chapter, Scott talked about initially feeling overwhelmed and intimidated by his son's needs. But now, he says, "Once you start to develop a relationship, he becomes a person. He's my son. I really enjoy taking care of him, giving him a bath or something. I think, *I get to spend time with Wes!* It's the little things that make it worthwhile, like Wes hopping up into my lap and giving me a hug, or the way he laughs when he gets tickled — just practical, love-type things. It's amazing."

Parenthood, in partnership with a loving spouse, is one of the deepest, most fulfilling experiences life has to offer. At the same time, given the adjustments involved, it's not surprising that for some men the adjustment to fatherhood is a bumpy ride.

David says, "I watched several of my friends go through shock when their kids were born. They became extremely selfish, spending all their time off work on the golf course or out with other guys instead of at home with their wife and child. It was almost as if reality hit but they weren't quite ready to acknowledge it."

Doug was one of those who went through "daddy denial," but the TV, not the golf course, was his escape of choice. He says, "I was completely uninvolved. I had no bad feelings toward our baby — I loved her — but my attitude was, 'What am I supposed to do with her? Julie's home with her all day. That's her job.' It didn't bother me that Julie was spending so much time with the baby — I only got bugged when she acted like *I* needed to pitch in. Julie was struggling with depression, and I was like, 'What's on TV?'"

He puts it bluntly: "I think I was pretty much a jerk. And I think I turned a corner when my wife said to me one day, 'You know, you're a jerk!' The suitcases were packed. She threatened to leave me. We've been married ten years now, and the more time goes by, the more I realize how much I was endangering. I was like a kid balancing along the edge of the Grand Canyon. I just did not know. I should have, but I didn't."

One of Doug's problems was a complete lack of role models — he was raised by a single mom and had no relationship with his father. So you'd think that young men from two-parent families would have it made in the fathering department, right?

Well, no. And that's what the next section is about.

How Not to Reinvent the Wheel

The fathers I interviewed acknowledge that they have been strongly influenced by their own fathers, but unfortunately, most of them see that as something not to celebrate but to overcome. One says, "My father was a very moral, hard-working person, but he came from a family that was not expressive of emotions. I never felt close to him while I was growing up, although I loved him and wanted him to spend time with me and talk to me and tell me he was proud of me. So even when he died, it didn't affect me that much. I regret that now. I'd give anything to have my father back and be able to tell him how much I love him. But because of that lack of contact and expression of love, we do a lot of hugging in our house now — even with the boys."

My husband, Jon, was a "Marine brat." His dad was a wonderful man, but he says, "Dad was hardly ever around. At the time, it was just a normal part of life. But I realize now how much I missed out on, and when we had Megan, I decided I was going to be there as much as possible."

Another dad says, "My father was gone a lot too, and I've also had some unpleasant memories of extremely harsh, cruel discipline that the Lord has had to heal me of. It's challenged me in some areas to be a better father than my father was. When my daughter looks back, she may see some mistakes I've made too, but I'm going to give it my best shot."

Still another young father says, "My dad was there, but I never had a close relationship with him when I was younger. I really envied people who had that. I looked at them almost with an astonishment, like, 'That's the way a family's supposed to be?'"

The mothers in this book had similar responses to the idea of using their parents as role models. In fact, most of the young parents I interviewed expressed hopes of surpassing Mom and Dad in the parenting department. I believe one reason for this is that new parents tend to be idealistic, with visions of avoiding Mom and Dad's mistakes without creating new ones of their own. Perhaps, too, some of their hesitancy to copy their parents has to do with personality differences; even when a child has a good relationship with her parents and shares their values, differences in their personalities may make her want to use a different parenting style. Besides, what young parent remembers how his own parents dealt with him as a baby? Because of all these things, the mothers and fathers in this book tend to look for role models elsewhere.

By far, other young parents were the most popular role models mentioned by the parents I interviewed. David says, "Dads of our fathers' generation weren't as involved as we are. My best role models are other young fathers slightly ahead of me. Watching how they do things and observing the results have been most instructive."

The drawback to this, of course, is that when you observe another young couple's relationship with their children, you're seeing only the short-term results of their methods — and a lot goes on behind the scenes. For a more complete picture, many of the young parents in this book have taken parenting and marriage courses, and most of them have turned to experts such as Dr. James Dobson of Focus on the Family for insight and advice.

No one would embark on a serious career without some kind of training, yet it's amazing how many young couples approach marriage and childrearing that way. Doug says, "You just kind of assume, when you make the decision to get married, that it's all about how much you love each other. Well, it's about a whole lot more than that. It's about making this complete adjustment of your life. You assume you know everything there is to know about being married, and you don't." The same could be said — with exclamation points — about parenting.

> No one would embark on a serious career without some kind of training, yet it's amazing how many young couples approach marriage and childrearing that way.

"I like to gather a lot of information," says Jennifer. "I can't really draw from my family because my parents divorced when I was ten. So I draw from a bunch of different sources and say, 'Okay, this is what they say about this issue. Where should we go from here?'" Some of these young parents read books together. Others have the wife serve as the family researcher, finding material and bringing it to her husband for reading and discussion. Stephanie says, "I highlight the books. I mark the pages, and Roy reads them."

Tom says, "It's an ongoing thing. You tend to slip back into old habits or things you think are right because they're what you saw growing up. You have

ly challenge yourself to read the books, take the classes — then you've
ll that in and decide as a couple how you're going to raise your child.
frustrating at times because you're the parent, you're the one who's
supposed to have the answers, and you're going, 'What? I don't know!'"

Loren adds, "Parenting doesn't come naturally. You can't see how your
action today is going to affect your kid next week, next month, next year, ten
years from now. What kind of patterns am I setting up? How am I going to work
on his heart, to train him to want to do what is right? It's just not something that
comes naturally for me. So Shannon and I are finding it really important to educate ourselves — lots of reading, getting all the different perspectives. No one
book has all the answers, but when you put a lot of different ideas together, you
find what works for your child. And of course, it's important to learn what the
Bible teaches about parenting. Education is just so important. If we hadn't been
doing that, we'd be doing things with Nathaniel and Alyssa simply based on the
way we were raised, without having any idea what the repercussions would be."

"One of the best things we did," says Scott, "was take an eighteen-week
Growing Kids God's Way course. Each week gave us something to talk about
together, proactively, way before it happened. It
also gave us a good foundation on biblical principles of parenting. It was like, 'Oh — I kinda get it
now. *This* is what parenting is about from God's
perspective!'"

Growing Kids God's Way is a course I heard
recommended many times while researching this
book. One of the biggest advantages mentioned,
aside from the practical, Bible-based instruction,
was that the weekly classes give young parents a
chance to connect with other young couples who
are working through similar issues. To find the
course, contact Growing Families International
(1-800-474-6264, www.gfi.org).

"Andrew attended Promise Keepers last fall,"
says Lisa. "He was reluctant to go at first, but the
Lord kept pushing him in little ways. It ended up
being a great experience for him. If he was a good
dad and husband with good intentions before he
went, he is an excellent dad and husband afterward, with an even clearer picture of who he is as

Proverbs 13:20 says,
"He who walks with
the wise grows wise."
The more time you
spend getting the per-
spective of wise and
experienced parents
through Bible-based
books, courses, and
study groups, the more
likely you are to make
wise decisions with
your own child.

a man, husband, and dad in the eyes of God." To learn more about Promise Keepers, visit their website (www.promisekeepers.org).

For good books and courses on marriage and parenting, check with your pastor or with a reputable organization such as Focus on the Family (719-531-5181, www.fotf.org). Another great resource is FamilyLife, a division of Campus Crusade for Christ (1-800-FLTODAY, www.familylife.com). In addition to conferences and books, FamilyLife offers the HomeBuilders Couples Series, an excellent, user-friendly series of Bible study courses on building a solid Christian marriage. Your local Christian bookstore is a great place to look for other family educational resources.

Even the best books, courses, and seminars have their limits. Since every family is unique, you'll still have to figure out the best ways to apply what you learn to your own home. But Proverbs 13:20 says, "He who walks with the wise grows wise." The more time you spend getting the perspective of wise and experienced parents through Bible-based books, courses, and study groups, the more likely you are to make wise decisions with your own child. Parents who neglect to learn from those who've gone before them are trying to reinvent the wheel — and there are an awful lot of lopsided, half-assembled wheels wobbling down the road of life as a result.

Recipe for a Thriving Family

Leo Tolstoy wrote, "Happy families are all alike; every unhappy family is unhappy in its own way." Tolstoy — a genius at observing and writing about human nature — wasn't claiming that all happy families are alike when it comes to frills such as hobbies and special interests, economic or educational backgrounds, or individual personalities. What he meant was this: At the heart of every happy family, whether they realize it or not, is a set of guiding principles that allows them to thrive. The family that departs from any of those principles can veer off the "happiness track" in various ways depending on where the departure happens.

The unfortunate upshot of this truth is that, since there's only one way to have a truly happy family and many different ways to have an unhappy one, happy families are in the minority. A study released in July 1999 by Rutgers University's National Marriage Project found that only 37.8 percent of people who were still in their first marriages reported being "very happy." The study went on to state, "Indeed, it has been estimated that after ten years only about 25 percent of first marriages are successful, that is, both still intact and reportedly happy ..." In other words, to paraphrase Jesus, the road to a happy family life is narrow, and few find it.

Because so few people grow up with strong, positive role models, many young Christian couples have no idea what a thriving family looks like from the inside. This section is an attempt to give a quick peek. We'll talk primarily about the marriage partnership, for two reasons: First, a thriving marriage is the first step to a thriving family. You can't have one without the other. And second, the application of many of the principles in this section to your relationship with your children can be found later in this book, in the chapters on discipline, spiritual training, and self-esteem.

As you read, you may feel discouraged if your marriage comes up short. Maybe you'll even wonder if your family has a chance. But take heart — few marriages start out looking this way. Mine didn't. But after a lot of talking and praying and learning and growing (and crying) together, it does now.

By the way, a thriving family doesn't mean a perfect family. As long as families are made up of human beings, there will be problems to work through. So what does *thriving* mean? A thriving family is one in which

1. each member is respected and valued — and knows it
2. the members stay in touch with what's going on in each other's lives and hearts
3. conflict is worked through in a positive way that leaves the members closer
4. time spent together is a priority and a source of joy
5. the parents see themselves as a team rather than as separate individuals with conflicting needs, and share a deep, firm commitment to the family's welfare.

Here are the essential ingredients: *respect, communication, time,* and *teamwork.*

Are you surprised that love isn't on the list? There's a good reason. The four ingredients above represent love in action. Feelings of love — those elusive, fragile things — are the result, not the cause, of demonstrated love. If both partners in a marriage are practicing active love, the emotions will come naturally (although they can never be depended on). If one or both partners are not, any feelings of love will be hard put to survive.

RESPECT

Every thriving family is built on the solid bedrock of respect: of the husband and wife for each other, of the children for their parents, and in a different way, of the parents for their children.

How does this character trait look in a thriving young family?

A *husband and wife who respect each other will choose to focus on each other's strengths.* Philippians 4:8 says, "Finally, brothers, whatever is true, whatever is noble, whatever is right, whatever is pure, whatever is lovely, whatever is admirable — if anything is excellent or praiseworthy — think about such things." Paul is saying, "Find something — *anything* — good, and focus on that!" It's no accident that this verse comes soon after his plea to two squabbling church members to get along better.

In any marriage, both spouses will be able to find plenty of flaws and quirks to pick at. But if they focus on trying to fix each other, neither love nor respect is likely to survive very long. The fascinating thing is that when we focus on encouraging our partners' strengths, we set them free to work on their flaws instead of trying to protect themselves from us. We also begin to see more and more things to admire, and we inspire them to become all God created them to be. This is what it means to be the wind beneath someone's wings.

Listen to this exchange between three men, all of whose wives describe them as "my best friend":

Tim says, "My primary role in Trudy's life is to be her encourager. It's my job to encourage her to keep going with the kids, to tell her she's doing a good job, to encourage her in how she looks."

"I have friends," says Jon, "who feel as if their main job is to make sure their wife does what she needs to do, based on their expectations. I don't see it that way. My role is to trust that Karen knows what God has called her to do — in the house, with the children, in her ministry, in her relationships with me and with him. My role is to support and encourage her. If I see problems, then we can work through them. But I'd never want to approach it from the viewpoint of, 'I've got all the answers, honey, and here's the way you need to do it.'"

"And if you see problems," adds Jeff, "especially in the way the housework is getting done, it's usually time to say, 'What can I do for you?' as opposed to, 'Golly — this place is a wreck! What'd you do all day?'"

Is it any wonder these guys' wives cherish them? (And one of these very special men — thank God — is mine.)

It can be hard to become an encourager if you weren't raised in an encouraging home. Loren says, "One of my biggest problems is that I reserve

> Loren says, "One of my biggest problems is that I reserve encouraging words until I think Shannon has actually achieved something. But housework is never really done."

encouraging words until I think Shannon has actually achieved something. But housework is never really done. It just keeps going and going — especially now that we have two kids. So I'm learning it's important always to encourage and not wait for some big achievement."

Tom says, "Brynn gives me praise even when I do small things to help her. It makes me feel good. You know, a lot of times guys get wrapped up in their jobs, at the expense of their families, because at work they feel satisfaction and control, and at home they don't." Brynn adds, "There is no glory in cleaning a toilet, but I give it to him. I go, 'Oh, gosh — *thank* you!'"

Expressing sincere gratitude and praise accomplishes two purposes: First, it makes your husband want to clean that toilet (or change that diaper) again, and second, it builds the attitude of respect and appreciation between you.

Brynn believes it's important for husbands and wives to encourage every-thing about each other. "Not just the daddy role but the husband role and his career too." The attitude of each spouse needs to be, "I appreciate you and what you do."

Here's a project to try if encouragement doesn't yet come naturally in your marriage: For one week, take a break from any criticism of each other — even mental criticism. Commit yourselves to give each other at least two sincere, spe-cific expressions of appreciation every day. Schedule a time at the end of the week to talk about how it went. I'm betting you'll want to continue the project.

A wife who respects her husband will never criticize or correct him in pub-lic, either to his face or behind his back. The same is true for husbands who respect their wives. Shari says, "There were times when I dreaded getting together with other moms, because all I heard was griping about what their husbands were or weren't doing. It was a real turnoff. It's important to respect your spouse, whether he or she is present or not. I know Jeff does the same for me." Save any correction for truly important issues and do it privately. When counsel is needed about problems in the relationship, a person who respects his or her spouse will go privately to someone who has proven trustworthy.

A husband who respects his wife will consider her work at least as impor-tant as his own and won't assume she's not as tired as he is simply because she's been home all day. These young parents shared some hilarious stories of how, when the husband was left home with the baby for a few hours, his view of what his wife should be accomplishing each day suddenly underwent a major shift.

Kim says, "Chris kept Natalie while I went to a baby shower. The house was pretty straight before I left, but when I came home she was in her high chair, and there were rags and food everywhere and toys all over the floor. Chris said,

'You would not believe what I went through!' and I answered, 'Really? I have no idea. Tell me about it.'"

Glenn says, "We did the same thing. Shelley was gone for a whopping total of about four hours. I met her at the door when she got home and said, 'Here's Wendy. I'm going to bed.'" Shelley adds, "He told me, 'All I got done today was I went through the mail! And I didn't even finish that!'"

"With Michelle, our third," says Trudy, "I had a C-section and had to stay in bed longer. Tim had to take care of things. I think he found out then how much work was involved, because after that it was like, 'It's okay if the house isn't clean — I understand. Dinner's not on the table? I understand.'"

🦋 A *person who respects his or her spouse will never dismiss the other's concerns with,* "Well, you shouldn't feel that way." (More about that in the next section.)

🐾 *Finally, a man who respects his wife (and vice versa) will be careful to treat her with courtesy at all times, even in the privacy of their home.* I've been a fan of author Judith Martin (Miss Manners) for years. Regarding courtesy in the home, she says, "Manners toward strangers are a fine thing, but in family life, they are essential. If you offend strangers, you can move on, but if you disgust members of your family — well, you can still move on, and many people do, but it is emotionally and otherwise rather expensive."

COMMUNICATION

While respect is the most important attitude in a thriving marriage, communication is the most important skill. All the love and respect in the world won't do your marriage much good if you don't communicate them.

At least three types of communication are vital to the health of your marriage: *keeping in touch, communicating needs and expectations,* and *working through conflict.*

Keeping in Touch

Keeping in touch can be hard to do when you have small children. "You're not focused on each other any more," says Chris. His wife, Kim, agrees, "You're focused on your child." Brynn adds, "The things you talk about change. We used to have wonderful conversations. Now it's usually, 'Let me update you on what your child did today.'"

What helps? Chris and Kim like to go for drives on the weekends. He says, "We're in a confined space, we can't watch TV, and hopefully the baby's asleep in the back seat. Anyway, she's locked in and can't get into anything. We just talk — about important stuff, unimportant stuff. If you're sitting there for a three-hour car trip, pretty soon you stop talking about the baby and start talking about other things."

"Nancy and I try to go for a walk with Hannah in the stroller after the evening meal," says David. "When we're unable to do that, we truly miss it."

Loren and Shannon are taking a marriage enrichment class that requires them to schedule a weekly date to talk about what they're learning. Loren says, "We usually discuss one of the questions on our homework, but often we stray to talk about things that are relevant to our relationship at the time. That's been a good tool to make sure communication happens. Because we've experienced that problem — you talk to each other, but you don't really communicate about important issues."

Jeff says, "We have something we're doing with our Growing Kids God's Way class called 'couch time,' where we just sit for fifteen minutes and talk. We haven't gotten it into the daily ritual, but it's prescribed. We're really working on that. Shari and I sit on the couch, Zachary's in his playpen, and Hannah's bouncing off the walls, going, 'Is couch time over yet?'" Phil and Cheryl follow this routine too, and Phil says, "Our kids know: Unless the house is on fire, don't talk to Mom and Dad until they're through."

Praying together is a wonderful way to get in touch with each other's needs and concerns — and with the One who can give you the wisdom to help meet them.

For many of these parents, evenings together are their best opportunities for communication. Stephanie says, "We do early bedtimes for the kids. And the night is ours."

"The best time Andrew and I have together is when we climb into bed at night," says Lisa. "It seems to be the only time there are no other distractions (no kids, no dishes, no laundry, no TV, no phone calls). We have some of our best heart-to-heart discussions lying side by side, staring up at the ceiling in the dark. I hope it won't always be this way. A romantic dinner would be nice, but there just isn't time or energy for it right now."

She goes on, "You have to prioritize communication. We've learned to talk whenever we get chances — in between chores, during chores. We do get disconnected at times. Usually I get upset if we go for a long time without communicating in a real way. I cry, we talk and do better for a while, then slack off again. It's a cycle. But each time we go longer between crys!"

Cil says, "Sometimes — not very often — I'll get up early with Marty. He'll say, 'You don't have to get up yet,' and I'll answer, 'I haven't talked to you in a week!'"

"We pray together every Sunday night," says Tim. "After the kids are in bed, Trudy and I kneel by our bed and pray for each other. It's hard to be mad at your wife while you're praying for her." Praying together is a wonderful way to get in touch with each other's needs and concerns — and with the One who can give you the wisdom to help meet them.

Knowing how to listen is as important to communication as knowing how to talk. Often when we share our problems and frustrations we don't want advice — we just want to know someone is aware of what we're going through, and that he or she cares. When her children were small, Lisa says, "Many times I didn't need answers or solutions to what I was crying about, just someone to listen. If Andrew had given me tons of advice, it would only have made matters worse. Instead he listened lots, hugged me lots, and pitched in with chores more so I could rest."

Communicating Needs and Expectations

Communicating needs and expectations is an area where new parents often struggle. Their lives have suddenly changed in a radical way. Each partner has a set of expectations about parenthood that may or may not be realistic, as well as needs he or she may or may not have communicated. It's helpful if you can bring these issues into the open before they start festering and turn into a full-blown conflict.

Before the baby arrives, your discussions will have to be pretty basic: How involved will Dad be in helping with the baby and the house during the first few weeks? Who will cook? Will you take turns with nightly feedings? And — most important — are you willing to adjust if your partner's or your baby's needs turn out differently than expected? A lot depends on your baby's unique personality and physical health, not to mention how the wife's body and emotions adjust to the fatigue and the hormonal changes of her first few months postpartum.

Because of the unpredictability involved in new parenthood, it's a good idea to declare the first month or so a grace period where you all simply adjust to each other. And Phil has a bit of advice for husbands: "Now's the time for brownie points! Help your wife out like you never have in your life — she'll brag on you for years to come."

Once you've adjusted to those first few weeks, schedule a meeting to talk about the things you feel you need from each other most. Scott says, "We did that a couple of times, out of desperation. We were getting frustrated, but Jennifer figured it out: 'Oh — we've got different expectations. Let's sit down and talk about it.' Defining what we expect from each other helps a lot."

Jennifer says, "Scott had a hard time with it at first; he didn't want to say, 'This is what I expect of you.' But I said, 'No, it would really help me. Because I'm running around trying to figure out what you want. If you would just tell me, I could set all the rest of this stuff aside and focus on what's really important."

Before the baby arrives, your discussions will have to be pretty basic: How involved will Dad be in helping with the baby and the house during the first few weeks? Who will cook? Will you take turns with nightly feedings? And — most important — are you willing to adjust if your partner's or your baby's needs turn out differently than expected?

"But be careful when you have that conversation," says Brynn. "Don't have it on a bad day, when your emotions are up. You have to do it when things are going pretty well and you're able to think clearly." That's the value in scheduling this meeting, rather than waiting until someone explodes and forces it. Kim says, "Some of our best resolutions have come when we've both just sat down calmly. Not when something's happened but maybe one of us feels like something's not working out right, and we talk about it. But when we're mad, that's when the worst things happen."

You should meet to talk about needs and expectations periodically, especially at the first sign that an issue needs to be dealt with. Jennifer says, "It's ongoing. My needs were different when Wes was six months old than when he was a year old. I need to keep communicating with Scott — 'Okay, I would really appreciate it if you could help me with this now, because we've got that other thing under control.'"

It can also be helpful to take a look at where your expectations come from. Tom says, "I've had to reexamine my expectations a couple of times. We husbands don't remember what it was like around our homes as young children. What we remember is when we were older and things were more in order. My mom admits it was pretty crazy around the house when I was little. But that's not what we remember, and that's not what we expect."

You'll also need to discuss your expectations of how you'll handle basic childrearing issues such as discipline and spiritual training. For these young parents, discussing these issues in advance — often in the context of taking a course or reading a book together — helped them avoid, or at least minimize, conflict.

What happens when a wife's needs and expectations clash with her husband's? *In a thriving family, both spouses will always seek a win-win solution.* A smart husband knows that what is good for his wife is good for him, and a smart wife knows that the reverse is true as well. If you come out of a discussion able to point out a clear winner and loser, or with no clear resolution at all, you've both lost. Lisa says, "As a general rule, Andrew and I try to put each other's needs before our own. It's hard, but it does make the other person feel cherished. If you both do it, no one gets left out or feels like a door mat."

Working through Conflict

Talking through your needs and expectations on a regular basis should help make conflict a rare occurrence, but it will probably still crop up from time to time. How you deal with it will determine whether the conflict is resolved in a positive way or merely pushed below the surface.

The parents in this book have a few tips on how *not* to deal with conflict:

Glenn says, "Don't try to deal with it when it's close to bedtime." (Brynn adds, "Which makes it hard, because that's often the only time our husbands have with us during the day.")

"Or when he's walking out the door in the morning," says Stephanie.

"Or on the phone when he's at work," says Jennifer.

"And not in front of the kids," adds Loren.

"And another thing," says Kim. "Don't try to deal with it when you're in the heat of anger. You can't think clearly."

"I always say things I don't mean when I'm mad," says Chris.

"Or tired," adds Tom. His wife Brynn laughs: "That's the hard part! When you're a new parent, you're always tired. And some women have hormone problems. Tom is very smart. He says, 'I'll never argue with a pregnant lady.'"

"Andrew and I usually argue the most when we're exhausted," says Lisa, "which is pretty often with little kids around. It helps just to recognize and

> Lisa says, "As a general rule, Andrew and I try to put each other's needs before our own. It's hard, but it does make the other person feel cherished. If you both do it, no one gets left out or feels like a door mat."

acknowledge it. Andrew will even say, when I try to argue about something, 'You're tired. I won't do this with you right now. What do you seriously need me to do to help you get through the evening?'"

The consensus that came out of our discussion is that it is much better, when conflict arises, to take a step back to give both partners time to calm down and think the issue through. Tom says, "My tendency was to badger Brynn to deal with it *now*. I've tried to learn not to push the issue but to be sensitive to the right time."

Christians are accustomed to hearing Ephesians 4:26–27, "'In your anger do not sin': Do not let the sun go down while you are still angry, and do not give the devil a foothold," as a biblical command to resolve conflict quickly. They tend to interpret this passage as meaning, "Talk it through right away. Hash it out, get it resolved." But let's look at these verses from a different angle.

Unresolved conflict has rightly been called "the marriage killer." Talking it through *is* crucial. But trying to talk it through before you've gained control over your own attitude can do more harm than good. I see the above Scripture passage not so much as a challenge to finish an argument before bedtime as a warning to examine my own heart and deal with my anger before God first. Notice the quotation marks in verse 26? The apostle Paul is quoting Psalm 4:4: "In your anger do not sin; when you are on your beds, search your hearts and be silent."

Brynn says, "It's time to pray, 'Open his heart, open my heart.' It could be that it's not him, it's me; I'm the one who needs to open my heart and see what needs to be done to have a better relationship." When I've taken the time to cool down and repent of my own wrong attitudes and actions, I have a better chance of dealing with conflict in a constructive way. And sometimes during these heart-searching sessions, I become aware of factors — hormones, stress, fatigue — that may be causing me or Jon to overreact to things that might not normally bother us as much.

Besides, everything looks darker at night. Scott says, "Once Jennifer and I start talking, my attitude is, 'Okay, we're not going anywhere until we resolve this.' But Jennifer is saying, 'It's 11:30 at night! I have to go to bed! You don't understand — I'm getting madder every second I'm awake!'" Jennifer adds, "It's hard, because we want to wait until Wes is asleep. But we've learned that discussing things at night is not for us." Shelley agrees: "I like resolution. I like closure. But I've learned there's going to be less anger if we wait until the next day."

Instead of debating into the wee hours, try making a breakfast or lunch or naptime appointment to discuss the problem, agreeing to pray and search your own hearts in the meantime. Find a babysitter if you have to. You'll be amazed at how much more quickly you can resolve issues when you're fresh and when you're each seeking not your own solution but God's. And remember — in a thriving family, the goal of your discussion is not to "win" or to vindicate yourself. A loss for one of you is a loss for both. Your goal is to answer the question, "How can we get through this with our differences resolved, so that we can move forward as a united and loving husband and wife?"

> In a thriving family, the goal of your discussion is not to "win" or to vindicate yourself. A loss for one of you is a loss for both.

What has to be agreed on by both of you is that you *will* get through it. When Jon and I married, we decided together to "burn our ships." Divorce was not an option. Any problems would have to be worked through, not escaped from. Tim agrees: "Trudy and I are committed to each other, till death do us part. If there's a problem, we're committed to work it out. There's no 'We can't.' Knowing we have that foundation makes it easier to talk things out."

So — you have a conflict looming. You've both taken a step back to think and pray about your own role in the problem. You've agreed together that you *will* get through it — no one's going to bail out of the relationship. You've made an appointment to get up before the baby does tomorrow morning to talk about it, or to get together during the baby's nap, or you've called a babysitter to come over for a couple of hours while you go for a drive together. Below are a few tips on how to come through it with a stronger, closer relationship.

But first, a quick note: Once you discover what following these steps can do for your relationships, you'll be highly motivated to continue using them. However, it will take determination and self-discipline to get started, especially if you have a tendency to be quick-tempered. Dealing with conflict in a positive way doesn't come naturally; most people tend to go into either "avoid" or "attack" mode when problems arise. It can help to read through these steps together and discuss them at a time when you're not in conflict. Then make a commitment to each other that when conflict arises, you'll pull them out again and follow them. You'll be very glad you did.

Before you come together, take an honest look at your own flaws. Understanding how much you need forgiveness is the first step toward learning to forgive others. As you do this, you may become aware of ways you've been contributing to the problem. If so, great! Confession and repentance are powerful keys to your spouse's heart. A sincere apology, coupled with a commitment to change, can work wonders to resolve conflict.

Pray together first. This is important, not only because God will hear and answer but also because the discipline of sincere prayer takes your mind off your own agenda and puts it on God's. Resist the temptation to pray "at" each other. Lay the situation in God's hands, praying what author Jan Karon calls "the prayer that never fails": "Not my will, but Thine, be done." Ask God to give both of you his perspective and to help you find a solution that's pleasing to him.

Now more than ever, show respect and courtesy toward each other. Offense and defense belong on the football field, not in family relationships. Don't raise your voice, and be careful of your facial expressions and body language. Watch your words carefully. You want your appearance, as well as your words, to convey the message, "You're important to me, and I'm willing to do whatever it takes to work this out."

Don't accuse. One husband says, "It's hard not to get sidetracked when my wife says, 'You never . . .' or 'You always . . .' I start thinking, 'Well, what about *this* time? What about *that* time?'"

Accusations raise your partner's defenses and can quickly become arguments about dueling memories. Instead, several young parents recommend "I" statements. Stephanie says, "It's easy to accuse. But when you tell your husband, 'I feel . . .' you have to think about what you're saying. You're not just lashing out." "It gives you an out, and it gives him an out," adds Shelley. "I could be feeling wrong. I could be taking it the wrong way. But you have to be honest — 'I do feel this way.' At least then you can talk about it. 'Why do you feel that way?'" Scott says, "That keeps me from getting defensive. When Jen says, 'I feel like this when you do that,' it gets me thinking about how to solve the problem. What can I change to help her not feel that way?"

Don't dismiss your spouse's feelings. I have a wise husband. I remember sobbing to him once, "I'm sorry, I know I shouldn't feel this way . . ." Jon stopped me gently and said, "Karen, whether you should or not, the reality is that you do. That's what we need to deal with." By his words, and by his actions that followed, he showed me that my emotional needs were more important to him than some ideal of how I "ought" to feel. He focused on my needs rather than on how those needs were inconveniencing him. (How could I possibly not love a guy like that?)

Stick to the subject. During your discussion, you may be reminded of another grievance against your spouse. Be very careful. It can be tempting to say, "While we're at it . . ." and try to clear the entire slate at once. But sometimes, the more you say, the less your spouse can hear. Being asked to correct one problem is painful, but doable. Being asked to correct an entire list may cause your spouse to wonder, "If I'm so flawed, why on earth did you marry me?"

It's usually best to deal with one issue at a time. If the grievance you've been reminded of truly is an issue, it will come up again.

Trust each other. In a thriving marriage, the partners are not hung up on issues of self-defense. Because they feel emotionally safe with each other, they can be quick to recognize and repent of their mistakes, as well as to forgive each other and move on.

It takes a lot of trust to bring up an area of conflict in a humble, approachable way. And it can be scary to humble yourself and say, "I'm sorry" (especially when you're afraid the response might be, "You sure are!"). But remember: Humility and trust build bridges between you. Pride and fear build walls.

Be worthy of your partner's trust. In order for your spouse to feel safe enough to bring up an issue, she has to be able to trust that you'll care, that you'll listen, and as one wife said, "that you won't make me feel stupid." Several spouses said it sometimes took them days, or even weeks, to build up the courage to bring up an issue. Handling a conflict badly can make it less likely that your spouse will feel able to come to you next time.

All the things we've already listed will help you earn and keep your partner's trust. Here are some other tips:

Really listen. It can be tempting to cut short a discussion you find unpleasant. But if you do, you miss a lot. You may hear your spouse's words but miss his or her heart. "I'm impatient," says one young husband. "I want it resolved. So I'm like, 'Okay. I heard it. You're saying the same things you just said. I understand, and I'm fine.'" Meanwhile, his wife may not be fine. She may be repeating herself not because she thinks he didn't hear her but because she needs reassurance that her husband understands how important the issue is to her. His cutting her off just makes her feel more insecure.

> Conflict is painful. In order for it to be worth the pain, your spouse needs to know you won't just shrug off what you've learned. In a thriving marriage, conflict is seen as a bugle call for action.

Give your spouse the benefit of the doubt. Don't assume you know his or her motives. If you want to know why your spouse said or did something, ask! If something hits you wrong, rather than reacting, try saying, "I know you would never try to hurt me, but here's how I felt when you said that . . ."

Act on what you've learned. Conflict is painful. In order for it to be worth the pain, your spouse needs to know you won't just shrug off what you've learned. In a thriving marriage, conflict is seen as a bugle call for action.

Respect your spouse's privacy. Tim says, "It's important to keep things between us. Not between Trudy and her mom, or between her and fifteen friends. Our conflicts stay at home, to work through by ourselves." Remember, though, we're talking about a thriving family. In a troubled marriage, outside counseling is often useful and even necessary. But be sure to find a qualified, trustworthy counselor.

Be faithful to each other. The people I've interviewed who are in thriving marriages tend to see this as a no-brainer, but it needs to be included. Jesus set a high standard for marital faithfulness: not just physical, but mental and emotional as well. In a thriving Christian marriage, the husband and wife aren't seeking fulfillment in romance novels or pornographic magazines or drooling over the latest idol out of Hollywood. They're focused on meeting each other's romantic and sexual needs. Problems in this area, as in any other, are worked through.

Invest in the relationship. "I believe a lot of problems can be prevented by doing things to make the relationship better," says Tim. "Get away every now and then without the kids. And Trudy and I pray together. The more things you can do like that to help build a healthy relationship, the fewer problems you'll have."

TIME

How do you spell love? T-I-M-E.

In the mathematics of human relationships, time plus attention equal love. "I think the number one mistake new parents make is they just don't realize how much time you have to devote to it," says Doug. "They want to squeeze it in, in the midst of everything else. That's the mistake I made." Doug calls the idea of spending small amounts of quality time together a myth. "Quantity has to come first."

Real quality time usually comes unexpectedly, in the midst of quantity time. The more oysters you open, the greater your chance of finding a pearl. The more time you spend together (TV time doesn't count), the more frequent those special, quality times will be.

Your time and undivided, positive attention are the most valuable gifts you can give your family. And of course, like any valuable gift, they will cost you. Saying yes to time together means saying no to something else. When asked what the best time is for uninterrupted talks with her husband, Brynn says, "Usually during Cole's nap on the weekends. Which can be really hard at this time of year. Football will be on, and Tom will turn off the TV and talk to me. Nothing tells me he loves me more than that."

The gift of your time and attention is really an investment that will pay off in a rich relationship with your spouse and children, as well as in the satisfaction of knowing you gave your family the very best you had to offer. Lisa says, "Andrew and I try to remember that we need to appreciate and make the most of the time we have as a young family right now. We will never be able to go back and reclaim these precious years!"

Since people interpret time and attention as love, it's not surprising that many new fathers are alarmed that they're suddenly getting a lot less of both from their wives. "Debby and I were married for three and a half years before Lisa was born," says Joe, "and we did everything together. After several months as a new father, I suddenly realized that the time I was getting from Debby had been, at its very best, cut in half. Talk about an adjustment! I'm not sure I can say how I handled it, other than sulking. My first reaction was to stay away. I felt really unsure of myself with Lisa, and I thought that if I could just continue providing for them, I'd be fulfilling my responsibility. I had no hands-on experience with Lisa."

His wife, Debby, says it wasn't until years later that Joe shared his feelings with her, probably because jealousy is not an attractive trait in a new father. But Joe says now, "Communication is the best route to healing. If you and your wife can just talk about why you're no longer getting all her attention, you'll work through it all right."

Our other dads claim that jealousy — or at least ambivalence — toward the new baby is normal. But it's interesting that the fathers who had little or no trouble with feeling displaced are the ones who jumped into fatherhood feet first and became actively involved in their children's care. "When Wanda was pregnant, there were times when she couldn't share with me how she was feeling," says Dennis. "And we didn't go through natural childbirth back then, but once Michelle was born, she became a focal point for our family. She became just one more thing Wanda and I had in common — something else to share. We became much closer and had more to talk about, especially since Michelle was so close to our hearts. I think we planned more and dreamed more."

Try to remember that your wife isn't focusing on the baby because she loves her more than she loves you; it's just that, in her mind, your baby needs her more than you do. Become involved with your child instead of dwelling on your hurt feelings. Of course, new mothers being what they are, you may have to pry your wife loose at times. Mothers can become so wrapped up in their babies' needs that they tune everything else out, but your wife really needs frequent breaks even if she seems reluctant to take them. Your involvement can help relieve that obsession and restore some balance to her life and to your family.

Stephanie has some advice for young mothers on this subject: Trust your husband, and don't hover. "Provide time for them to be alone together, without you anywhere near. I was so controlling when Rachel came home! Everything Roy did, I'd tell him, 'This is how you have to do that.' When I finally left her alone with him for a few hours at around six weeks old, he freaked out. After that, I had to go back to work for a couple of months, and he had to take care of her. It was the best thing that could have happened. They got so close during that time. And it was okay if she woke up in the morning and had her pajamas on backwards." Yes, babies do have special needs, especially in the safety department, and you need to make sure that both you and your husband are aware of them. But remember, your baby is his child too.

Nurturing tasks — feeding, diapering, bathing — are good ways for a new father to spend time with his baby. Several dads also said they enjoyed lying on the floor or couch with the baby on their stomach. A nursing mother gets plenty of cuddle time simply by feeding her baby, but a daddy has to go out of his way to hug and hold his child — something that doesn't come naturally to many fathers. Tim says, "It's important to have that close contact, and it's something I neglected at first, expecting Stella to do it all. The children need it, but *I* need it too, not only to help Stella but also to get to know my children. I'm still working on it."

Of course, a newborn won't be able to react to you as much as she will when she grows older, but those early interactions are important to help you bond with each other. And it will get easier as your baby's personality develops. One of our dads, who shall remain nameless, said, "Our daughter was a slug until about six months." (Speaking of slug, that's what his wife did to him when he said that. Actually, a baby's personality starts peeking through long before she's six months old!)

David is a music director whose ministry frequently keeps him out at night. He says, "I work during the day and am home for maybe two or three hours in the afternoon, and I'm rarely there when Ashley goes to sleep at night. I've had to learn to make the time I do have with her of good quality. It's extremely important when I walk in the door to put everything else aside." To other new fathers intent on building their careers — but not at the expense of their families — he says, "Make the most of your time at home. If you come home tired, put yourself aside for a while and interact with your child. The floor is one of the best places. Don't make whatever you do halfhearted — make it valuable time, something that will fulfill your child's need for a father."

"Fathers are at a disadvantage in the war against time," says Phil. "We're gone eight to ten hours a day, then comes the nighttime routine of dinner, bath, cleaning up, and bedtime. Where's the time for actual father-child interaction? ('Sit up straight!' and 'Don't put that in your nose!' don't count.) I have to fight the natural urge to sit on the couch after dinner and watch the news. Cheryl and I tag-team the nightly routine, then make time to snuggle and read with the kids on the couch. I spend a lot of quality time with my kids, but I can often look back and see missed opportunities." Phil says one of his favorite activities with his children is to turn on the stereo and dance in the living room.

"I really enjoy playing with Wes," says Scott. "One of the things Jennifer taught me early on was, 'Pay attention to him. Watch what he's doing.' When I do that, looking into his eyes instead of being focused on how tired I am or what I'd rather be doing, it becomes more fun to be with him."

Tom says, "I used to think quality time meant sitting down and helping my kids learn the alphabet or studying the Bible together — which is all fine — but some of the most special times I've had with Aaron, who is three now, have been just doing yard work. He'll ask me how the lawn mower works, or why you change the oil in a car — just ordinary, everyday things you wouldn't think would be important to a child. He was fascinated by the way I repaired the lawn mower. He has a toy one, and now he never uses it without turning it over and checking to see if the blade is 'sharp.'"

> "I really enjoy playing with Wes," says Scott. "One of the things Jennifer taught me early on was, 'Pay attention to him. Watch what he's doing.' When I do that, looking into his eyes instead of being focused on how tired I am or what I'd rather be doing, it becomes more fun to be with him."

All of these fathers recommend that you *not* have the TV on while you play with your baby. Your child needs and deserves your undivided attention. Mike says, "If I'm going to watch any TV, it's going to be after they're in bed. Until then, it's got to be off, or I'll be distracted."

"Andrew used to have to make a conscious effort to put aside his agenda," says Lisa, "and sometimes I know he didn't feel like it at all! But in the last few years,

I've seen it become increasingly easier and more natural for him to focus on the kids and prioritize their needs. I even see them help him relax and enjoy himself after a long day. It's a two-sided blessing — good for the kids, and good for him."

Playing together and caretaking are not the only ways a father can grow close to his children, of course. As head of the household, it's vital that he participate in the more serious side of his child's life as well. "Being there for teachable moments is important," says Lisa. "It lets the kids know that Daddy is not only the financial provider but also their teacher and confidant. It sets the stage and develops the relationship to help them be comfortable coming to him in future years with their questions and concerns." (In chapters 8–11 we'll talk about ways to help a young father stay involved in his child's character development.)

Jennifer says, "I tell my husband that every minute he spends with our little girl is a treasure she'll have for the rest of her life." What legacy do you want to leave your children? You have no way of knowing how long you'll have to build it. "I lost my father when I was five," says Wayne, "and Mom never remarried, so I've been without a father for practically my whole life. My fondest memories are of the days I spent with my dad. I remember that he always had time for me, and anytime he went somewhere where he could take me, he would. So I've purposed in my heart that I'll always be there for my kids and that I'll never be too busy for them."

How much you value your family time will be shown by how carefully you guard it. "We're very protective of our evenings," says David. "We limit church meetings, telephone conversations, and anything else that threatens to invade the few precious hours we have together."

David and his wife Nancy are both active at church — David in music ministry, Nancy in drama. But, he says, "We constantly work to keep things balanced. With any new requests for our time, we discuss whether it's wise to take on that increased responsibility. We've rejected the notion that 'Somebody has to do it, so I guess I will.'"

One of the biggest thieves of quality family time sits right in the family room (and maybe in the bedroom and kitchen as well) — the TV. Stephanie says, "That's the worst mistake we ever made. For our first two years of marriage, we didn't even have a TV. Then we got one. Then we got cable. Now I want to shoot the thing. But it's hard to convince my husband to give it up. And it's so tempting to get up in the morning and go, 'I'm exhausted!' and *click* — the kids are occupied. Getting a TV is the worst thing we ever did."

The television can become a real point of contention, especially if one spouse is emotionally hooked while the other isn't. (I consider a person emotionally hooked on the TV if he or she feels a need to have it on to relax. And yes, I've been there too.) We'll talk more about TV in chapters 8 and 10. Meanwhile, see the earlier section on communicating needs and expectations.

Many of the men and women I interviewed struggle with the Mary-Martha syndrome — acknowledging that their family relationships are important, but feeling pulled toward business or housework that brings them results they can actually see. Shelley says, "I was starting to use evenings to do my housework. It was like, 'I've got to do one more load of laundry,' or, 'I didn't get that done today because of Wendy, so I'll do it now.' I thought, *This is really good — I'm starting to get some things done!* But I was taking the time away from Glenn. One night we got angry with each other because of it. It was a big wake-up call for me. My priority in the evening has got to be getting my child in bed on time and not doing laundry or vacuuming or whatever after Glenn gets home. Because we need time together."

Glenn adds, "One of my commitments to Shelley is to come home on time. This is the same thing." She agrees: "I would be really aggravated if he were working late all the time, and that's exactly what I was doing. But I didn't realize it."

"My father told me this," says Tom, "and I try to do it: If you need to spend extra time at work, try to go in early rather than come home late."

David says, "Fortunately for Nancy and me, I gave up looking for fulfillment in my career several years before Hannah was born. I adopted the philosophy, 'This company was running before I got here, and it will keep running after I leave. It won't hurt them if I leave on time.' Nancy supported me by saying she valued my being at home more than my reaching some lofty position at work."

"Andrew works in the food industry," says Lisa. "He could easily have a job that requires weekends and holidays as well as late nights. He purposely sought out a job that is Monday through Friday, no holidays — which was difficult to find — so he could spend time with us."

By realizing the issues involved and making the decisions they have, these people are telling their families, "You're more important to me than a clean house, more important than gaining more power and money and prestige at work."

Making family time a priority is a challenge for these young couples. Making time to be alone together is an even bigger challenge. And yet, according to them, it's crucial.

"Probably the most difficult thing I've had to adjust to regarding our relationship is the infrequency of truly 'alone as a couple' time," says David. Nancy adds, "When we do make time for each other, we can hardly stay awake long enough to do anything fun!"

This is another area where you'll need to communicate. Resist the idea that your time alone together has to look like some conventional view of a "date." What you do isn't important. What's important is that you both enjoy it and that it provides you with quality time where you can focus on being not Mommy and Daddy but husband and wife. Lisa says, "Andrew and I are both of the opinion that it's usually harder than it's worth to go out. We do have home movie dates and sit by the fire together. Or we sit outside on the porch during nice weather."

> Resist the idea that your time alone together has to look like some conventional view of a "date." What you do isn't important. What's important is that you both enjoy it and that it provides you with quality time where you can focus on being not Mommy and Daddy but husband and wife.

At the same time, it can be helpful to schedule your dates in advance to make sure they happen, especially if a babysitter will be needed. Nancy says, "We bought season tickets to the theater to insure a special date on a regular basis."

"Cheryl and I set aside two Fridays each month for a date night (which just happen to coincide with paydays)," says Phil. "It was definitely hard to keep that commitment when Emily was a newborn, and we missed some Fridays. Now that the kids are older, though, they know Mom and Dad have a date every other Friday. We may just eat a cheap meal and walk around Wal-Mart, but it focuses us on each other at least twice a month. It also encourages Cheryl to see my determination to keep our husband-wife relationship healthy."

What about babysitting? If you've got a couple of sets of eager grandparents close by, your problem is solved. If not, you may have to do a little hunting. The first place to check is with your friends who have children — do they have a babysitter they've been particularly pleased with? Or if your church has a bulletin board, check it to see if anyone is looking for babysitting jobs. Or ask your church nursery workers. But be sure you get ironclad references for any potential sitters from people whose judgment you trust. Patty says, "Never leave your baby with someone you don't know, or who isn't recommended by someone you know and trust."

Patti and Sonja were both able to figure out ways to have their babysitting done free. Patti formed a babysitting co-op with several other young mothers, in which points were gained by babysitting for one of the involved moms and spent by having one of them babysit for her children. Sonja developed a similar arrangement involving only one other couple: "When our children were four years and fifteen months old, we made arrangements with some friends who had children the same ages to switch off babysitting duties with us on alternating Friday nights. We've been doing it for nine months now — our marriages have blossomed, and our wallets aren't flat."

TEAMWORK

Finally, in a thriving family the husband and wife see themselves not as two solo players in separate arenas but as a team. And while the game is in progress, all the players are on the field.

Here are some characteristics of a thriving family team:

Common Goals

Good communication, reading and discussing books together, and taking marriage and parenting courses can help you establish common goals. Paul and Phyllis, a wise couple of my acquaintance, have come up with a mission statement for their marriage and family. Each year on their wedding anniversary, they take time to look at their purpose and discuss how they're doing.

Having common goals means that everyone in the family is on the same side. Can you imagine the chaos if the members of a basketball team suddenly started ignoring the real opponents and playing against each other? The spectators would think they'd lost their minds, and any chance of winning would fly out the window.

Such a thing could never happen on a championship team, where the members have learned to work together toward their common goal of winning the game. In the same way, on a thriving family team no adversarial relationships — husband versus wife, kids versus parents — are allowed to develop. Problems are talked through and worked out. And as the children grow, the parents work hard to help them see that they, too, are on the same team. (More about that in chapter 10.)

Common Effort

It's not uncommon for a new mother to feel as though she's been pushed out onto the playing field by herself, with her husband munching hot dogs and yelling, 'Atta girl!' from the stands. Or maybe he's working in the box office or out mowing the grounds. The point is, he's not on the field with her.

As you may already have discovered, this doesn't work too well. The mothers I interviewed whose husbands were actively "on their team" valued them tremendously, and those whose husbands weren't found themselves fighting resentment. One said, "Life will never be the same for a woman after she has a baby, and her husband needs to understand that it's not going to be the same for him either."

Feelings of fear and awkwardness—especially when the baby is very young—can stand in the way of a new father's involvement. A brand-new father of my acquaintance says that his main feeling is one of helplessness: "I don't know what to do with this baby!" he says. "I don't know how to hold her or feed her or change her diaper. I've been buttonholing the nurses in the halls and asking, 'Show me how to change my baby's diaper.'"

To tell the truth, most new mothers feel as inept as new fathers do when presented with their babies for the first time. It's just that they have no choice. Somebody's got to change the diapers and give the baths, and they're the most likely candidates. The involved fathers I've interviewed say that the way to overcome your feelings of awkwardness is to do what new mothers do: jump right in. Read the little how-to pamphlets your wife brings home from the obstetrician and collar the nurses and ask if there are any training films for new fathers offered at the hospital. The more knowledge and experience you gain, the more confident and competent you'll feel with your child.

Watch the way your wife and the nurses hold and diaper the baby. And David recommends asking your wife for instructions, or at least being tolerant when she inevitably starts to give advice. But relax. You do have to be careful when handling your baby, but he's not as fragile as he seems—and he won't stay that little for long. Tom says, "Our boys went through that stage so fast—Pene and I hardly remember it."

Another thing that can stand in the way of a new father's involvement is confusion about what his role "ought" to be. It can be hard to remember that the true standard for a Christian father is not his own father, or what he's seen on TV, or other young fathers (although the dads in this book are unanimous in their opinion that the current cultural trend toward fatherly involvement is a healthy one). The true standard for a Christian husband and father is this: "Husbands, love your wives, just as Christ loved the church and gave himself up for her" (Eph. 5:25).

Verses 26 and 27 explain *why* Jesus gave his life for the church: *to enable her to become all God intended her to be*. Without his sacrifice, that would have been impossible. The same is true in Christian marriage. My husband, Jon, is a great example — if not for his strong support and sacrificial love, this book would never have been written, and I'm sure I would not be who I am.

The scriptural command for husbands to love their wives "just as Christ loved the church" is a command to demonstrate sacrificial and redemptive love. Jesus' love for the church took him to Gethsemane, then to Golgotha. For young husbands intent on following his example as the spiritual head and Christ-figure in their homes, this rule of thumb applies: If it doesn't hurt, at least occasionally, you're probably not doing it right. The payoff, and the balance, is that your loving sacrifice inspires your wife to respond with loving respect and enables your marriage to become a true reflection of Christ and the church (not to mention a really great place to be).

This is serious stuff, because the husband's servant-leadership of the "home team" is, I am convinced, the single most crucial factor in determining whether his family will thrive. There are many reasons for this, but here's one of the most important: Your wife is physically and emotionally vulnerable after childbirth and may also feel isolated. Your involvement — especially when it means stepping in to meet her needs as well as the baby's — makes her feel cherished and lets her know she is not alone.

Look at the example of these young fathers:

David says, "The first four months were extremely difficult for us. It wasn't uncommon for Ashley to wake up ten or twelve times a night, or to cry for forty-five minutes and then sleep for forty-five minutes all night long." Ashley suffered from colic, an ailment we discuss more thoroughly in chapter 6. Fortunately, most babies don't have colic, but David's advice to new fathers with a colicky baby is to hang in there: "I tell everybody who approaches me with the same problem, 'This, too, shall pass.' And it did. She grew out of it. But there were times in the middle of the night when Christine just couldn't take any more, and I would have to step in and take over. The Lord really helped us get through those difficult times, and I felt it was very important as the head of the home to minister to Christine and keep building her up, especially since she tended to get depressed about it and think she had done something wrong to give Ashley colic."

"Wanda and I took turns getting up," says Dennis, whose daughter, Michelle, also suffered from colic. "The Lord always made sure one of us had

> The scriptural command for husbands to love their wives "just as Christ loved the church" is a command to demonstrate sacrificial and redemptive love.

just a little more energy or patience or understanding when the other one didn't. I was both working and going to school back then, and I missed out on a lot of sleep, but the Lord pulled me through."

Wayne says his active role in fathering has been good for his marriage: "Karin and I had to pull together as a team," he says. "She lost her mom right after Matthew came, and that made things even rougher on her. We did a lot of extra praying and seeking God, and the Lord brought us through some hard times. It really brought us closer."

Teamwork sometimes means carrying more than your share of the load when your teammate is exhausted or sick or stressed, but in a thriving family, both partners are aware that the condition is temporary and that the favor will be returned when the need arises. Lisa says, "It's been a blessing to all of us that Andrew is an involved father. Not only has it been great for him and the kids, but he has rescued me on more than one occasion from overwhelming exhaustion and frustration with sick or teething children who were not sleeping. The Lord always makes sure one of us has just enough energy to cope with the situation. It has been very comforting to know that if I'm 'losing it' with the kids, I can go to Andrew and say, 'Here — take him. I can't do this anymore.'"

Jennifer has a bit of advice for new mothers on this subject: "Ask for help. My husband will do anything I ask him to. If I don't ask, he feels like I don't need him." Husbands do tend to assume (aargh!) that we're doing okay without their help unless we speak up. Besides, as the manager of the home, you'll probably always be more aware of what needs to be done than your husband will. This isn't a shortcoming on his part; it's just reality. You'll need to delegate to him, and later to your children, what they need to do around the house as part of the family team. As you communicate your needs in a positive way and express appreciation afterward (even if it was something your family members were supposed to do anyway), helping becomes a positive experience for all involved.

A note to new fathers: Don't be offended if there are times, especially with a nursing baby or when the baby is sick, when only Mommy will do. "There's an emotional quality that only a mother can give a child," says Dick, "especially from, say, newborn to one year. I notice this when Adrienne goes to choir rehearsal or somewhere and I'm home watching the children. Stephanie will become fussy, and I just can't quiet her down or meet her emotional needs the way Adrienne can. Of course, the more time I spend with her, the more relaxed she is with me." Joe adds, "But there are emotional needs we fathers can meet for our kids too, especially as they grow older, that Mom can't."

How does common effort in teamwork play out in the daily life of a young family? Probably the most obvious example is in the evenings, when dads of an earlier generation would have been sitting with their pipes and slippers, reading the newspaper. The philosophy of the young parents I interviewed is pragmatic: "You've been working all day and so have I. Let's finish what needs to be done together, so we can both relax."

"That way no one feels like they're always getting the short end of the chore stick," says Lisa. "Andrew quickly learned it was not to his advantage to sit down when I still had a lot of things to get done. I would be miserable and let everyone know it—and if Mama ain't happy, ain't nobody happy! Teamwork is the only way for us. We usually get a few quiet moments to ourselves at the end of the day, which we can use to communicate. We wouldn't have that time, and I wouldn't have the energy, if Andrew wasn't such a big help."

Just as the way to a thriving career is to give more than people expect and to give it cheerfully, so is the way to a thriving marriage—but both partners have to be willing to do it. Mike says, "I get better results if I'm proactive about helping around the house. That's when Elizabeth really appreciates it. Sometimes I'll ask, 'Do you want me to change Hallie's diaper?' and I'm hoping for a no." He laughs. "Just go change the diaper! It'll take five seconds."

Brynn says, "When Tom helps me, it makes me think, *Oh, thank you, God!* He doesn't realize how just unloading the dishwasher takes this huge load off me. Sometimes I feel like, 'Do you realize I've still got to do this, this, this, and this?' When he steps in and helps, it makes all the difference in the world."

"We started a system," says Shannon, "I usually had supper ready when Loren got home, then afterward one of us would put Nathaniel to bed while the other did the dishes. Then the next night we'd switch. It worked out really well. Now, with two children, it's a little different. We each put one child to bed." One advantage of this system is that it prevents your child from becoming dependent on being put to bed by a certain parent.

Her husband, Loren, adds, "After Nathaniel was born we were always struggling with this idea of expectations. Finally we decided that since we're both working during the day [Loren at his job and Shannon at home], when I got home we'd divide the work exactly in half. That's where the alternating system came from. I think it worked well, because we both felt it was fair. It wasn't always exactly equal, but we at least had something to shoot for that we both thought was reasonable."

Common Commitment

Lisa says, "I think our success as a family comes from a simple, basic commitment Andrew and I have equally made. We made the choice to have a family and are both committed to doing whatever it takes to survive, and hopefully to thrive." There, in one sentence, is the real secret to a thriving family: A husband and wife who are both committed to doing whatever it takes to see their family succeed. When that commitment is in place, success becomes largely a matter of learning what it takes. But it's vital to begin learning those lessons early in your family's life, before major mistakes are made.

It's also vital to stay alert and recognize each new lesson as it comes along. After more than twenty-two years of marriage, Jon and I are still learning from each other and from our children, as well as from mentors and peers. I suspect we always will be.

o o o o o

HAVING YOUR FIRST CHILD drops a stone (some might say a boulder) into the pond of your marriage. The ripples go on forever, and each new child introduces new ripples of his or her own. But as you work together to put the principles of this chapter — respect, communication, time, and teamwork — into action in your relationship, you'll find your marriage becoming deeper and richer than you ever dreamed possible. And you'll give your children the happiest of all possible legacies to pass on to the generations to come: a thriving family.

Diaper Duty — and Beyond

Poets and greeting card companies like to use flowery adjectives to describe motherhood: warm, tender, giving, loving. But beneath all the sweetness and light and baby powder, motherhood is something else: *earthy*.

Before long you'll be more familiar with your baby's anatomy than you ever were with your own, and you'll be able to tell what your husband fed Junior for lunch by the color and texture of your child's next dirty diaper. And you'll find, probably to your own amazement, that what was disgusting in the diaper of your neighbor's baby is just a natural part of life when it's your child who's done it. It can even be beautiful — ask any mother who has just seen her baby's first normal dirty diaper after a bout with diarrhea!

Handling their babies' dirty diapers didn't bother most of the parents in this book. All the same, Connie, who has three girls, feels it's important not to make your baby think he's been bad for filling his diaper — especially when he does it as you're walking out the front door or, worse yet, all over you. (Both of these things, by the way, *will* happen at some point. Possibly at several points.) After all, he's just performing a natural function in the only way God gave him to do it. "Sing to your baby and smile while you're changing him," Connie says.

Patty recommends disposable diapers for your baby's first three months at least: "Newborns, and especially breastfed newborns, 'go' continually! Disposables are a very practical gift if anyone asks what you need."

Stephanie warns against stocking up on newborn diapers. "They grow out of those so fast! I just bought regular diapers and flipped them down in front to avoid the umbilical stump." Linda cut a V in the center front of Philip's disposable diapers during his first few weeks to keep his umbilical stump from becoming wet or irritated.

Before Megan was born, I bought a package of each brand of disposables I planned to try. After she arrived I quickly found out which ones worked best for her, and we stuck with those brands from then on.

Save your receipts. Most stores will accept returns on unopened packages. Some will even accept returns on opened packages if you're unsatisfied with the product.

"Try the cheap diapers first," says Stephanie. Christine agrees: "Some store brands are just as good as national brand diapers, and they're much cheaper." Do use diapers with elastic around the legs, though. You'll be sorry if you don't, and so will anyone who happens to be holding your baby when she wets.

Other ways to save money on disposables: clip coupons, stock up during sales, buy diapers at discount warehouse stores.

Most of our babies didn't mind being a bit damp — and those who did, such as Donna's little girl April, let their mommies know about it in no uncertain terms — so you needn't feel your baby's diaper every few minutes. Before each feeding, at bedtime, and whenever you notice that she needs changing is enough. And if your child won't tolerate a damp diaper for even a few minutes, take solace in this: Donna is convinced that April's aversion to soggy drawers is what made her potty training go so quickly later on.

> If your child won't tolerate a damp diaper for even a few minutes, take solace in this: Donna is convinced that April's aversion to soggy drawers is what made her potty training go so quickly later on.

Cheryl discovered that masking tape works well to reseal Jason's and Brian's disposable diapers. Even though her boys are both toddlers now, she still keeps a roll handy for emergencies, such as when Brian manages to pull the diaper tapes loose. It happens. Julie, mother of brown-eyed, curly-haired Sean, says you've never known true horror until you open your child's door in the morning to find him finger painting his crib with the fragrant brown stuff that used to be in his diaper. Megan learned this trick at about fifteen months, and after two or three days of walking in and seeing her grinning at me stark naked from her crib, I took my brilliant husband's suggestion to reinforce her diaper tapes with masking tape *before* I put her down for a nap.

I found disposable diapers especially useful when Megan had diarrhea. The superabsorbent gel in a disposable has a better chance of holding in what might run right out the sides of a cloth diaper. Overnight disposables give even more protection against leaks. Of course, your baby's diaper needs to be changed immediately after each bowel movement when he has an intestinal upset. Also, call your doctor for medical instructions and be extra alert for diaper rash at such times.

When making cost comparisons between cloth and disposable diapers, consider the fact that a baby who needs eighty cloth diapers each week will probably use only fifty or sixty disposables. "With cloth diapers," says Cheryl, who used both, "you have to change the baby more often. Not only does the wetness stay right next to his skin, but you get a strong ammonia smell if he's at all wet. Plus disposables hold more, so you don't have to change the baby every time he wets a little bit."

A friend gave me a dozen cloth diapers before Megan was born. Even though I used disposables, the cloth diapers were great for putting on my shoulder when I held Megan, for draping her face while she nursed, and for mopping up little messes.

If you use cloth diapers, Christine suggests you also use diaper liners, which are available at large discount stores. When your baby has a bowel movement, you just lift the liner out of the diaper, dump the contents into the toilet, and throw the liner away. No rinsing! Even if you use disposables, it might be a good idea to use liners so that you can easily flush your baby's bowel movements rather than putting them into plastic bags for the trash collectors. In many areas it's illegal to dispose of human waste in the same manner as regular garbage.

Connie kept a diaper pail half-filled with detergent and water in her bathroom. As soon as a cloth diaper left her little girl's behind and she flushed whatever extra was inside, Connie dropped it into the pail. When wash time came, it was a simple matter to carry the pail to the washing machine, dump the contents inside, spin dry to get rid of the soapy water, then wash.

"Don't soak cloth diapers in chlorine bleach," says Cheryl. "It'll eat right through them." That's not the only problem with soaking diapers in bleach; several mothers pointed out that the ammonia in your baby's urine, combined with chlorine bleach in a closed diaper pail, creates dangerous fumes.

Most of our cloth-diaper moms washed their children's diapers in detergent and chlorine bleach, then double-rinsed them to make sure no residue was left to irritate their babies' behinds. "Use a wooden spoon to poke the diapers down into the wash water when you're using bleach," says Kristy. "It'll keep your hands from becoming irritated."

A friend of Kristy's received sample foil packets of baby wipes when her child was born. After the wipes were gone, she refilled the packets from the large economy-size tub on her changing table and kept them in her diaper bag.

"Baby wipes are great for trips and outings," says Cheryl, "but if you can't afford them or don't have any on hand, wet a washcloth, wring it out, and put it into a plastic bag." Or take several damp, sturdy paper towels in a plastic bag.

Elizabeth adapted this recipe for homemade baby wipes from one she found in the book *Miserly Moms* by Jonni McCoy: Cut one white Bounty Big Roll in half with a very sharp, heavy (not serrated) knife. Remove the cardboard tube from the center of each half-roll. In a Rubbermaid 2.4-liter round container, mix 2-1/4 cups water, 2 tablespoons baby shampoo, and 2 tablespoons baby oil. Pour one cup of the mixture into another container. Put one of the half-rolls of paper towels into the Rubbermaid container, cut side down, and pour the remaining cup of mixture over the top. Put the lid on and allow to sit for twenty minutes.

In cool weather, warm the baby wipes between your hands before cleaning your baby's bottom, or use a cloth rinsed out in warm water. The same goes for baby lotion — rub it between your hands to take the chill off before applying it to that warm little behind.

It takes just a few hours for a mild case of diaper rash to blossom into a full-blown one, so start treating your baby's diaper area with medicated ointment at the first sign of irritation. With a very bad case of rash, your baby's behind needs as much fresh air as possible to heal. Our pediatricians recommend letting children with diaper rash go without a diaper, but that's not too practical if you value your carpet and furnishings. Try putting your baby into a cloth diaper with no plastic pants and changing him immediately each time he wets.

"Don't use alcohol-based baby wipes on your baby's behind when he has a rash," says Mary Ann. "They sting. Use a soft washcloth wrung out in warm water instead." Once when Megan had diaper rash during a visit to Grandmommy's, my mother showed me how to change her diaper without making her cry. While she was wiping the irritated skin, she blew on it gently — no tears!

Stock your changing table carefully, since unnecessary items just collect dust and create clutter. If a month or so goes by and you realize that something isn't being used, put it away. And be sure to put hazardous items — such as alcohol, lotion, pins, and thermometers — in a cabinet out of reach when your child becomes old enough to crawl and climb.

As she diapered Zachary and Ashley, Terri pointed out to them the diaper pins, lotions, and other changing table items. She says it's also good to get into the habit of explaining, very simply, what you're doing as you give your baby her bath, change her diaper, dress her, or prepare for her feeding. Not only will it be a learning experience for her and help keep her entertained; it'll help prepare you for the thousands of questions that come when she starts to talk.

Megan initiated a contest when she was four or five months old that was still going strong at one year. Her objective was either to sit up or flip off the

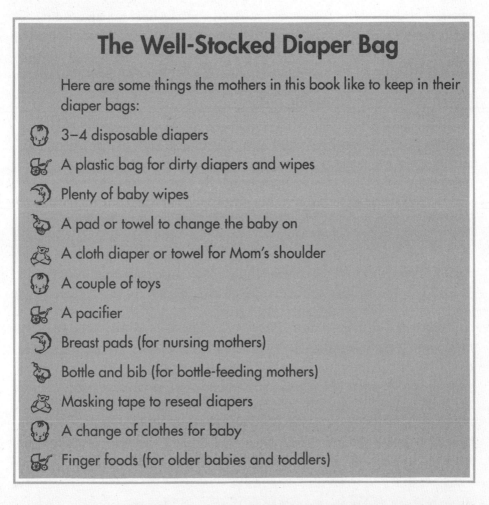

The Well-Stocked Diaper Bag

Here are some things the mothers in this book like to keep in their diaper bags:

- 3–4 disposable diapers
- A plastic bag for dirty diapers and wipes
- Plenty of baby wipes
- A pad or towel to change the baby on
- A cloth diaper or towel for Mom's shoulder
- A couple of toys
- A pacifier
- Breast pads (for nursing mothers)
- Bottle and bib (for bottle-feeding mothers)
- Masking tape to reseal diapers
- A change of clothes for baby
- Finger foods (for older babies and toddlers)

changing table before I got her diaper fastened; mine was to keep her from falling on her head. I found that keeping a couple of special toys at the changing table helped occupy her attention. A piece of waxed paper worked well when I could keep her from eating it, and she also liked playing with the colored ribbons tied to the open woodwork at the top of the table. "We sing songs," says Jennifer. "That distracts Wes."

Several parents said that for safety's sake they began changing their children on the bed or the floor when these wrestling contests began.

It's a big help if you can keep your diaper bag stocked so that all you have to do is pick it up with your baby and walk out the door.

"I went through three diaper bags before I found one that could hold everything I needed," says Lynda. "I'm the typical overprepared mother. When I take Grant to the sitter, I take an extra pair of shoes, extra socks, and two changes of clothes. In a regular diaper bag, the plastic liner was always attached to the handle, and the weight of everything in the bag would tear out the bottom of the liner in just a few weeks. I discovered that an athletic bag — the type you'd take to the gym — works much better. It's sturdier and holds more."

Graduation Day: Using the Potty

The mothers I interviewed are emphatic about *not* trying to potty train a child too soon. Some of their little girls caught on as early as eighteen months, although that was unusual. Most of their children (especially the little boys) were at least two, and often almost three, before they were ready. Pressuring a toddler to potty train too early results in more stress than the Lord ever meant a little child to have to deal with. Christine tells the tragic-comic tale of her little niece waking in the middle of the night sobbing, "But I don't *want* to poo-poo in the potty!" (Her parents got the message and postponed her potty training for a while after that.) Patti, who successfully potty trained her children Keva and Joel and is now working on toddler Jonathan, puts it this way: "When they're ready, it's easy. When they're not, it's a struggle."

Before you start potty training your toddler, realize that it's going to take him a little time to get used to this wonderful new idea. "I don't know how I could have been this dense," says Christine, "but I thought that if you waited until the child was ready, she would catch on the first day you put panties on her, with maybe a couple of accidents. So I tried it, and Ashley did not go in the potty *one time* the first day. So I put diapers back on her for three months. Someone finally told me, 'Chris, it takes a few days.'" Try setting up the training potty in the bathroom and giving your child a few days to become accustomed to its presence before encouraging him to use it.

Potty Training Pointers

Little boys need to see Daddy using the bathroom; little girls need to see Mommy.

Wait to start toilet training until age two, or until your child shows interest (whichever comes first).

Introduce the training potty and let your child get used to having it around before asking him or her to use it.

Look for fun books to read to your child about using the potty. Check your library and bookstore.

Expect and be prepared for accidents. *Never* punish your child for them. Accidents are a normal part of potty training.

Make it fun! Offer rewards for just sitting on the potty at first, then for successful urination and bowel movements. Give lots of praise and encouragement.

Learn your child's "personal potty schedule."

Encourage your child to spend time in the bathroom with other children who are potty trained.

If it becomes a power struggle, take a break from potty training. This is not something you can force your child to do.

An important part of potty training is allowing your toddler to watch you in the bathroom. Children are great imitators, and it's much easier to persuade them that using the potty is wonderful if they see you doing it. In fact, several mothers reported that their children *asked* to start using the potty because it was something their parents did.

Julie, who has two boys, adds: "It's important for little boys to see their daddies in the bathroom. If all they see is Mommy, they'll never understand what's going on."

Don't expect your child to tell you when she has to go. By the time she gets around to telling you, it'll probably be too late. Most of the mothers in this book used a method similar to the one Christine used with Ashley. First, she showed Ashley the training potty and made sure she understood what they were going to do. "Then, when I got Ashley up in the morning, I asked, 'Do you want to go potty?' Yes. So she sat down; nothing happened. Thirty minutes later she wet her pants. I didn't make a big deal of it. I just said, 'Oh-oh, we didn't make it to the potty,' and changed her pants.

"About thirty minutes later, I said, 'Let's see if you can go to the potty, okay?' I had some miniature marshmallows, and I gave her one if she would just try. If she really went, I gave her two or three." With her four children, Joyce used raisins, pineapple chunks, apple pieces — any special treat that your child really likes will do, but be sure that it really is a special treat and not one your child can have any time for the asking. Mary Ann kept a jar of brightly colored jelly beans and let her little boy choose two or three when he was successful.

Shannon's husband, Loren, sat in the bathroom with Nathaniel and read him stories. "That helped him get used to sitting on the potty," she says. "He loves books. The more he went to the potty, the more stories he would get. Also, we used M&M's. Every time he urinated in the potty, he got one, and if he had a bowel movement, he got two."

Encourage your child when he uses the potty successfully. Applaud and tell him how proud you are, how proud Grandma and Grandpa will be. Children really do want to please their loved ones.

The sound of running water helped many of our children to start urinating. For Megan, the sound of water from the tub faucet was more effective than the sound of water from the sink tap.

The most important ingredient to potty training success, according to these mothers, is consistency. "You have to stay on a schedule," says Rita. Standard potty times are first thing in the morning, a half hour or so after each meal or snack, before naps, and right before bedtime, with a few extra times in between. Each child's digestive system is different, and it won't take long for you to learn when your toddler needs to visit the potty in order to train successfully.

When Christine was first trying to potty train Ashley, she had a hard time getting her to sit on the training potty. She says, "Finally, a friend told me, 'It's never going to work if you keep wanting it so badly. Just relax. Tell her very lovingly, "Ashley, I don't care if you're not potty trained until you go to school. As long as you learn before you're six, and when you get into first grade you're not wetting in your seat, it's okay with me." If you'll relax and just keep trying it every now and then to see if she's ready, she'll do it eventually.'"

What finally got Ashley started was that bane of parents everywhere: peer pressure. "We had company. There were four or five kids her age in the house, and they all used the potty except her. The next day after they left, I asked her, 'Do you want to start using the potty?' She said yes." Ironically, Ashley in turn inspired another little friend, Tiffany, to potty train. But be careful that *you* don't pressure your child. Just let her watch her little friends and relatives. She's bound to develop the idea that if they're doing it, it must be fun.

Carol is a former science teacher with four children. She says, "Instead of asking my little boy, 'Do you want to go potty?' because of the pressure involved there, I ask, 'Do you want to empty your bladder?' It works!" Evidently, some toddlers hear the question, "Do you want to go potty?" as a demand for a performance, with all the fear of possible failure such a demand entails. Carol discovered that asking her child if he wants to empty his bladder has really taken the pressure off him. (Of course, it helps to explain very simply to your child what a bladder is.)

Carol's children were more willing to sit on a sturdy wooden training potty with a plastic seat than on a flimsier all-plastic one.

Joyce has some unique advice on potty training boys: "My older sister discovered that her two little boys liked the noise it made when they 'went' into a tin can," she says. "She also discovered that they were always dry when they first woke up. So if their mother came quickly with the little can, the problem was solved. This worked beautifully for me with my two boys. The little tin potty went with us in the car too." Be sure to blunt any sharp edges on the can.

Cil potty trained her twin boys just before they turned three. She said, "We'd write with a marker on the potty and tell them, 'Aim for the spot,' or we'd put a sticker on it. We used lots of stickers." She also found that her boys felt more secure urinating while sitting on the toilet seat, facing backward (straddling it). That way, they could use one hand to hold on to the toilet tank and the other to point their penis downward. This method also helps minimize accidents resulting from poor aim.

Lisa is wondering if modern technology may be contributing to almost-three-year-old Robert's reluctance to potty train. She says, "Diapers these days are very good at keeping wetness away from babies' skin. Robert's 'diapies' are so comfortable and convenient for him that he hasn't had much interest in using the potty." If you suspect this may be true for your child, try the method Terri used with Zachary and Ashley. She put them in two pairs of training pants with plastic pants over them. This gave them protection against wetting but still let her children feel as if they were wearing "big boy (or girl) pants." If you do this, try to make the switch in a positive way. It's best if your child can see it as a privilege and a promotion, not a punishment.

Take note of the time your child usually has a bowel movement each day and schedule your bowel training around it. It was common for our toddlers to take anywhere from a few days to several months to start using the potty for their bowel movements, even after they stopped wetting their pants. Try not to be impatient; for the parents I interviewed, getting angry didn't help at all. Just keep allowing your child to practice after each accident and he'll see the light eventually.

Some children find having a bowel movement in the toilet frightening. Jennifer says, "Wes had a bowel movement in the potty, and it scared him so much! I was on the phone, and I had to hang up because he was crying — 'What happened, Mommy?' It's hard to explain to him, 'It's the same thing you do in your diaper.'"

It wasn't uncommon for our children to continue wetting the bed at night for some time, although some stayed dry through the night as soon as they were potty trained. Nighttime wetting is something your toddler probably has no control over, so don't make him feel guilty for it. Many mothers found it easiest to continue using diapers at night for a while even though their children were in training pants during the daytime.

On the other hand, an older toddler may continue wetting at night simply because she's wearing a diaper and thinks she's expected to use it. Try putting her into regular underwear (or no underwear) at night and explaining, "Honey, you're not wearing a diaper, so if you need to go potty, call me and I'll take you to the bathroom." (And make sure she has a waterproof mattress pad!)

Patti points out that it's unrealistic to expect your toddler to stay dry through the night if you give him liquids at bedtime. "I give my children their last fluids an hour or two before bedtime and then have them visit the potty right before bed." If your child wants a bedtime drink of water, it's probably a good idea to make it a small one.

If your child suddenly starts wetting the bed again after having been potty trained for a while, it may be because of emotional stress. With the parents I interviewed this happened most often when another baby came into the family, but with Scott, Sylvia's little boy, it happened when he started school. "About midway through the school year, he began wetting at night," she says. "Now that I look back, I think probably he could see the difference between what he was doing and what the other kids were doing." Scott was later discovered to be dyslexic and received special tutoring. Mary Ann's son Joseph reverted to bedwetting when his baby brother died. In both cases the wetting eventually stopped.

On the other hand, if your child just can't seem to control herself enough to potty train, don't overlook the possibility of a medical problem. Carol's daughter Kristie was still having trouble when she reached her fifth birthday, and after changing pediatricians was finally diagnosed with a kidney dysfunction that would have resulted in kidney failure had it been allowed to continue.

For an older child whose bedwetting is not caused by a medical problem, check with your doctor about getting an alert system that sets off a buzzer when your child wets the bed.

o   o   o   o   o

A FINAL WORD ON this subject: When at last your toddler is potty trained and you're breathing a sigh of relief, don't throw away those diapers. In his infinite wisdom and sense of humor, the Lord designed children in such a way that by the time they're toilet trained they're also just about old enough to start asking for a little brother or sister.

Chapter 4

Breast and Bottle

When baby formula was introduced to the public in the first half of the twentieth century, it was hailed as technology's best for the modern baby. But in recent years, science has realized what many wise moms knew all along; namely, technology ain't got nothing on God.

Give serious thought to your decision of whether to breast- or bottle-feed your baby. It's more than just a matter of preference. God designed every part of your body for a reason, and when you use your breasts to feed your child, you're fulfilling the primary purpose for which they were created. If your baby is already here and you're bottle-feeding, don't despair. Many of the parents in this book were raised on formula and are now healthy adults. We include tips on bottle-feeding later in this chapter, but please do go ahead and read the first sections. My hope is that you'll be encouraged to nurse your next baby. "Breast really *is* best" for many reasons, as the next few paragraphs will show.

Even the baby formula manufacturers today admit that breast milk is the perfect food for your baby, and they include a disclaimer to that effect on their labels. Breast milk is more easily digested and less apt to cause stomach upset than formula. And of course, formula contains none of the antibodies present in breast milk, which researchers now believe can help protect your child from many different kinds of infections. In fact, the American Academy of Pediatrics claims that breastfeeding may continue protecting your child from various illnesses into adulthood.

There are other benefits to breastfeeding as well. Did you know that a woman who nurses her children is less likely to get breast cancer and that the longer she nurses, the greater the protection? Also, according to *The Complete Book of Breastfeeding* by Marvin S. Eiger, M.D., and Sally Wendkos Olds, new ingredients are constantly being discovered in mother's milk: "One recently discovered component in breast milk is a fatty acid known as DHA (docosahexaenoic acid), which appears to be vital for newborns' brain and eye development. As of this writing, in the United States DHA is not added to formula, which means that the only way babies can get it is through their mothers' breast milk." Add to all these benefits the fact that, since breast milk is such a complete food, most pediatricians agree that your baby needs no other sources of nourishment — not even water — until he's four to six months old.

Now, it's only logical that anything *that* good for your baby — and for you — has got to be hard to do, right?

Wrong.

My paternal grandmother was a smart, sturdy country woman who nursed nine healthy children. She took pride in the fact that her babies all gulped to keep up with the flow of her milk, and while visiting paid me the compliment of observing that Megan was doing the same thing. Yet before Megan was born, when folks asked whether I planned to nurse, I would reply, "I really want to. I hope it works out."

> Just as I was, most expectant mothers I've talked with are nervous about nursing. Part of it has to do with fear of the unknown. After all, the idea of producing food in your body for someone else is pretty strange.

Just as I was, most expectant mothers I've talked with are nervous about nursing. Part of it has to do with fear of the unknown. After all, the idea of producing food in your body for someone else is pretty strange. But I suspect that another reason for our nervousness is centered around the horror stories we've been told by mothers who "tried to nurse, but couldn't" — mothers who themselves probably went into nursing filled with fears and misconceptions and without adequate emotional and practical support.

The truth is, there's just not that much to it. Nursing is much less complicated and requires less effort than bottle-feeding, though it does take more time.

Try thinking about it this way: The past couple of generations notwithstanding, nearly every baby ever born has been breastfed. A lot fewer of us would have survived if it were all that difficult.

But this is not meant to paint an overly rosy picture of breastfeeding. It's easy to feel like the Lone Ranger while you're nursing, since it's a serious responsibility no one else can take for you. Also, most of our nursing mothers went through an adjustment period of about four to six weeks. The major contributing factors were the fatigue and readjusting hormones resulting from pregnancy and childbirth, as well as some initial breast tenderness and nipple soreness. Add to all this an overanxious nonnursing grandma or two, and a baby's first few weeks can be pretty difficult for his new mom. Lynda says, "I was so gung ho about nursing before Grant was born, but when I got home from the hospital, everything changed. One of my friends encouraged me, 'Give it at least two weeks.' If she hadn't, I probably would have given up."

Jan is another nursing mother who had a difficult adjustment period: "When Jordan David was a week old, I was so engorged that I could hardly stand having a nightgown touch me, much less a bra or my baby's sucking. There were a couple of times when I cried through the first few minutes of the feeding because it hurt so much. During those crying times, I just kept reminding myself of the advantages to Jordan David and me, and that I really wanted that special time with my baby. Everything is going great now — still nursing at six months."

Engorgement can be painful, but it doesn't last long, and it doesn't happen to all nursing mothers. (I know, because it didn't happen to me.) It does, by the way, happen to many nonnursing mothers, since a new mother's breasts naturally gear up to produce milk. For the nursing mother, her baby's feeding relieves the pressure. The nonnursing mother has to wait it out until her breasts stop producing milk, usually within a few days.

Remember, you would go through some kind of adjustment period even if you weren't nursing, and then you'd have to be washing and sterilizing bottles and nipples, boiling water to mix with powdered formula, and warming your baby's bottles at feeding time. The nursing mother has no bottles to wash, no nipples to scrub, no water to boil, no formula to mix. When her baby is hungry, she just plugs him in.

One of the most important benefits of nursing, though — more important than its ease and lack of necessary paraphernalia, more important than its considerably lower cost, and nearly as important to these mothers as its nutritional superiority — is the sense of oneness it gives you with your baby. Without exception, our nursing mothers (even Jan and Lynda) feel they developed a closeness with their children through nursing that nothing else could have given them.

Getting Started

Read everything you can about nursing. It will help take the mystery out of it. One excellent resource has already been mentioned: *The Complete Book of Breastfeeding* by Eiger and Olds. It contains a checklist to help you determine whether your baby is eating enough. This is a huge concern for young mothers — after all, you can look at a bottle and tell how much formula a baby has drunk, but you can't do the same with a breast. You can't even tell by the amount of time a child spends nursing. *The Complete Book of Breast-feeding* lists ways of "judging intake by output" — in other words, using your baby's diapers as evidence — as well as what to look for in terms of your baby's behavior and weight gain.

Along with reading, it's very important to ask questions. "Ask anything," says Cheryl, "even if you think you're supposed to know the answer already." A local La Leche League leader can be a great resource for information, encouragement, and advice. Here's how to find one: (1) Ask your doctor for a list of leaders in your area, (2) look in your phone book, (3) call 1-800-LALECHE (in the U.S.) or (4) check out their excellent website (www.lalecheleague.org).

Basic tips from the experts: Don't go on a diet while you're nursing. Drink at least eight eight-ounce glasses of water a day. Continue taking your prenatal vitamins. Avoid caffeine. Take note of the foods you eat that cause your baby gastric trouble and avoid them. (You'll learn that one quickly!) Finally, check with your doctor or a good medical reference book before taking any medications while nursing.

Expect success, but be prepared in the event of complications. Ask your doctor to recommend a lactation consultant and don't hesitate to call on her. Even if your insurance won't cover the consultation, your money will be well spent if it helps you nurse your child successfully. (Think of it as paying the consultant with the money you're saving on baby formula.)

Surround yourself with support. Find a friend (or several) with positive nursing experience and ask for permission to call if you need advice or encouragement. Most successful nursing mothers are eager to help others succeed. Probably the best place to find these women is in Sunday school classes for young married couples or small group Bible studies targeted to young marrieds. Or ask the nursery workers at your church to recommend a positive nursing mother who might be open to giving advice.

The issue of support is crucial. It was typical for the young mothers I interviewed to be the first nursing mother in their family for several generations. Because of this, not only could they not seek advice from the women in the family, they often faced active opposition. One mom says, "My mother-in-law told me, 'She's not getting enough! You need to quit!' and my mom said, 'I don't know how to help you because I never did this.'" Without a network of friends to encourage and support them, the temptation to throw up their hands and turn to the bottle was too great for several of these mothers.

Fear and concern are factors in family opposition to breastfeeding. But another young mother adds, "I think guilt is part of it. Now all the doctors are saying breast milk is best, and my mom, and my husband's mom too, are feeling like, 'I didn't do it right, then.'"

It can help to be sensitive to the emotional issues involved and to adopt a philosophical attitude. "With my first baby," says Patti, "I was really uptight about everything Grandma did. But I finally realized that the baby won't die if she gives him a bottle, and if it makes her feel better, it's okay — especially since Grandma sees him only once in a while." And take heart. Once Grandma sees that your baby really *is* thriving on breast milk, she'll relax.

Our nursing moms agree that having a husband who supports you in your decision to nurse — and isn't afraid to say so — is essential if you're to withstand opposition from other family members. Milk production is intimately tied in with a woman's emotions. The mother who lacks emotional support from her husband may fail to produce enough milk to nurse or may give up in despair during her adjustment period. By choosing to be a strong source of support and encouragement, a new father can help his nursing wife succeed.

Lisa says, "When I first told my husband I was planning to nurse, he thought I was crazy. He came from a family of bottle-feeders and had never known anyone who had nursed a baby before. It's ironic, but I think from his lack of experience and knowledge at the time, he even thought there was something unnatural about breastfeeding! I talked him into it by telling him

> Fear and concern are factors in family opposition to breastfeeding. But another young mother adds, "I think guilt is part of it. Now all the doctors are saying breast milk is best, and my mom, and my husband's mom too, are feeling like, 'I didn't do it right, then.'"

about all the advantages. It was amazing how quickly he became accustomed to it. He would sit with us sometimes and watch, marveling at how natural and perfect nursing was. He even thanked me later for being willing and able to do this for his children. I'm so glad I stood my ground. And it was great to have Andrew's wholehearted support in front of other uncertain family and friends, who also learned to adjust and accept in time."

Jeff says, "I was never more appreciative of Marilee than when she breast-fed our kids. There's a warmth that's transferred from mother to child that can be lost if she doesn't do it. We assigned so much importance to it that everything else took a distant second place."

Several of the fathers I interviewed say they found the sight of their wives breastfeeding their babies a pleasant one — not only emotionally but sensually as well. "I thought it made Kathy sexier," says Hugh, "and I think somehow it made her feel more womanly. It was a very beautiful thing, especially with our first child."

Elementary as this sounds, a newborn needs help finding the spout where the milk comes out, so make sure you get your baby plugged in at the right spot. Kristy laughs about her experience with this now, but it was very *un*funny to her at the time: "They brought my baby in for her first nursing at about nine at night. Everyone was gone, and the room was dark. I was so naive — I stuck the baby up there and thought everything was fine.

"But it *hurt*, so I pushed the beeper and the nurse came in. I was crying, and I told her, 'This is killing me!' 'Let me check it,' she said. She pulled the baby away, and she hadn't even been on the nipple. There was a big ol' hickey on the side of my breast!"

It can help to have a lactation consultant stop by while you're in the hospital to help get you off on the right foot. Or find the most compassionate nurse around and ask for some pointers.

Sometimes inverted nipples or some other irregularity can make nursing difficult for your baby. Cindy recommends asking your obstetrician before your baby is born whether your nipple shape might pose a problem. "I was having trouble nursing Lindsey in the hospital," she says, "but I didn't realize there was anything abnormal about my nipples until I saw the girl who shared my hospital room nursing her baby." With a little patience, Cindy overcame her problem and was able to nurse Lindsey without further difficulty. Using a special shield or "breast shell" in your bra during your last months of pregnancy can help correct the shape of your nipples. For sources, check with your doctor, a lactation consultant, or the La Leche League.

Any nipple soreness you have should be mild and temporary. If it's not, you need to check your technique, or possibly call the La Leche League or a lactation consultant for advice.

Also, how you attach and disengage your baby will have an influence on nipple soreness. Make sure your child takes as much of the colored portion of the nipple into her mouth as possible. Lisa says, "I had problems with nipple soreness and cracking. My daughter latched on enough to get the milk, but she wasn't taking in enough of the breast to disperse the force of her sucking." When you're ready to remove your baby from your breast, don't just pull her off. Slide a finger into the corner of her mouth to break the suction.

To relieve soreness, try warm or cold compresses, or blowing warm (not hot) air from a hair dryer on your nipples.

Cleaning your nipples with soap or alcohol will dry them out and make them more likely to crack, so just keep them clean with clear water.

"Breastfeeding mothers are told that our milk flows better when we're relaxed," says Cheryl, "but it's hard to relax when your baby is tense and crying. I found that if I took a minute before I picked Jason up and took some deep breaths, put on some quiet music, and said a quick prayer, I could immediately unwind a little."

A wise mother warned me before Megan was born that there would be days when I seemed to do nothing but nurse, and she was right. Breast-fed babies eat more frequently than formula-fed ones — as often as every two hours at first, and sometimes even more often than that. But if you keep your priorities clear, your nursing times become God-given opportunities to relax and cuddle your baby, not interruptions.

Jan says, "I feel breastfeeding is God's way of slowing Mommy down. Sometimes I do absolutely nothing while Jordan David is nursing but watch him. Other times I read the mail or a book, pray, watch TV, or jot down a 'things to do' list."

You're doing so many wonderful things for your baby while you nurse — feeding him the very best food available, meeting his emotional need to be cuddled, and building your relationship. What other activity allows you to accomplish so much in an armchair with your feet up?

Try "treating yourself" while your baby eats. Keep some books you've been wanting to read next to the chair where you nurse. (Joining your local library is an inexpensive way to keep yourself supplied with good books.) Pour yourself a glass of milk or juice before you sit down. Put your feet up. You deserve it! You're doing so many wonderful things for your baby while you nurse — feeding him the very best food available, meeting his emotional need to be cuddled, and building your relationship. What other activity allows you to accomplish so much in an armchair with your feet up?

Nursing even the lightest baby without support will make your arm feel as if it's about to fall off. A thick pillow underneath your elbow will keep your arms and back from becoming tired.

Our nursing moms found that after their milk came in, one breast usually leaked while their baby was nursing from the other, so take breast pads and an extra nursing bra to the hospital with you. You'll probably need to wear breast pads constantly during your baby's first few months, and several companies make disposable ones. Christine, though, made her own reusable pads from cloth diapers, and Terri made inexpensive emergency breast pads by cutting up a disposable diaper. She got about twenty pads from each diaper, and the plastic backing kept her milk from soaking through to her clothing. Linda used thin terry washcloths as breast pads. She just folded them and tucked them into her bra cups.

During your first few weeks of nursing, carry a cloth diaper or a receiving blanket in your diaper bag when you go out, in case you soak through your breast pad. More than once, having a blanket to drape over my shoulder saved me from acute embarrassment.

Several of our nursing moms discovered that when they felt their milk letting down while they weren't wearing pads, they could stop the flow by crossing their arms in front of their breasts and pressing in firmly. In fact, when Megan was a few months old, I eliminated my need for breast pads, except at night, by pressing in on one breast for a minute or so while she began nursing from the other.

You'll need to help your husband understand that all nursing mothers leak at times. It's the way God designed them. Especially during your first weeks of motherhood, stimulation of the nipple is what triggers milk letdown — whether it comes from scratching an itch, your baby's sucking, or your husband's caresses.

Julie wears a front-closing underwire bra instead of a nursing bra. It gives her more support than a regular nursing bra and is easier to unhook discreetly. "Plus it's a whole lot easier to get back into," she says. "You don't have to reach all the way up to your shoulder to rehook it."

"Hallie was a month early," says Elizabeth. "They would only let me go into the NICU at certain times, and every time I went in, she wouldn't eat.

I love nursing, and I was afraid Hallie wouldn't nurse because they were supplementing her with bottles of formula and breast milk. But when we got home, it was fine. I finally realized that she'd been poked and prodded so much in the NICU that she just wanted to sleep when they let me in to nurse. If I have any advice for moms with preemies, it's this: If you really want to nurse, set your mind to it, and it'll probably be okay once you get home. I set my alarm every night and pumped while she was in the hospital."

Nursing babies need to be burped between breasts and at the end of the feeding. I gradually learned that when Megan started to squirm during a feeding, chances were she either (1) needed to be burped, (2) was filling her diaper, (3) was taking a play break (as she grew older), or (4) was full.

Several moms suggest this method of keeping track of your baby's weight between checkups: Weigh yourself, then step back onto the scales holding your baby. The difference between the two weights is your baby's weight. Do this only every couple of weeks, not every day. Babies gain weight in small increments, and worrying day by day about whether your baby is getting enough nourishment can make your milk production go down. Call your pediatrician if you feel your baby isn't gaining weight normally.

Jan warns that just because your baby wants to suck doesn't necessarily mean he's hungry. "I nursed Jordan David for two hours straight one night and he still wanted more. I called my husband's cousin, who's a doctor, and he told me, 'You've overfed him, and his stomach probably hurts. Give him a pacifier and let him suck while you hold him.'"

Be careful, though. Eiger and Olds, in *The Complete Book of Breastfeeding,* warn against offering a nursing baby a pacifier before breastfeeding is firmly established. This is to avoid "nipple confusion," in which the baby rejects the breast in favor of the rubber nipple. For this reason, they recommend no bottles or pacifiers until your baby is six to eight weeks old.

If you're concerned about the possibility of nipple confusion, or if your little one won't take a pacifier, cut your nails short and let him suck on the end of your finger.

Long before your baby starts teething, he may bite down and arch his back, pulling his head away — and your nipple with it. That's an easy habit to nip in the bud, though. Julie did it by tapping Ian on the cheek; Megan responded to a gentle thunk on the back of the head. "Anything to break the baby's concentration," Julie says. "You have to explain to him that your nipple isn't portable; it stays with Mommy."

Several of our nursing mothers, including me, learned the hard lesson that a baby who becomes too accustomed to feeding from only Mommy may refuse to take a bottle at all, which makes it very hard for you to leave her with Grandma or the sitter for an evening out with your husband. To keep that from happening, let your husband give the baby a bottle of expressed milk or formula several times a week after your baby is six to eight weeks old. If you're desperate for sleep, ask your husband to do his feedings at night while you rest. Be careful not to rely on bottle-feedings too much, though, or your milk production will go down.

If you've already gone too long between bottles and your nursing baby refuses to take one, try offering it to her at the beginning of each feeding, while she's hungry. Be persistent — it took Christine a month to retrain Ashley this way. Kathy breastfed her three children, and she says they took their bottles more easily when she rested her hand against their cheek as they drank.

If your baby won't drink from one type of nipple, try another. Cil says, "We tried every nipple on the market. We finally found one that worked." Brynn adds, "Try different formulas, too." (Check with your doctor about which formulas to try.)

Megan flatly refused a rubber nipple but would drink at six months from a hard plastic sip-tip. There are now sip cups available for babies that young.

Don't buy a bulb-type breast pump — not one of our nursing moms had success with it. Hand expressing is much easier. The technique takes a little practice, but according to a nursery worker of my acquaintance, babies who refuse to take a bottle of formula from a stranger will often gulp down their mother's milk. Your obstetrician or his nurse can show you how to express.

The only breast pump that got good reviews from our mothers was the Medela electric pump, which can be rented from some hospitals and pharmacies. Lisa used this method to stock up on expressed milk: She rented the pump for a month, during which time she stored as many bottles as possible in the freezer. When she began to run low on bottles after a few months, she rented the pump again.

Expressed milk will stay fresh for up to two days in the refrigerator or for several months in a freezer below zero degrees Fahrenheit. If you're expressing for long-term storage, keep the bottle you're filling in the freezer, tightly capped. Express into a clean bowl, then immediately pour the milk into the bottle and put it back into the freezer, where it will freeze in layers and stay fresh. I found that expressing an hour or so after a feeding yielded more milk for storage and still allowed me plenty of time to produce milk for

Megan's next meal. Or try expressing from one breast while your baby nurses from the other.

🛒 Don't warm expressed milk in the microwave. Overheating can destroy antibodies and nutrients. Use a bottle warmer, or place the bottle in a pan of warm water until it reaches the desired temperature. Shake the bottle gently and check the temperature carefully before feeding your baby.

🌙 Nursing is more difficult if you must return to work full time, but it's not impossible. Luellen found a nursery close to her workplace and left work twice a day to nurse Benjamin. She also left the nursery workers a small emergency bottle of expressed milk.

Lynne did it this way: She breastfed baby Michael during the weeks she took off after his birth but gave him a small bottle regularly to keep him accustomed to it. When she returned to work, she was still able to nurse Michael for his morning, evening, and late-night feedings, and she expressed several times during the day to keep her milk production up and to prevent her breasts from becoming too full. "Take extra breast pads and a cloth diaper to work with you," she says. "No matter how neat you are when you express, you're going to drip." She also stresses the importance of having a refrigerator nearby if you plan to save your expressed milk for your baby's midday feeding the next day.

🧁 One of the most common arguments against nursing is that it's too restrictive for the mother, but it has been my experience that the nursing mom can go just about anywhere the bottle mom can. All it takes is a little planning. I was able to leave Megan with my parents and go with Jon to Disney World's Epcot Center for a full twelve hours by freezing four feedings in advance and expressing several times (which took only five minutes or so each time) while we were there. Leaving behind plenty of frozen bottles of milk and taking a high-quality breast pump with you would even allow you to leave your baby with Grandma for a weekend alone with your husband.

🛒 Taking your nursing baby with you makes getting out of the house even easier. But you'll need to revamp your wardrobe in case you have to nurse while you're out. The consensus of our nursing moms is that the best blouses for nursing are pullovers and sweaters that you can lift from the bottom. Your baby's face and the folds of your blouse cover your breast, and your baby's body hides your exposed midriff.

> It has been my experience that the nursing mom can go just about anywhere the bottle mom can. All it takes is a little planning.

By the way, *all* (yes, even the most modest ones) of our nursing moms nursed in public at one time or another — and usually no one knew it except the person they were with. Julie says, "You *can* nurse in public. Just take a shawl with you to put over your shoulder and drape the baby's face. And when your baby is older, use a safety pin to attach the shawl to your shoulder, since older babies love to pull it off." Our moms have used this method to nurse discreetly in movie theaters, crowded restaurants (booths work best), and friends' living rooms.

Do be sensitive, though, about nursing in mixed company where everyone will be aware of what you're doing. Husbands whose wives have nursed are usually very comfortable around other nursing mothers. But single men and husbands who've never been around nursing mothers can feel intense discomfort just knowing that a woman in the room has a baby at her breast.

Give your baby the freedom to play at your breast. Feedings are great times for building your child's self-esteem and establishing a healthy liking between you. If your baby likes to pull on your necklaces, try stringing some brightly colored wooden beads and hanging them around your neck for her to play with at feeding time.

A word of warning: Don't depend on nursing as a method of birth control, unless you want another baby right away. Several of our moms learned this by experience.

If your little one suddenly starts waking up ravenous in the wee hours after sleeping through the night for a while, it may be time to ask your pediatrician about giving him some cereal for dinner. This happened with Megan at about four months and will probably depend on your baby's weight.

There's no set rule on when a child should be weaned. The American Academy of Pediatrics recommends nursing through the first full year of your child's life, but there's no reason why you can't keep nursing long past that deadline if you want to. Let your child, your pediatrician, and your own wishes be your guides. Karen nursed Josh, now a two-year-old he-man, for eleven months and wishes it had been longer. "Nurse your baby for as long as you can," she says. "Those are very special times."

Bring on the Bottle

This book is unabashedly pro-breastfeeding, and indeed most of our contributing moms are breastfeeders, although it wasn't planned that way. But there's no need to feel as if you've failed your baby if you can't nurse for some reason. As we said at the beginning of this chapter, many of the parents in this book were raised on formula and did just fine. Also, even the most devoted nursing mother will probably praise God for the invention of the bottle every now and then.

The bottle-feeding mother is, however, faced with a temptation from which the nursing mother is spared; namely, to prop a bottle in her baby's mouth while she takes care of something "urgent" — like housework. Don't do it! The Lord designed your body so that you'd have to cradle your baby in your arms while nursing him, and bottle-feeding needs to approximate this posture as closely as possible. "That time is very important for both of you," says Rosemary, and Wanda recommends that you continue holding your baby during feedings for as long as he'll let you: "That closeness is great, and they grow up way too fast!"

> The Lord designed your body so that you'd have to cradle your baby in your arms while nursing him, and bottle-feeding needs to approximate this posture as closely as possible.

The mothers I interviewed had definite preferences regarding brands and models of bottles and nipples. (In many cases, so did their babies.) When starting out, it's a good idea to buy one or two of each type you might want to use, then stock up once you see which ones your baby responds to best.

After your baby is a month or so old, you may not need to sterilize his bottles and nipples and the water for his formula. Ask your pediatrician; a lot depends on the water in your area.

Powdered formula is less expensive than premixed formula, but it takes more time to prepare. Connie made things easier for herself by mixing enough formula for twenty-four hours at a time and refrigerating the extra bottles.

Some baby-bottle manufacturers don't recommend using a microwave to heat formula because of the need for extra precautions. If you decide to use one, be very cautious. Microwave for only five seconds at a time until you reach the desired temperature. Avoid overheating (which can reduce the nutritional value of the formula), and remove the nipple to keep the bottle from exploding (as it will if the formula becomes too hot). Also, avoid glass bottles, which can shatter if the chilled formula is heated too quickly. Shake the bottle and test the temperature carefully before feeding the baby. Warn your husband and any babysitters to do the same.

As your baby grows older and no longer needs to have the water for his formula sterilized, measure a couple of days' worth of powdered formula at a time into individual bottles. When feeding time comes, just add warm water and shake. Several of the mothers I interviewed used room-temperature water, which made preparing the bottles even simpler.

"A newborn needs to be burped gently after each ounce or so of fluid," says Connie. "Drinking too much at once can cause her to spit up, usually on you." Air bubbles can also give your baby a tummyache, which will in turn give you an earache. Connie found that the best position for burping her little girls was to sit them on her lap facing left. She gently supported the baby's chin with her left hand while tapping her back with her right. Remember to keep a cloth diaper or a towel handy in case your baby spits up.

Cow's milk was meant for baby cows, not baby humans, and it can lead to problems if you feed it to your child too soon. Ask your pediatrician before switching over from formula.

Many of our children refused to drink water, preferring milk or juice. Vicky solved the problem by diluting Lauren's juice with an equal part of water. A couple of bottles of this each day gave Lauren the equivalent of one bottle of juice and one bottle of water. Again, though, check with your pediatrician or a good, up-to-date baby health-care manual before adding anything — even juice or water — to your baby's diet.

Most of our bottle mothers are emphatic about not putting a baby into bed with a bottle. "It's bad for his teeth, causes ear infections, and makes it harder to get rid of the bottle later," says Christine. According to the American Academy of Pediatrics, Christine is right on target. Their website (www.aap.org) states, "If you bottle-feed your child, hold his or her head above stomach level during feedings. This keeps the eustachian tubes from getting blocked. . . . Do not give your child a bottle while he or she is lying down in the crib or playpen." Wanda adds, "It's the hardest habit to break."

"When I went out," says Lisa, "I would use a container I bought at the supermarket that had three sections, into which I put measured amounts of powdered formula. I also took clean bottles with warm water in them. When feeding time came, the water would still be slightly warm, and I would simply add one section of the formula powder and shake." Several moms recommended these sectioned powdered formula containers. Look for them in stores that sell a good variety of baby supplies.

Don't feed your baby in a moving car, especially when the two of you are alone. If he starts to gag, you could cause an accident trying to stop and help him, and the bottle itself could injure him if you're involved in a collision.

Breaking Away

Several mothers in this book were surprised at how easy it was to wean their babies. In fact, some, like Stella's little girl, Dina, weaned themselves. For our bottle mothers, weaning was usually easier if the toddler wasn't accustomed to taking a bottle to bed and if weaning was accomplished at or shortly after the age of one, before the toddler had time to start looking at the bottle as a security blanket.

Both bottle- and breast-feeding moms usually followed a similar procedure: Long before they were ready to wean, they acquainted their little ones with the training cup by allowing them to drink water and juice from it. Then, when Mommy decided the time was right, she very gradually started substituting a cup of milk or formula, one feeding at a time, for the breast- or bottle-feeding. This gradual method worked especially well for our nursing moms, since it allowed their milk production to dwindle slowly.

Cheryl allowed her boys an occasional bottle until they were two years old, but eventually the time came to break with it completely. "The best way I've found to break any habit," she says, "is to encourage the behavior I do want. We gave Jason a cup when he was a year old and praised him when he drank from it without spilling. As he approached his second birthday, we were preparing to toilet train him, so we told him, 'You're really getting to be a big boy now — you're almost two years old! You're going to learn how to go potty all by yourself, and you're not going to need a bottle anymore.' With his birthday, that was it — no more bottle. It was fairly easy."

Patty recommends putting only water in your toddler's bottle if he refuses to give it up: "He'll be more willing to part with it, since most babies aren't too crazy about water."

Giving up the last feeding before bedtime can be hard emotionally for both of you — especially if your baby is accustomed to being nursed to sleep. It helps to substitute a new bedtime ritual for the breast- or bottle-feeding. Megan continued to ask for and enjoy her "nurse and night-night" right up until I weaned her at two years old, and I delayed weaning her several times, fearing

For our bottle mothers, weaning was usually easier if the toddler wasn't accustomed to taking a bottle to bed and if weaning was accomplished at or shortly after the age of one, before the toddler had time to start looking at the bottle as a security blanket.

it would be traumatic for both of us. But Christine, Ashley's mom, gave me an idea that made Megan's weaning almost painless.

For her second birthday I bought her a small cassette recorder designed especially for children. I showed her how to push the buttons, and it was such a novelty that she wanted to carry it around the house all day.

But an hour or two before naptime and bedtime, I loaded the recorder with a cassette of Christian nursery rhymes, put it into her room, and told her, "We'll listen to the recorder later when we go night-night."

When bedtime came, I cuddled her and sang to her for a few minutes, then turned the recorder on with the volume low and put her to bed. She was so eager to listen to the recorder that she hardly noticed the fact that we hadn't nursed. By the time the recorder's novelty wore off, she was no longer accustomed to being nursed to sleep.

If you don't want to spend a small fortune on recorded tapes, check your public library for children's cassettes. Even if your local branch doesn't have a good selection, they may be able to request tapes from other libraries in your county network. Or buy some blank tapes and record your child's favorite stories, songs, and nursery rhymes.

Weaning your little one may feel bittersweet. It's a big milestone, but it means he's growing up and becoming more independent. After the cutting of the umbilical cord, weaning is the first in a progression of parent-child separations. Next comes independence in the areas of toilet habits and eating, then before you turn around he's off to school and the house is suddenly very quiet (except for his little siblings, of course!). But each successful separation leads to the next, and each age has its blessings.

Whether you bottle- or breast-feed, my hope is that in future years you will look back on those precious feeding times with rich memories of cuddling and enjoying your baby.

Chapter 5

Solid Food

The Adventure Begins

Your baby's entrance into the fascinating world of solid food is one of the first signs that he's growing up. It's also one of the first places where his budding personality will start to shine.

Jennifer Joy showed herself to be a fastidious young lady who hardly ever misplaced a drop of food—a trait that Patty, her mom, says mercifully carried over into the months when she began eating finger foods and feeding herself. Kimmie, on the other hand, sucked her thumb furiously after each spoonful of cereal, using it as a plunger to ram the food down her little gullet and squirting cereal out the sides of her mouth in the process. Still other babies used mealtimes to assert their independence, refusing to take food while Mommy was holding the spoon and insisting on feeding themselves at the ripe old age of eight or nine months.

Starting Out

The first solid food your pediatrician will probably tell you to give your baby is rice cereal mixed with formula or breast milk, to which you will gradually add pureed fruits. There are a couple of ways to make preparation of these meals quicker and easier.

Mix enough cereal for a day or so and keep it in the refrigerator, in a container from which you can ladle out one serving at a time. If you use a microwave to heat your baby's cereal, be careful. I liked to heat Megan's cereal in a sturdy

For Julie, the time-honored tradition of turning a spoonful of food into an airplane or train still serves its purpose: "It works. Ian's attention is so distracted by what I'm doing that the food could taste like soapsuds and he wouldn't care. He opens his mouth and I shove the food in."

Pyrex custard cup, since a cold baby food jar can shatter if the contents are heated too quickly. Remember, overheating can destroy nutrients, so it's best to heat in very short (five-second) bursts, stirring the food each time. Also, stir the cereal and test the temperature before spooning it into your baby's trusting little mouth. Such caution is necessary because microwaves heat those tiny servings very quickly and may heat them unevenly, causing hot spots that will burn your baby.

Here's an alternate method: Measure enough cereal and powdered formula for one serving each into clean baby food jars. When mealtime comes, add warm water and fruit.

Don't refrigerate "used" baby food. It can go bad quickly. Throw out any leftovers your baby's spoon has touched.

Before their babies were old enough to sit up, several mothers fed them in their bouncy seats or infant carriers. Brynn, though, recommends getting a high chair that will recline: "I could put Kaylie in the high chair as soon as she was a couple of months old." Using a reclining high chair eliminates the safety concern that your baby might fall from a table or countertop while in her bouncy seat.

Most of our moms occasionally had trouble getting their children to sit still and look up during feedings. Babies would much rather examine their belly buttons or grab the spoon or stick their fingers into their mouths and then anoint their heads with cereal. At such times a jangling set of keys or a noisemaking toy can be a great distraction. "I held the toy up in front of my baby and jangled or squeaked it," says Connie. "While she was occupied with looking at the toy, I spooned the food in." For Julie, the time-honored tradition of turning a spoonful of food into an airplane or train still serves its purpose: "It works. Ian's attention is so distracted by what I'm doing that the food could taste like soapsuds and he wouldn't care. He opens his mouth and I shove the food in." On the other hand, from Patti: "I tried that with Jonathan, and he shoves it back out."

When your baby's doctor prescribes vitamin drops, try putting them into her juice or cereal after it has been warmed, or into a small serving of pureed fruit. Megan refused to take her vitamins straight. They dribbled down her chin and all over her clothes. (The same method can be used to give medication when your baby is ill, but do check with your doctor or pharmacist to see whether there are any foods with which your child's medicine should not be mixed.)

If your baby tries to grab the spoon while you feed him, try giving him something to hold while he eats — a teething ring, a simple rattle, another spoon. Just make sure it's something that washes easily. Or try Brynn's method: "From the very beginning, I would gently hold Kaylie's hands down with one of mine. That way she didn't get used to being able to grab the spoon. She's learned now, 'Mommy's going to hold my hands while I eat.' When they're older, though, you have to say, 'Now *you* do it.'"

"Wendy would never take cereal from a spoon," says Shelley. "We tried and tried. She did okay with fruits, but not cereal. Family members suggested putting cereal in her bottle, and finally we did. But I didn't know what to do about the nipple! Cereal wouldn't go through the regular hole, and of course all the labels say, 'Do not tamper with this nipple!' I just worried and worried. Finally my friend Stephanie told me, 'Get a crosscut nipple, and get scissors and cut it.' That worked." Stephanie adds, "I just enlarged the X on the nipples. You gotta do what you gotta do!" If you do this, enlarge the X just a little at a time, and watch your baby carefully while she eats to make sure too much cereal isn't flowing through.

Most babies hate having their faces wiped, so try making it a game. I dabbed playfully at Megan with a damp paper towel while making funny noises, then followed up with several quick, gentle wipes. I was usually finished before she had a chance to become upset.

If you have to feed your baby while you're out, you can keep her cereal from spoiling by measuring the cereal and powdered formula into a plastic cup and adding water just before serving. If you're not sure whether there's a water supply at your destination, take along another container with the right amount of water. At mealtime, dump the cereal-formula mixture into the container and stir.

If your baby makes frequent visits to Grandma's house, buy extra baby food, along with a spoon and bib, to leave there. You'll have less to pack each time you go.

"Remember that for the first year a baby's main source of nourishment is breast milk or formula," says Stephanie. "If they're not eating a lot of food, it's no big deal. My mom used to panic because Rachel would eat only a quarter of a jar." Again, it's a good idea to check with your pediatrician regarding the types and amounts of food your baby should be eating at each stage of development.

When your pediatrician gives you the go-ahead to start feeding your baby vegetables and meats, you'll have fun watching your little one's expression as you spoon green beans into his mouth when he was expecting peaches. Debby, who has three girls, says that when her babies were reluctant to try a new food, she put a bit of an old favorite, such as the aforementioned peaches, on the tip of the spoon. The little girl would taste her favorite food first and eat the whole spoonful.

Introduce new foods one at a time, leaving a gap of several days between each one. That will make it easier to pinpoint the source of any food allergies.

Never give honey to a child under twelve months old. Its use has been linked to infant botulism, a potentially fatal form of food poisoning. For this reason it's best to check with your pediatrician before adding honey to your child's diet.

Commercial baby food is often sold in stages for different age babies. Elizabeth says, "I've found that stage 2 is usually the same as stage 1 — it's just in a bigger jar. You can save money by buying those second-stage jars. Add a little water to thin it if that makes you more comfortable. The third stage, though, has a lot more texture."

Other ways of saving money on commercial baby food: Stock up during sales. Watch for coupons in newspapers and on checkout tapes. Check prices and varieties at your local discount warehouse store. And don't keep food your baby won't eat. Several mothers said they sometimes returned baby food to the store for a refund.

Making Your Own

I was surprised to find that making your own baby food, when it involves meat, is not any less expensive than buying commercial baby food. I still preferred to make Megan's food, though, for a couple of reasons: It gave me control over which ingredients, and how much of each, went into her tummy, and it tasted much better than the bland, unidentifiable chicken pudding sold by the baby food companies — even though it contained no added fats or seasonings. The recipe calls for chicken, but as I began to make baby food on a regular basis, I found it much easier to bake a large turkey, skin and bone it, make broth from the carcass, and freeze the meat and broth separately in two-cup batches to be used either in her food or in casseroles.

And so, without further ado, I submit to you my recipe for Hull House Baby Stew, which Megan loved, and which I began feeding her at around six months, as soon as her pediatrician okayed meats and vegetables.

Hull House Baby Stew

1 2-½-lb. chicken (or 2 cups chopped, cooked turkey meat)
4 cups water (or 4 cups turkey broth)
1-½ cups chopped carrots
2 10-ounce packages frozen green peas
1-½ cups rice cereal

Rinse the chicken and put it into a large pot. Add the water (it should cover the chicken) and heat until the water comes to just under a boil.

Reduce heat and simmer, covered, for one hour or until tender.

Remove and cool the chicken, discard the skin and bones, and cut the meat into one-inch pieces.

Strain the broth and skim off the fat, then use the broth to simmer the vegetables until tender.

Add the chicken, and puree the mixture in batches in a food processor or blender, using more water if needed to make it blend smoothly. It's important that this mixture contain no lumps to make your baby choke, so check it carefully. The puree should be a bit soupy.

Add the cereal and mix thoroughly. Adjust the consistency by adding more water or cereal as needed.

Baby stew can be frozen several ways: in ice cube trays (when frozen, pop the cubes out and store in plastic bags), in clean baby food jars (leave room for expansion at the top and check the lids after the stew is frozen to make sure they're still tight), or in plastic containers. Do whatever works best for you. As your baby grows older and his digestive system matures, you can vary the recipe by using a pound of stew beef instead of the chicken, and green beans with the strings removed or broccoli instead of peas. Use your imagination. For an older baby with a good number of teeth, process the mixture more coarsely, use less broth, and substitute chopped, cooked noodles for the rice cereal.

🥄 Plain meat pureed in broth was too grainy for Megan to swallow, so I learned to smooth the texture by adding rice cereal and a little extra broth.

🧁 Freezing vegetables for your baby is simple. Just cook until tender, puree, and freeze in ice cube trays or baby food jars, smoothing the texture with a little rice cereal and cooking liquid if necessary. Sweet potatoes, carrots, squash, green peas, green beans with the strings removed, and broccoli are all easy to prepare this way. If your vegetables turn out to be stringy, strain them through a sieve.

> Until your baby is at least a year old, Cheryl recommends double-checking with your pediatrician or a good, current baby health-care book before giving new foods. "Some foods that seemed like healthful snack ideas to me caused real problems," she says, "like serious diarrhea."

If you decide to freeze pureed fruit for your baby, you can keep it from turning brown by adding about a tablespoon of lemon juice to each quart of fruit. Apples, pears, bananas, and peaches are good fruits to preserve this way; a little corn syrup can be used to sweeten them if need be, and straining them will remove any strings. When Megan grew old enough to eat bananas as a finger food, I kept from wasting the ones that became too soft by mashing them, adding a little lemon juice, and freezing them in half-cup portions. She loved eating them half-thawed as "banana ice cream."

Instead of freezing Jonathan's food in advance, Patti fed him pureed table food. "With my first baby, feeding seemed like a real challenge," she says, "but by my third, I was just giving him spoonfuls of whatever we were eating. I just took some out before I added the spices."

Several of our moms caution against adding seasoning or fats to food destined for your baby's tummy. They're not needed, and they could give him a stomachache.

Fantastic Finger Foods

Our moms hailed finger foods as a real blessing. "Finally, Mommy can have a hot meal," says Julie, "since the baby can eat while you eat." Cheerios were the number one favorite of moms and babies alike. They're easy to pick up, don't make a mess, and are extremely portable. They're also easily gummed into mush by babies who are late sprouting teeth. (Megan was so late we thought about having her fitted for dentures.) As their babies cut more and more teeth, our moms started feeding them fish sticks, American cheese, vanilla wafers, pieces of banana, pear, or apple, chopped seedless grapes . . .

As you may have guessed, finger foods are another area where you can use your imagination. Just about any food that's not too spicy and is firm enough for your baby to hold yet soft enough for him to chew easily can qualify. But proceed with caution when you start your baby's journey into the marvelous, messy world of finger foods. Cut the food into small pieces to lessen the danger of choking, and never give your baby a round food, such as grapes, bananas, or hot dog slices, without first cutting it into halves or quarters. Even more important, never feed nuts to a young child or let him eat unattended. And of course, if you give your baby a Cheerio and she gags, fish it out. She's not ready yet.

Until your baby is at least a year old, Cheryl recommends double-checking with your pediatrician or a good, current baby health-care book before giving new foods. "Some foods that seemed like healthful snack ideas to me caused real problems," she says, "like serious diarrhea."

When Ashley began eating finger foods, Christine put an old beach blanket underneath her high chair at mealtimes. "After she finished eating, I just picked up the blanket and shook it outside. It saved me from having to sweep and mop the floor after each meal." Other mothers use a vinyl shower curtain. Patti, though, has the ultimate solution for messy floors: "We have a dog."

Stephanie recommends using your high chair's tray instead of a plate or bowl for finger foods: "I don't think I used plates and bowls until we moved Rachel to a booster seat. I knew a bowl would hit the floor." Just remove the tray and wash with hot, soapy water after each meal.

Brynn, a teacher, warns against worrying too much about messy eating: "God made these children washable for a reason. Remember, they're not just eating. They're learning and experiencing. Feeling hard and soft. Experimenting. Don't get all upset and mad about it."

Depending on how many teeth their children had, most of our moms began feeding them table food at about one year of age.

Picky, Picky

There's a big difference between a reluctant eater and a truly picky (or as I lovingly call my daughter Anna, a "highly selective") one. Reluctant eaters can often be persuaded to eat a small serving of something they're not crazy about by the promise of a favorite food to come later. Picky ones will wail about losing out on the favorite food but are so repelled by the one they're rejecting that they still won't eat it.

"There should be a support group — Mothers of Finicky Toddlers," says Lisa. "At three years old, Robert eats absolutely no meat! Ever since I put him on solid food two years ago, his diet has consisted of fruits, some veggies, yogurt, string cheese, crackers and peanut butter, macaroni and cheese, rice, and pasta. What's a mother to do? I used to stare into the cupboards before each meal, hoping something new and nutritious would jump out at me. Mealtimes were very stressful. I felt like a failure for not being able to get my kid to eat a nutritious and varied diet. It encouraged me greatly as I spoke with other mothers of finicky toddlers and realized I was not the only one!

"Now," she says, "I have mellowed out. Robert likes what he likes. I continue to offer him new foods and encourage him to try meats, but I have come to accept his unique personality. I have also stopped blaming myself. I did all the same things with him as I did with my daughters, who both eat everything."

With the understanding that there are no magic remedies for seriously finicky eaters, here are some tips several moms found helpful:

Keep portions small. Elizabeth says, "If you put too much on their plates, it overwhelms them."

"I've found it helps to let them dip," she adds. "Stewart loves to dip his food in ketchup. Or carrot sticks in ranch dressing. Anything he dips, he likes."

Debby goes by the slogan, "If they hate it, grate it!" She grates vegetables and hides them in soups, breads, spaghetti sauce, meat loaf, and other foods she makes.

Several mothers mentioned that their children won't eat casseroles. Try setting aside the separate ingredients (chicken, rice, and so on) on a plate for your child before you assemble the casserole for the rest of the family.

"I insist that my kids eat at least one bite of a new food," says Patti. "If they don't like it, I don't make them eat it. After all, I don't eat foods I don't like."

Many vegetables have a similar vitamin content. If your child won't eat peas, maybe she'll like green beans, or vice versa.

Patti has found that sometimes the dinner table becomes yet another area where her toddlers test their disciplinary limits: "If my two-and-a-half-year-old says, 'Yuck, I don't like that,' none of the others will eat it, so I've had to be very strict about their commenting on my delicious cuisine."

"You can't force them to eat something," says Shannon, "but you can keep trying. Don't give up. Keep introducing new foods. And if something doesn't work one day, try it again a couple of days later."

Finally, keep your attitude as positive as you can. A highly selective eater is nobody's fault — not yours, and not your toddler's. Be thankful for vitamin supplements! If your child is

> "Now," she says, "I have mellowed out. Robert likes what he likes. I continue to offer him new foods and encourage him to try meats, but I have come to accept his unique personality. I have also stopped blaming myself."

seriously finicky, you may want to check with your pediatrician about giving her one.

👶 Wanda's daughter Michelle has been intolerant of sugar and allergic to artificial color since birth, which has prompted Wanda and her husband, Dennis, to do some in-depth research on sugar and additives. "Artificial color, we discovered, was in everything from medicine to shampoo, both of which affected her," says Wanda. "We learned a lot through trial and error and now have a built-in radar for food, drinks, and snacks." Something else Wanda and Dennis discovered: "Any juice made from concentrate may have sugar in it—concentrate is made with an allowable amount of sugar. The company doesn't have to state 'sugar added' unless it exceeds those limits." Some juice concentrates are now being marketed that claim to contain no added sugar. Just to be sure, check with the company before giving them to your child.

For older toddlers who need to avoid sugar, Wanda recommends these snacks: "Natural applesauce, raisins, cheese, dried or fresh fruit (stay away from pineapples and oranges, since they have a high natural sugar content), natural juices, and natural peanut butter. Michelle loves to make 'smashed banana jelly' for her sandwiches." Smashed bananas also make good "butter" for toast. "Natural juices or plain yogurt mixed with fruit can be frozen in popsicle molds as a nice summer treat; you can also make 'jello' from natural juices and an envelope or two of plain gelatin." ("Natural" in this context means without sugar or other additives.)

o o o o o

PLANNING NUTRITIOUS MEALS THAT everyone in the family can eat may seem like the impossible dream at times. But don't give up. Involve your children as much as possible (within safety considerations) in the meal planning and preparation. When your little one can say "I helped!" with dinner, he may be more likely to accept a helping on his plate. As you make his kitchen experiences positive ones, you'll be making memories along the way, and maybe—who knows?—creating a budding chef.

Chapter 6

Crying, Teething, and Other Fun Things

It's a puzzle why otherwise tenderhearted, sensitive Christian parents take such glee in scaring their friends who are about to enter parenthood, but they do. And if your baby hasn't yet made her grand entrance, your friends who beat you into the baby business are probably having a great time terrifying you with stories of how their babies screamed for hours on end with colic, or how two-year-old Hilary *still* isn't sleeping through the night, or how little Joshua had diarrhea all over Pastor Sternhagen. When they really want to be cruel, they tell you how much a good pair of walking shoes costs and then twist the knife by pointing out that a growing baby needs new ones every two months.

Terror, though, is usually just fear of the unknown or unfamiliar, and the best remedy for it is finding out what to do about the situation. So here, in this chapter, you will learn what to do about a variety of circumstances, along with practical tips on some miscellaneous topics.

Hush, Little Baby

There are several things all babies do regardless of their color, cuteness, or socioeconomic bracket. Four of them are eating, sleeping, burping, and going to the bathroom. Can you guess what number five is? That's right—crying.

No matter how sweet and placid your baby is, she's going to cry occasionally. It's the only way God gave her to tell you she needs something. "If I had just one piece of advice to offer new mothers," says Stella, "it would be, 'Relax!' The more relaxed you are, the more relaxed your baby will be." Lisa agrees: "Mothers start from day one setting the atmosphere of their homes." The parents in this book have all experienced the frayed nerves caused by a baby who continues to cry for a reason only she knows but can't tell. But they've also learned that getting upset does more harm than good. When the unexplained crying times come, just take a few deep breaths and ask the Lord for wisdom, patience, and — above all — love.

You'll be relieved to know that colicky babies were in the minority among our children. Your relief will be short-lived, though, if your baby proves to be among the vocal few. But don't despair. Since colic is generally thought to be caused by abdominal pain, there are, to a certain extent, things you can do about it.

The first step, if your baby's crying seems abnormal or excessive, is to visit your pediatrician to rule out possible medical problems.

Several mothers mentioned that a warm bath helped soothe their fussy babies. Wanda's daughter, Michelle, suffered from colic until she was four months old. Her problem was aggravated by an underdeveloped digestive tract and a severe intolerance of the sugar in her baby formula — a condition it took several doctors to uncover. "She cried for hours at a time," says Wanda, "and when you have a baby in pain, you try to learn quickly what makes her feel better." One of her favorite soothers: "I supported her on her tummy in her little tub, with her head resting in my palm. As she lay there, I rubbed her tummy gently. I suppose it relaxed her stomach muscles and helped the pain go away." Of course, don't try this until your baby's umbilical stump has fallen off.

> "If I had just one piece of advice to offer new mothers," says Stella, "it would be, 'Relax!' The more relaxed you are, the more relaxed your baby will be."

Something else that helped Michelle was having her mommy walk her or rock her while singing softly. "Even when she was tiny, songs about Jesus watching over her and loving her soothed her more than any others," says Wanda.

"When Ashley had colic," says Christine, "it sometimes helped for me to lay her on her stomach across my knees and pat her back. And occasionally just riding in the car would calm her down — we did that in the middle of the night a couple of times."

Several mothers mentioned that simethicone "baby gas drops" (Myle-con is one brand name) helped when given just before a feeding. Check with your pediatrician before giving your baby any new medication.

"I breastfed one of my babies and didn't breastfeed the other, and they both had colic," says Kristy, "so I couldn't blame it on the way they were fed. What helped me most was remembering the phrase from Scripture, 'And it came to pass . . .' A child is in one phase or another until he's married, but whatever he's in now is going to pass. It won't last forever." True enough — colic usually goes away by the time a baby is around three or four months old. Do check with your pediatrician, though, if your formula-fed baby is having trouble with colic. A change of formulas could help.

I found nursing to be a wonderful pacifier, especially when Megan was very young. The warmth, closeness, and ability to suck nearly always soothed her and usually put her to sleep. The few times she had colic, she seemed to feel better when I nursed her while reclining with her tummy pressed against mine. I spent a couple of nights that way, in fact.

Baby swings were often mentioned as good soothers for fussy babies.

Cheryl found fresh air to be the best way to calm her little boys when they were colicky or fussy: "Walking settled both baby and Mommy, and the exercise didn't hurt either."

If you're pretty sure your baby doesn't have colic, but he's still crying even though he's been fed, burped, and changed, the time has come for Mommy to play detective. *How long ago was his last nap?* Many babies become cranky when they're tired. *Has he been overstimulated by too many visitors or strange surroundings?* With several of our babies, it helped to take them to a quiet, darkened room and rock or nurse them when they were crying. The hum of a fan helps to mask outside noises. *Could his clothing be causing discomfort?* Grant, Lynda's usually placid little boy, cried nonstop during a visit to his aunt's house until Lynda took off his shoes. When his daddy had dressed him that morning, Grant curled up his toes, and his foot had gotten stuck in that position inside his shoe. *Have you introduced a new food to his diet that could be causing gas? Or if you're a nursing mother, have you eaten a food that could be causing the problem?* If your baby's crying is due to gas, try one of the colic remedies already mentioned or try laying him on his back and gently bending his legs several times so that his knees touch his tummy. "It helps release the gas," says Cindy. *Is it possible that your baby is bored or just plain having a grumpy day?* If so, diversion is probably your best bet, and chapter 7 is full of diversionary tactics. *Is your baby ill?* If your child's crying is accompanied by a temperature above 100 degrees Fahrenheit, diarrhea, vomiting, pulling on the ears, or other abnormal symptoms, call your pediatrician for instructions. *Last, but probably first, does your baby simply want to be held?* If so, hold him.

"I was an anxious mother who panicked when Jessica cried," says Jennifer. "I finally wrote a list of all the things that usually made her cry and posted it in a prominent place. It was great. I could just look down the list and figure out what she needed, even in my mind-numbed panic."

When Megan was tiny, on the rare occasions when she was overly tired or too wound up to nurse, I discovered that if I put her into her crib and let her cry for a few minutes — say, ten or fifteen — she would release enough tension so that when I picked her up again she would nurse and fall asleep. A few times she even fussed herself to sleep before the time limit was up. "If a baby is fed, dry, and healthy, it won't hurt her to cry for a little while," says Rosemary. Our other moms agree. Keep a sharp eye on your baby if you're letting her fuss, though — while kicking in her crib, Megan once rubbed a blister on her toe and popped it. Also, burp your baby when you pick her up, since she's probably swallowed some air.

"Don't think you're not a good mother if your baby has a fussy time of day," says Christine. "Sometimes your baby will cry no matter what you do, whether you hold him or not." Cheryl adds, "Start preparing dinner early in the day so you won't have as much to do during your baby's fussy period, which will probably be in the early evening." Sure enough, most of our moms report that their babies were grumpiest during the late afternoon or early evening.

For mothers who can't think that far in advance, Julie recommends the cloth baby carriers that snuggle the baby against your stomach or back while you work. If you want to use a cloth baby carrier, be very careful working around hot foods. Also, start using it while your baby is still very young. Several mothers found that their little ones wouldn't tolerate the unaccustomed confinement because they had waited too long to try it. Make sure the carrier you choose gives your baby's head and neck adequate support.

Babies have a strong sucking urge that isn't always satisfied at the end of feeding time, so some mothers in this book encouraged their children to use a pacifier. When Connie's baby girls refused the rubber nipple, she made it more acceptable to them by putting a dab of corn syrup on the end at first. (Remember what we said in chapter 5: Never give honey to an infant.) Christine didn't separate Ashley from her pacifier until she was almost two, but when the time came, she used an interesting method that was completely untraumatic for Ashley: "I cut off the tip bit by bit, a little more each day, until it was down to a nub. She didn't even notice when I finally took it away."

🐿 Carol has this comment about babies crying in public: "There will be times when you're halfway finished buying groceries and your baby will start screaming, and none of your distractions will work. Grin and bear it — it's part of being a mother." LeEtta adds, "Most people have had a child in that situation, though, so they understand." And if they haven't, they'll understand when they do get around to having children.

👶 The last resort in crying remedies comes from Kristy: "If all else fails," she says, "try cotton." She explains, "You gently put the baby into his crib, then you go into your room and put the cotton in your ears."

Lullaby and Good Night

For your baby's first few weeks, unless he's very unusual, he'll be paging you nightly to come and open up the 2 A.M. buffet — or more likely, the 10 P.M., 2 A.M., and 6 A.M. buffets. He has to — his little tummy can't yet hold enough to get him through an eight-hour stretch. And besides, he has no way of knowing that you've been sleeping through the night ever since you were eight weeks old and don't just love coming into his room for a visit and a snack two or three times a night.

🍼 Steel yourself mentally to get up at least once a night for your baby's first couple of months. That way you'll have a wonderful surprise if he starts sleeping through the night earlier than expected. And don't get your hopes too high when your baby finally does sleep through the night for the first time. Nearly all our babies went through phases when they slept through the night for a week or so and then began waking again.

🐣 Several moms found the sleep method recommendations in Gary Ezzo and Robert Bucknam's *On Becoming Babywise* (revised and updated edition) helpful. After reading it, I wished this book had been around when Megan and Anna were born. Ezzo and Bucknam's advice on helping babies learn to go to bed without "sleep props" (such as being rocked or nursed to sleep every time) makes a lot of sense. You need to know, though, that some of the views in this book are considered controversial. No book contains a foolproof formula, and you'll still have to discern what is best for your child.

> Steel yourself mentally to get up at least once a night for your baby's first couple of months. That way you'll have a wonderful surprise if he starts sleeping through the night earlier than expected.

If you can, put your baby to bed as soon as she starts acting sleepy. Believe it or not, becoming overly tired can result in your baby's taking shorter naps, not longer ones.

On the other hand, when Julie was trying to teach her babies to adhere to a sleep schedule, she used warm baths in the early evening to help them stay awake until bedtime. She says, "They came home with their days and nights mixed up. The baths really helped."

Keeping a very dim night-light in your baby's room will let you check on her without turning on any other lights. But if she refuses to go to sleep, try extinguishing all the lights, including the night-light. At about seven months, Megan wouldn't sleep with a light on in her room. The light gave her too much to look at.

Lisa has found it handy to double-make her baby's bed. She says, "Every time I wash and change my baby's crib sheets, I put on a mattress pad and sheet, then another waterproof pad and another sheet. This has been very helpful, especially for middle-of-the-night changes when the sheet gets wet or the baby is sick. All you have to do is remove the top sheet and pad, and you have a clean sheet."

"At only a few weeks," Glenda warns, "our baby could roll off a double bed, even with pillows surrounding him. After a real scare, we learned to put him on a mattress on the floor when he wasn't in his baby bed." Putting pillows around a young baby is a bad idea anyway because of the risk of suffocation. Probably the safest away-from-home bed for a baby is a playpen or portable crib.

All our moms checked their sleeping babies to make sure they were still breathing, but some of their little ones breathed so softly that it was hard to tell. Several mothers solved the problem by gently holding a mirror in front of their babies' lips when they wanted to check on them. The baby's breath fogged the glass, and Mommy's mind was set at ease.

If your little one just can't sleep, try turning out all the lights and walking or rocking him in a completely quiet room. That way there's no visual or audible stimulation to keep him wound up. Walking him will keep him from trying to stand up on your lap, which can become a problem as babies pass their first few weeks.

If your baby starts crying the instant she hits the crib, she may just not want to be left alone. A soft bear with a windup music box inside helped Megan at such times.

Lynda keeps toys in Grant's crib so he can play quietly if he wakes in the night. She says, "I figure that sometimes I wake up in the middle of the night and have to read until I get drowsy, and this is pretty much the same thing. Grant usually plays with his Busy Box for a while and then goes back to sleep."

🌙 As our mothers' babies grew older, their naptime habits changed — both in length of the naps and in going-to-sleep methods. Ashley's favorite method of going to sleep was for Christine to rock her. Grant played quietly in his crib until he became drowsy and nodded off. Megan preferred to be nursed at naptime until she was about nine months old, when suddenly she refused to take naps unless I just put her into her crib and let her grump her way to dreamland. To quote the editors of *American Baby* magazine, "It's not uncommon for a baby to cry himself to sleep. The crying seems to rid him of tensions that otherwise prevent his transition from waking to sleeping."

So don't be thrown off-balance or frustrated by the sleep phases your baby passes through. They're just another sign that he's growing and changing, and they're common to all of us. "Every time I thought I finally had Philip's schedule figured out," says Linda, "he changed."

🐻 As each of her two little boys passed the age of six months, Cheryl found it best to try to have their naps at the same time each day. "It helped me develop consistency in discipline and scheduling," she says, "but it also made naptime a special time." She recommends loving firmness as a way to get this schedule started: "Tell your child it's time to rest and perhaps rock him and nurse him, or read a story or sing, or lay him down and massage his back, or as he gets older, say a little naptime prayer. But then say good night, close the door, and let him go to sleep. This will give you the time you need to nap, do housework, have devotions, or do whatever else you need to do."

🐻 Almost inevitably, there will come a time when you'll have to start letting your baby fuss himself back to sleep when he wakes up in the night. I resisted the thought when other moms warned me about it and didn't become desperate enough to try it until Megan began waking every two hours when she was eight months old. I was petrified. I wanted to do the right thing for Megan, but I also desperately wanted to start sleeping at night and feeling like a human being again.

So Jon and I prayed for wisdom, and that night, when she woke only an hour and a half after I had put her to bed, we let her fuss. When she realized I wasn't coming, she became very upset and cried hard for about twenty minutes. Then, suddenly, silence. "Oh no," I told Jon, "she's choked to death." I tiptoed to her door and peeked in. The wail started again and I backed off. After about five minutes, more silence. Ten minutes later she resumed crying, but it was only a minute or so before she finally gave up and slept the rest of the night. The next night she again woke a couple of hours after I had put her down, but cried for only ten minutes or so before giving up. The third night she let out a single "Yaaa!" before settling back down, and she's slept through the night ever since, with the exception of a few bouts with the flu and various childhood illnesses — which brings us once again to the cardinal rule of parenthood: *Be flexible.* Even after your baby starts sleeping through the night consistently, there will be times when he needs you to offer some nocturnal solace — when he's sick or having teething pain, or during those fun-filled nights when he has learned to stand up in his crib but hasn't yet figured out how to get back down, or when he's older and has obviously been frightened by a nightmare. The trick is to know when the problem has been solved, then go back to your policy of no after-hours service.

Some experts recommend the following method of convincing an older baby to sleep through the night: First, pick a night when no one has to get up early the next day. Then when your baby wakes and begins to cry, go in and say gently, "It's okay. Mommy's here, but it's time for you to sleep." Perhaps pat her on the back for a minute, then leave quietly. Don't turn on the light, don't pick her up, and don't stay longer than a minute. Repeat the procedure every ten minutes or so until she goes back to sleep. (Several nursing mothers said their babies went back to sleep more quickly if their fathers did this, since the little ones knew they couldn't expect Daddy to nurse them.)

Your child will probably cry for quite a while the first night, but the crying spells should become shorter and shorter each night until they stop completely. Lisa, who used this method with her son Robert, says, "It was tough, but afterward I wished I'd had the courage to do it sooner. I thought it would be mean to let him cry, but I actually did him a favor by teaching him how to get a good night's sleep."

"When your toddler reaches the size and age when he's inclined toward and able to climb out of his crib," says Patty, "he's probably ready for a child's or twin bed. If you have enough space, put the bed in the same room with the crib and use it for naps at first, then gradually nights as well. And do buy a guardrail. They're very inexpensive, and your child will fall out of bed without it. It'll make him feel more secure just to know it's there." A few mothers started out by letting their toddlers sleep on the mattress on the floor with the guardrail, adding the box springs a few weeks later, and the frame a few weeks after that.

When your child graduates from the crib, make sure his room is thoroughly toddler-proofed and add a gate at his door to keep him from roaming the house unsupervised.

Most of the parents in this book use bedtime rituals (stories, lullabies, short prayers) to help their children wind down and prepare for sleep. These rituals not only make bedtime a special time of togetherness, they also serve as a signal to their children that it's time to rest. Jennifer says, "Even if we have to change Wes's bedtime for some reason, as long as we do the bedtime routine — the songs, the prayer — he'll go to sleep."

After all this advice on putting your baby to sleep, here's some from Connie on waking him up: "When you need to wake your child," she says, "do it gently with soft words and an easy rub on the back rather than by flipping on the light and announcing, 'Time to wake *up!*' The way you wake your baby can determine his mood — calm and happy versus jumpy and irritable."

Jennifer says, "Even if we have to change Wes's bedtime for some reason, as long as we do the bedtime routine — the songs, the prayer — he'll go to sleep."

Time for a Bath

After seeing pictures in catalogs and advertisements of babies happily splashing away in bathtubs filled with rubber duckies and toy boats, it comes as a shock to new mothers that newborns don't enjoy their first baths. The little ones usually cry from fear and cold — especially since their bodies can't be immersed in warm water until the umbilical stump falls off. Sofie's husband, Paul, a pediatrician, has some advice on making those initial baths less traumatic: Wrap the baby in a receiving blanket and gently sponge-bathe one part of his body at a time with comfortably warm water, keeping the other parts covered. Remember not to bring the wet blanket into contact with your baby's umbilical stump. Jennifer adds, "Turn off the air conditioner and any fans."

Gather all your bath supplies before you undress your baby for her bath. This will help prevent "wetting" accidents on the way to the tub.

For the first few months, a molded bath sponge is wonderful for your baby to lie on in the tub. It supports her head up out of the water, leaving both of your hands free to bathe her. After your baby is old enough to sit up, a rubber bath mat or a thick towel will keep her from sliding around in the bathtub.

Lisa says, "I used a common gardening kneeling pad at the side of the tub so I could stay close, keeping one hand on my baby at all times."

Never, *ever* leave your baby while he's in the bathtub, even if he's lying on a bath sponge. Ignore the phone and the doorbell, or wrap your baby in a towel and take him with you. Several mothers in this book have bathroom horror stories, all of which occurred because they left their babies or toddlers alone to take care of something "urgent."

New parents tend to be petrified of the soft spot (fontanel) on their baby's head, but there's no need to be. The skin covering the fontanel is very tough, and washing your baby's hair thoroughly won't hurt him. In fact, if you don't, and allow dead skin and oils to collect on his scalp, your baby can develop a crusty skin condition called cradle cap.

Keep a firm grip on your baby as you take her out of the bathtub. Wet babies are slippery!

A cotton swab works well to clean your baby's ears, but don't do any deep cleaning with it. It's unnecessary and dangerous to stick a swab down inside your child's ear. Unlike what your mother always taught you about housework, "Just clean what shows" is a good rule of thumb here.

Hang a mesh bag in the tub for your baby's toys. When bathtime is over, rinse the toys and put them into the bag to drain. This will keep the rest of the family from tripping over them in the shower.

Cover the bathtub faucet with a spout protector or a washcloth secured with strong cord to keep your baby from bumping her head, and make a strict rule against standing or crawling around in the tub.

Shelley recommends bath visors (sold in the baby department of large discount stores) for babies who hate getting water in their eyes when their hair is washed. On the other hand, Cil says, "I pretty much doused my kids from the beginning. They've never known anything different, and I've never had any trouble." She believes getting them accustomed to having water in their faces has helped them with swimming as well. (Getting young children to put their faces in the water is often a big hurdle in beginning swimming lessons.) Of course, if you're going to try this, be sure to use a shampoo that won't sting your baby's eyes. And don't let water get up into his or her nose. That feels awful!

Connie recommends blunt nail scissors to trim your baby's fingernails, since nail clippers can pinch and biting the nails off can leave a jagged edge or pull the nail off into the quick. Lynda keeps blunt-tipped scissors on Grant's changing

> Several mothers in this book have bathroom horror stories, all of which occurred because they left their babies or toddlers alone to take care of something "urgent."

table. She says, "Every few days, I check his toenails and fingernails while I'm changing him." "I did it while my boys were sleeping," says Cheryl. "They slept right through it." I usually found it easiest to trim Megan's nails while she nursed. If I did it while she was up and active, she stood in grave danger of losing her fingertips along with her nails. I supported her head on a thick pillow, which left both of my hands free.

Keeping Up Appearances

The havoc that can be wreaked in a family room by a six-month-old baby who's just beginning to crawl is one of those things you have to see to believe. And believe me, you will.

As your baby grows older and more mobile, his potential for strewing toys from one end of the house to the other increases dramatically. So unless you want to spend your child's toddlerhood up to your neck in toys, it's important to have some kind of system whereby the clutter gets put into its proper place at natural breaks in the day — for instance, naptime, bedtime, and before meals and outings.

"We have a couple of small laundry baskets that we keep in the rooms where the boys play," says Cheryl. "At naptime, or when I receive news that unexpected company is on the way, I just carry the basket around the room and toss the toys in, to be put away in the boys' bedroom or in their big toy chest at a later time. Now that they're toddlers, Jason and Brian enjoy helping me put the toys into the basket."

When Megan outgrew her yellow plastic bathtub, I kept it to use as a portable toybox since it matched her bedroom and slid easily underneath her crib. When we took it out into the family room, she liked to unload all the toys and sit in her little "boat." I even used the tub as a spare laundry basket when the need arose.

With the great-room concept in homes becoming more and more popular, fewer families have a separate family room or playroom where the children can keep their toys. If you're particular about your decor, get a big, covered wicker basket or a pretty wicker clothes hamper to use as a living-room toybox.

Keep only about ten toys in your living-room toybox, since the number you have in it is inevitably the number your toddler will drag out. And keep four or five books on a low bookshelf, the rest out of reach. Rotate the toys and books every week or two.

"If we didn't have a system, we would drown in toys," says Lisa, who has three children. "We have upstairs toys and downstairs toys, regular toys that stay out all the time and project toys that are messy and come out only on special occasions or rainy days. Even my three-year-old understands that if he brings an upstairs toy down, he must put it back upstairs that same day. All the toys have a place, too. Some go in a toybox, others belong in the playpen, others on shelves. I don't think it's as overwhelming for my kids to clean up if they know each toy has a certain place and all they have to do is take it there, not decide for themselves what to do with it."

Several mothers found plastic tubs and bins helpful when sorting toys into categories.

If you have more than one child, there will be inevitable confusion about what toys belong to whom. I found it helpful to mark each child's first initial on the bottom of her toys or on the tags of her stuffed animals with a black permanent marker. Even a small child can learn to recognize the first letter of his or her name. (We still do this with CDs and identical gifts.)

"Watch the wall about two feet off the floor once your child starts crawling and walking," says Cheryl. "Handprints there are easy to miss since they're not in your line of sight. And if your baby manages to get hold of a crayon or pen and marks the wall with it, a plastic scouring pad will sometimes clean what a cloth or sponge won't. An art gum eraser will take care of pencil marks."

Teething Isn't Fun

"When I cut my wisdom teeth," says Virginia, "I finally understood why teething made my babies so grumpy." Your child will be teething off and on for most of his first two years, so it's important to come up with ways to soothe his itching, painful gums. Our babies responded better to many of the following teething ideas than they did to commercial teething rings.

Terri says, "A washcloth wrapped around an ice cube and tied with strong cord worked well for Zachary and Ashley. The cloth absorbed the water as the ice melted, along with any drooling from the baby."

Cold vegetables and fruits were favorite teething tools for our little ones. Several moms found that a peeled, refrigerated carrot was a good soother for their babies' sore gums. Jan let Jordan David teethe on celery sticks; Julie gave Sean and Ian thick, cold cucumber slices with the seeds removed; and Wanda used thick apple slices as a sweet way of soothing Michelle's gums. Linda came up with a unique way of helping her teething babies: frozen bagels.

Make sure any pieces of fruit or vegetables you give your baby aren't small enough to fit all the way into his mouth, or he may choke. Also, your baby will probably go through a transition period when he has enough teeth to gnaw off a chunk of food but can't yet chew it up. To avoid the danger of choking, don't let him teethe on food during that time. And of course, never leave your baby alone when he's teething on food.

"Even a soft children's toothbrush can be rough on your baby's gums," says Patty. "When he first starts cutting teeth, put a dab of toothpaste on a damp washcloth and rub his teeth gently with it once a day. When it's time to switch to a toothbrush, make it fun. Buy a cute children's toothbrush for your baby and let him brush his teeth along with you when you do yours. Times like that create a feeling of togetherness."

Of course, you'll need to help your child brush his teeth for several years, since a toddler doesn't have the manual dexterity to do a thorough job. And never let a child climb or run with a toothbrush in his mouth.

Safety Always

The best safety device you can give your baby is a set of constantly vigilant parents. True, it takes quite an effort to make sure your baby is always within sight or earshot and to buckle him in every time you go out in the car, even if he cries, but it's well worth it.

It would be impossible in a few pages to give warning of all the predicaments babies get themselves into, and after you read even this incomplete list, you'll probably wonder how any babies manage to grow up. Don't let these potential horrors cause you to live in fear. Your responsibility is to do your very best to make your child's world safe and to trust God for the things you can't foresee.

As diplomatically as possible, insist that your baby's grandparents read and observe the following safety tips if you let your child spend much time alone with them. The safest home in the world won't help your baby if Grandma's house is full of hazards.

Starting the day you bring your baby home from the hospital, *use a car seat*. This is vital to your baby's safety, but for some reason many otherwise good parents don't see the need to buckle their babies in *every* time they go somewhere in the car, even though almost all state laws now require it. Find a way to buy a good, new car seat or put it first on your list of potential baby gifts.

Although you may be tempted to borrow a car seat from a friend, Nancy points out, "The Highway Patrol recommends getting a new one. An old car seat may have been in an accident at some time and might not be structurally sound anymore, or the manufacturer might have recalled it and you would never know. New seats are safer than old ones."

Things You Should Know about Car Seats

According to the National Highway Traffic Safety Administration:

- Used correctly, child safety seats are 71 percent effective in reducing fatalities in children under the age of five and 69 percent effective in reducing the need for hospitalization.

- About 50 percent of children under age five who died in crashes were unrestrained. Of the remaining 50 percent, 26 percent were in adult seat belts, which do *not* provide effective protection for most children under age five. Others were in a child restraint system but had not been restrained properly.

- In studies conducted by the NHTSA, *nearly 80 percent of the child seats observed were misused in one or more ways.* In some cases, the seat was not properly attached to the vehicle; in others, the child was not appropriately buckled into the seat.

Jennifer adds, "Read and follow the directions on your car seat carefully. I read some shocking statistics about how most people are using their car seats wrong!"

A final word on the importance of buckling your child in *every* time, from the very beginning: You may have to endure some crying if your baby is not one who does well in the car. (Megan — *sigh* — was one of these.) But as time goes on, your child will learn that being buckled into her car seat is a necessary part of going somewhere. If you ever give her the option of getting out and crawling around or sitting in your lap, you're setting yourself up for some earsplitting, mind-frazzling battles, not to mention endangering her life and health. Don't do it! The car seat is not optional. Ever.

Patty says, "If you don't have a cloth cover for your car seat, put a towel or small blanket over it when you have to leave the car — it can get pretty hot in the sun." Wanda remembers a friend whose baby cried every time he was put into his car seat until finally Wanda noticed that the hot straps were making angry red marks on his shoulders. Also, if at all possible, get a quilted cloth seat cover to keep your baby from sweating against the warm plastic.

Babies' actions are largely reflex at first. Your child can grasp the side of his changing table and flip himself off before you know it, so don't turn your back on him for even an instant while he's on the changing table. If he does manage to flip off, don't panic, but do call your pediatrician. He or she can give you danger signals to watch for if your baby has had a fall.

Before allowing your baby to play with a new toy, examine it for sharp edges, pointed tips, or loose parts — eyes, ears, nose, tail. Stay away from cheap toys made with brittle plastic — which can break into sharp pieces — and toys with small parts on which your little one can choke. Most toys nowadays carry labels that indicate what age level the toy is made for. No matter how brilliant your baby is, stick with toys at his age level.

Balloons are fun, but they carry some important safety concerns. For advice on playing safely with balloons, see chapter 7.

Dolls with yarn hair can be a problem for teething babies. Megan had a Raggedy Ann doll she played with constantly, until one day I discovered a wad of red yarn in her mouth.

Hanging your baby's pacifier around her neck with a ribbon sounds like a cute, handy idea, but don't do it. She can be strangled or seriously hurt if the ribbon becomes caught on something. Jennifer says, "Snap-on straps for pacifiers are available and work great." Check your local large discount store.

Once your baby is old enough to push up on his hands and knees or sit up by himself, take his crib mobile down and don't tie anything across the top of his crib or playpen. Otherwise he could become entangled and hurt himself.

The time to babyproof your home is when your child first shows signs of creeping. Cheryl got down on her hands and knees when babyproofing for Jason and Brian to give herself a baby's-eye view of her house: "It gave me a better idea of what tempting things were in their sight range," she says, "and showed me small items in the carpet or under the chair or sofa that I would otherwise have missed."

Babies, especially teething babies, put everything in their mouths and are fascinated by small objects, so keep the floor well picked up once your little one is old enough to creep. If you sew or do handicrafts, be meticulous about picking up dropped pins and buttons. They can be deadly if your baby manages to get one into her mouth.

You will most likely need at least two childproof "baby gates." These make wonderful baby gifts, or you might try borrowing from a friend with older

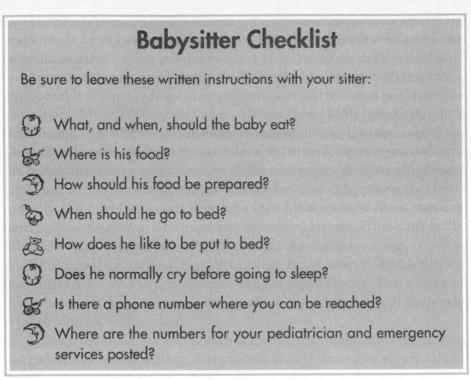

Babysitter Checklist

Be sure to leave these written instructions with your sitter:

What, and when, should the baby eat?

Where is his food?

How should his food be prepared?

When should he go to bed?

How does he like to be put to bed?

Does he normally cry before going to sleep?

Is there a phone number where you can be reached?

Where are the numbers for your pediatrician and emergency services posted?

children. "I invested in a good childproof gate, the kind older kids and adults can open and walk through, to go between the family room and the kitchen," says Lisa. Several mothers mentioned the importance of using baby gates at the top and bottom of stairs, at the door of a toddler's room, and in other places to keep your little one from wandering off and getting into trouble. The gates are also handy to have at Grandma's house.

Julie stresses the need to put plastic plugs in the electrical outlets. She says, "An accident can happen so easily. Those little wet fingers that the baby just took out of his mouth or that little tongue that does most of his exploring can find the wall outlet, and you may not even notice that your baby is near the outlet until it's too late." Also, I noticed when Megan began roaming around in her walker that the electrical outlets were just about at her eye level.

Put plugs in the outlets above your kitchen and bathroom counters, too, against the time when your child learns to climb.

When your child starts to crawl up to furniture and pull himself to a standing position, a well-padded playpen is a good place for him to practice standing up and sitting down. Remove most of the toys from the playpen, leaving only ones that won't hurt your child if he falls on them.

Lisa invested in a fireplace hearth pad to keep her toddlers from knocking their teeth out on the family room hearth.

Know the names of your houseplants and call your local poison control center or county agricultural extension office to find out whether any plants within your baby's reach are poisonous. You'd be surprised how many common houseplants are. Sooner or later your baby is bound to grab a leaf and put it into his mouth, and you can save him from illness or death by eliminating hazardous plants until he's older.

Terri suggests using a twist tie to corral electrical appliance cords. "A small baby can reach a lot more than you think," she says. Patty goes even further, suggesting that electrical cords be taped to the backs of table legs. She says, "It's so easy for a crawling baby's legs to get caught on a cord and pull a lamp over."

"Make sure you know what your baby is doing all the time," says Karen, "especially if things are quiet. Babies get into things you'd never dream of."

Donna stresses the importance of childproof latches on drawers and cabinets that contain medicines, cosmetics, pesticides, cleaning supplies, and sharp objects. Even better, put such items in high cabinets and then put latches on those cabinets in case your little one learns to climb up and reach them. "Especially now that I have two children," she says, "I can't have my eye on both of them all the time. While I'm with one, the other child can get into my cabinets before I know it."

Buy a small bottle of ipecac syrup in case you ever need to induce vomiting after an accidental poisoning. Also, purchase a bottle of activated charcoal, which can absorb poisons a child has swallowed and give you time to get to the emergency room. (Check with your doctor or pharmacist. This is *not* the kind of charcoal used to grill steaks.) Check with your pediatrician or poison control center for instructions on how to use these medications.

Stephanie points out the need, before you give ipecac syrup, to call the poison control center and read the warning label of any substance you believe your child has ingested. Some caustic substances can cause even more damage, or death, if they're vomited up.

According to Megan's pediatrician, a leading source of accidental poisonings is the medicine in Grandma's purse or Grandpa's coat pocket.

Keep the doors closed to rooms you don't want your baby wandering into, especially bathrooms. Toilets are fascinating to older babies and toddlers, and believe it or not, children have been known to fall in and drown. Terri says,

More Babysitter Hints

"If you're going to be more than twenty or thirty minutes away," says Patty, "leave the number of a nearby friend or relative who could get there while you're being called."

If there's any chance your babysitter — especially Grandma or Grandpa — will need to take the baby out while you're gone, go ahead and install your car seat in their car and give instructions on how to use it.

If you're leaving for a weekend with your husband, be sure to write and sign a medical release form authorizing the sitter to obtain medical treatment for your baby in the event of an emergency. Leave the number and address of your health insurance policy as well.

"When your toddler is big enough to pull doors open, tie bells to the ones you don't want her to touch. That way you'll know when to come running."

The bathroom is one of the most dangerous rooms in the house. Donna says, "One day when April was two years old, she was playing in the bathtub when I had to leave the room for a second. My husband had left the blow dryer on the counter by the sink. April got out of the bathtub, got the blow dryer, got back into the bathtub, and turned it on. Praise the Lord, she did not drop that thing into the water. I ran in and jerked the plug out of the wall." Linda left eighteen-month-old Philip alone in the bathroom for a moment only to be summoned back by bloodcurdling screams. Philip had gotten out of the tub and grabbed the hot end of Linda's curling iron.

The moral of the story is, don't leave your baby or toddler alone in the bathroom, especially when there are small appliances in the room. And make sure the door is kept securely closed.

Secure the cords of curtains and venetian blinds to the wall or drape them over the curtain rod out of reach. Babies have been known to accidentally strangle themselves while playing unsupervised with long cords.

Cook on back burners whenever possible, and keep the handles of pots and pans turned to the back of the stove. Also, don't allow your baby to play near

Crying, Teething, and Other Fun Things · The Mommy and Daddy Book a hot stove, and never lift a pot of hot food or liquid over your baby. Always go around him.

Make the stove knobs a strict no-no, and don't leave near the edge of the counter sharp objects, knives, or glasses that can shatter. A baby in a walker can reach farther than you might think. In fact, throw out your walker and get an Exersaucer. They're more fun and less dangerous. "Lots of action," says Jennifer, "but they can't go anywhere."

Keep all plastic wrap and plastic bags out of your child's reach, and don't leave them in your wastebaskets when she becomes old enough to crawl around.

Patty recommends keeping your ironing board either put away when not in use or in a room where your baby isn't allowed. "Even a cool iron will hurt your baby if she pulls it off onto her head," she says.

Also from Patty: "When your baby starts walking, make it a habit that he always holds your hand when you go out together. If you make exceptions, your little one will take advantage of it. They're faster than we think." To give Michelle a feeling of freedom, Wanda used a baby harness and leash on walks and shopping trips. "I got some nasty comments from people who told me I was treating my little girl like a pet animal," she says, "but I always replied, 'Well, I love my child too much to let anything happen to her.'" Having the courage of your convictions is a great help at times like that — and a good-sized stubborn streak doesn't hurt either.

Patty says, "As early as possible, teach your toddler his first and last name, his parents' names, city, and street name — if not his street number and phone number. No mother wants to think about her child's getting lost, but precautions can't hurt." It's a good idea, as soon as your child can understand, to teach him not to get into a car or go with anyone Mommy or Daddy hasn't certified as okay. Sad though it is, a child playing outdoors should be either in a fenced yard behind a locked gate or within a supervising adult's sight range — preferably both.

Don't dress your toddler in clothes embroidered with his name. A stranger coming up, calling his name, and saying, "Your mommy told me to come and get you," is very convincing.

Your library or bookstore has simple storybooks available dealing with such problems as kidnapping and sexual abuse. Use these resources to teach your child to protect himself.

Holiday Hazards

Keep your carpet free of dropped Christmas tree needles, which when dry are as sharp as pins. Also, make sure none of the hooks used to hang ornaments become stuck in your rug.

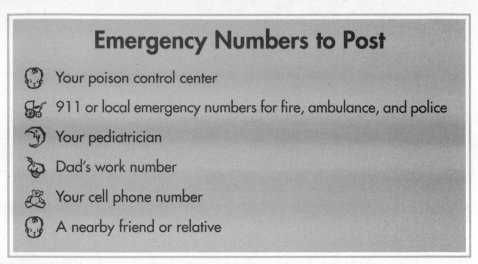

Emergency Numbers to Post

- Your poison control center
- 911 or local emergency numbers for fire, ambulance, and police
- Your pediatrician
- Dad's work number
- Your cell phone number
- A nearby friend or relative

Keep glass ornaments high on the tree, with only safe, soft ones within the baby's reach.

It's generally best never to leave your baby unsupervised in the room with the Christmas tree. Its bright colors make it irresistible, and your child can pull it over on himself in an instant.

Holly and mistletoe are poisonous, so put them up out of reach or avoid buying them until your baby is older.

Family parties can be dangerous for young children. Adults often assume that someone else is watching the children, with the result that no one is. Add to this the swimming pool in the back yard, or the front door that's left open because so many people are going in and out, or the fact that those interesting purses and coat pockets may contain hazardous substances, and you have a recipe for disaster.

Try designating adult-child buddies, specifying which adults are responsible to keep an eye on which children. (If your childless friends and family members are willing to help you in this way, you'll know they really love you!) Or assign child-watching shifts to several responsible adults. At the very least, be aware of the danger and stay alert.

The Well-Dressed Baby

Experience with her four children taught Sofie this lesson: "Never, never, *never* buy clothes that fit perfectly. I always buy clothing that I have to hem up a few inches or that needs to have the button moved over."

Lisa adds, "I wash all baby clothes before I ever put them in the baby's dresser (except for fancy outfits she'll only wear once anyway). Some outfits will shrink a great deal, others not so much. Then I sort the clothes according to approximate size. With my first child, I found out the hard way that if you wait until a kid grows into things, then wear and wash, you may get only one wearing!" It's best to wash your baby's clothes before she wears them anyway, to get rid of the chemical sizing that makes the clothes look so fresh and crisp in the store but that can irritate your baby's skin.

The age sizing used on babies' clothes isn't standard from manufacturer to manufacturer, so these mothers tend to ignore it and go by their children's height and weight instead. For example, at four months Megan was wearing twelve-month sleepers.

If you're like most of the parents in this book, birthdays and Christmas are the two times of the year when your baby's wardrobe will receive its biggest boost. "When people ask what your baby needs," says Patty, "ask them to consider department store gift certificates. That way you can buy the things your baby really needs, in the right sizes. And ask them to limit dressy clothes. Sleepers, playsuits, and undershirts are much more practical."

Several mothers have found yard sales and consignment shops to be good places for finding children's clothes, especially dressy outfits that are usually worn only once or twice before they're outgrown or play clothes that must fit but don't need to look brand new.

Pene's skill at sewing keeps her children in inexpensive clothes: "Especially when they're little, it doesn't take much material at all to make a pair of shorts or a sundress."

Check carefully for quality when buying everyday play clothes, especially once your baby starts crawling. An outfit isn't a bargain if it has to be replaced before it's outgrown. Christine says, "You can buy good clothes at discount stores, and you can buy shoddy clothes at expensive department stores. You just have to look carefully at what you get. Check the seams and the fabric to make sure clothing is made well." Make it a habit to check the clearance and sale racks before looking at higher-priced clothes.

Christine started a habit when Ashley was born that's still yielding benefits now that her little girl is three: "Anytime I dress Ashley to go out," she says,

> **Check carefully for quality when buying everyday play clothes, especially once your baby starts crawling. An outfit isn't a bargain if it has to be replaced before it's outgrown.**

"I change her back into play clothes — clothes that already have stains on them — as soon as we get home. That way if I feed her or give her a drink, it doesn't get on her good clothes. As a result, I hardly ever have to wash most of her nice out-fits." This keeps Ashley's good clothes from wearing out prematurely.

I went through Megan's closet and dresser when she was about six months old and weeded out the clothes she had outgrown. I was amazed at how many there were and how much extra storage space I ended up with. The out-grown clothes can be given away or saved in plastic bags for your next child. Repeat the process a couple of times a year.

"Since children's clothes are small," says Lynda, "we had Grant's closet made with shelves for stackable clothes above and the rack for hanging clothes about halfway down." Having the shelves on top keeps Lynda from having to stoop while putting Grant's clothes away or finding an outfit for him to wear. Although Lynda had Grant's closet custom made when she and her husband were building their new house, it would be simple to adapt an existing closet with wooden or plastic-coated wire shelves. Such customizing yields so much extra storage space that a dresser in the baby's room isn't necessary. Kristy also points out that the low rack for hanging clothes makes it easier for you to teach your toddler to hang up his own clothes later on.

The mothers I interviewed are all for getting good children's clothes as cheaply as you can, no matter where you find them, but they're not willing to take any chances in the area of shoes. "A cheap shirt can't hurt your baby's body," says Christine, "but a cheap pair of shoes can ruin his feet." Luckily for our pocketbooks, though, babies don't need shoes as soon as the shoe manu-facturers would like us to believe they do. Until your child begins to stand and try to toddle, shoes are merely for decoration and warmth unless your pediatri-cian has told you that your baby needs corrective shoes. And even when he starts walking, the best shoes for your child to wear while he's at home are none at all. In cold weather, a footed sleeper-playsuit with nonskid rubber pads on the feet will do just fine, with maybe a pair of thick socks underneath for extra warmth.

When your baby is old enough to walk outdoors and in public, high-top shoes or good quality sneakers are a good way to start, and these mothers insist that nothing can take the place of a professional fitting. If you find that your baby is a standard size, you can then feel free to buy his shoes at discount stores.

Before their babies began to stand and walk, several mothers got away with buying their children's shoes too big and letting their feet grow into them. But that was no longer possible when their little ones began to toddle. Shoes that are too big don't give a baby the stability he needs, and they can rub blisters on his feet. If your budget won't allow for new shoes every couple of months, buy them *slightly* larger than needed and let your baby wear thick socks until he grows into them. Feel the toes and sides of his shoes every week or so, and buy new shoes the minute the old ones start to become tight.

Patty says, "To help your toddler learn to put his shoes on the correct feet, put a small piece of colored tape on the bottom of his right shoe."

Christine found that a good way to keep Ashley's shoes tied — especially as she began to stand and toddle around — was to tie the laces in a bow, then tie the loops of the bow in a knot.

Terri and Connie were both proud mothers of little girls with no hair. They made sure everyone knew their children were girls by sticking bows to their peach fuzz with tape. Keep an eye on your little one, however, when she's wearing bows and take them out when you're at home. Your baby can choke on a bow if she manages to pull it off her head and stick it into her mouth.

If your baby's shirt won't stay tucked in, use a piece of masking tape in the front and back to stick his shirttail to his disposable diaper or plastic pants. Keep a roll at your changing table and in your diaper bag, since the tape sticks to disposable diapers so well that you may have to change it each time you change a diaper.

God's Name Doesn't End in M.D.

Children's health care is far beyond the scope of this book, but the mothers I interviewed do have some definite ideas about dealing with your baby's doctor.

Your pediatrician may someday literally have your child's life in his hands, and the yellow pages are not the place to find him. Ask for references from your friends with children or from your obstetrician.

Even after you've chosen a pediatrician you respect and trust, remember that he or she is human. If you suspect something is wrong with your baby, go with your instincts. "You live with that child every day," says Carol. "The doctor doesn't." You may never have to face this situation, but don't hesitate to get a second or even a third opinion if, after you've thoroughly discussed your concerns with him, your pediatrician can't seem to identify the problem or insists that there isn't one. "Even if you turn out to be wrong," says Christine, "at least you'll know!"

A hearing problem with Rita's son Brian, a severe foot problem with Vicky's daughter Lauren, and even a life-threatening kidney dysfunction with Carol's little girl Kristie went undiagnosed by the first doctors to see them. Lindsie,

LeEtta's little girl, went untreated with bronchitis for three months because her doctor kept saying she'd get over it. LeEtta says now, "I'm not going to be so sentimental about my pediatrician next time. If I don't see results, I'm going somewhere else."

These mothers are much in favor of finding a comprehensive, up-to-date manual on children's health care to refer to when problems arise. "I have several medical books," says Carol, "and I try to read up as much as I can when there's an illness. Then when I take my child to the doctor, I can point out the symptoms. Believe me, it helps." Obviously, you should never try to diagnose and treat an illness at home, with the possible exception of a head cold. The purpose of a health care manual is to help you communicate with your child's doctor, not to replace him.

Most important, of course, is to trust the Lord for your baby's health and ask him for wisdom if she shows unusual symptoms. Hard as it is to conceive, he loves her more than you do.

> Even after you've chosen a pediatrician you respect and trust, remember that he or she is human. If you suspect something is wrong with your baby, go with your instincts.

Chapter 7

A Busy Baby Is a Happy Baby

We'll begin this chapter by bursting yet another bubble: We're not going to tell you how to make your baby occupy himself all day long so you can go about your business and not spend time with him. Even if that weren't impossible, it would be awful for his development. According to medical research, the most important factor in your baby's intellectual development is the amount of time he spends interacting with you, his mother. It's absolutely essential that you talk to him, play with him, cuddle him, read to him, explain things to him, and provide new experiences for him—especially during the crucial time between the ages of eight and eighteen months.

Having said that, we'll add that it's not necessary for you to entertain your baby all day long. He learns much by playing alone and by watching you go about your daily activities. In this chapter, you'll find tips the mothers in this book use to keep their little ones occupied and happy at home and abroad, as well as ways to have fun together.

One word of caution: All babies—even those who play well on their own—require constant supervision. Catastrophes can happen quietly. (In fact, several mothers said that when the house gets quiet, that's when they start to worry.)

Early Days

Beg, borrow, or buy an infant swing if you haven't received one as a shower gift. It's a great invention. Babies are often much more willing to sit and watch Mommy work if they can swing at the same time.

Two other contraptions the mothers in this book found helpful for keeping their babies content are bouncy seats and Exersaucers. Both allow the baby to jiggle himself. Nancy says, "We got a combination vibrating bouncy seat-hammock swing. It was about twice the price of a regular bouncy seat, but worth it." In the Exersaucer (which looks like a walker but doesn't go anywhere), a baby can bounce, rock, or spin. Plus it has a tray for toys or finger foods.

Let your baby sit in his swing or infant seat and watch while you do dishes or cook. He'll enjoy touching the dishes as you put them away — cool smooth glass, rough wooden spoon, shiny metal pan. Tell him the name of each item. "I put my little girl's swing in the kitchen while I worked," says Carol, "and gave her gadgets that didn't have small parts and weren't pointed — a metal tea strainer, plastic measuring cups, everything possible — to let her touch and feel them."

Put your baby in her infant seat and carry her around the house with you. She'll enjoy watching you work, especially if you talk and sing to her while you do it.

"Wendy loves the stroller," says Shelley. "Sometimes if we come back from a walk and she's really cranky and it's the wrong time of day, I'll leave her in the stroller and roll her around the house while I work."

"Make sure your baby has plenty to look at in his crib and playpen," says Lynda. "Grant loves to look at his Busy Box or listen to his windup musical crib toys." Babies also love mirrors, and there are some good unbreakable ones for the crib and playpen on the market. Your little one will have fun looking in the mirror and trying to figure out who the other baby is.

Sofie learned by hard experience that it's important to start using the playpen *before* your baby is old enough to creep. If she becomes too accustomed to wide, open spaces, she may refuse to stay in a playpen. Be careful not to depend on the playpen too much, though. "A playpen can be bad if you constantly use it as a babysitter," says Carol, "and if you don't keep stimulating toys in it. You know your baby is bored if she stops crying when you take her out and put her on the floor."

Don't clutter your baby's playpen with too many toys. They make it hard for her to maneuver, and she can play with only one or two at a time any-

> Let your baby sit in his swing or infant seat and watch while you do dishes or cook. He'll enjoy touching the dishes as you put them away — cool smooth glass, rough wooden spoon, shiny metal pan. Tell him the name of each item.

way. Just put two or three interesting toys in with her and set the rest aside. Change the toys every few days. I did find an exception to this rule. When Megan reached the age of six months or so, she became very interested in putting one item inside another. Now and then I would put a whole box of toys into her playpen with her, and she occupied herself for long periods of time taking all the toys out of the box and then putting them all back in.

A friend of mine claims he'd be a millionaire if he could invent a toy as fascinating to babies as a paper bag, but more durable. Infants love the crackly noise paper makes, plus the fact that a small paper bag is light enough for them to wave around. Watch your baby carefully when she plays with paper, though. She can quickly gum a piece off and swallow or choke on it.

Several mothers have finally discovered a use for junk mail. They give it to their babies to play with. Megan's favorites were the crackly cellophane window envelopes, colorful flyers on card stock, and catalogs — especially those with pictures of children. The best part of this play idea is that it's free, and it renews itself daily. It is still important, though, to supervise your baby when she plays with paper, especially if she's teething.

Vicky's daughter Lauren loves soap bubbles. "I used to blow bubbles for her in the kitchen while she sat in her carrier," says Vicky. "Now I do it while she's in the bathtub. She loves it! She tries to pop them."

Tear off a sheet of aluminum foil and hold it in front of your baby. You can't let him have it, of course, but you'll have fun watching him react to his reflection and to the noise the foil makes when he bats it.

As They Grow

As your baby develops, he'll continue to enjoy many of the above ideas, but abundant new possibilities open up as well. Here are a few of them:

Many of our children love playing with balloons, especially if the balloon has a short cord (about five inches) so that it can be dragged or held. (Not longer — you don't want your baby to get entangled in it.) "I have a whole bag of balloons in my kitchen," says Carol. "They do pop, and it scares me but not my children."

Any balloon play should be closely supervised, and popped balloons should be confiscated immediately. Also, never allow your toddler or young child to try to blow up a balloon. It's too easy for him to suck in at the wrong time and inhale it. Vicky says, "My brother choked badly on a balloon when he was about two. I still remember it." Another potential danger is that a teething child might chew on an inflated balloon, then gasp when it pops, sucking the balloon into his windpipe. For this reason, the safest balloons for small children are probably the Mylar (metallic) ones that don't pop. These can be bought cheaply at party supply and craft stores, and they hold air much longer than latex balloons. To make them easier to play with, try simply blowing them up rather than having them filled with helium. (Use a straw to blow up a Mylar balloon.) Again, though, keep a sharp eye on your baby and confiscate deflated balloons right away.

When babies are about six months old, they learn a delightful game called "Mommy Pick Up." They drop their rattle or toy again and again and expect you to pick it up each time. You can help short-circuit this by tying the toy to your baby's high chair with a short piece of strong cord (not yarn, which your baby will gnaw through). Remember to supervise any play involving cord to make sure your child doesn't become entangled. There are also plastic chains on the market for attaching toys to your baby's high chair or Exersaucer.

When their babies became old enough to crawl around and explore, several mothers gained peace and quiet as they worked in the kitchen by giving their children their own special kitchen cabinet filled with plastic cups, bowls, lids, and unbreakable plastic cookie cutters. "Ashley loves those plastic bowls," says Christine. "She takes them all out and stacks them inside each other and sees which lid fits on which bowl. She's learned a lot about sizes that way."

Carol uses the plastic cups in her children's cabinet to teach them independence: "My three-year-old can go and get his own cup and water because our refrigerator has a spout for cold water on the front. Even the neighbor kids do it now when they come to visit."

Wanda recommends keeping two boxes of toys — one for your baby to play with now, and one to put away for the time when he tires of the toys that are out. This way your child can have "new" toys from time to time without your having to pay for them. In fact, it's a good habit to put away one of your baby's old toys each time he receives a new one. By the time he tires of the new toy, the old one will be interesting again. Wanda also suggests a rainy-day play box of toys, games, and craft ideas for when your child is old enough to chafe at being kept indoors by bad weather or illness.

> Wanda recommends keeping two boxes of toys — one for your baby to play with now, and one to put away for the time when he tires of the toys that are out. This way your child can have "new" toys from time to time without your having to pay for them.

Several mothers mentioned that it's helpful to keep baskets of toys in various parts of the house. Not only does this make toys available, it also keeps you from having to continually return them to a central location.

When Megan was about eight months old, I bought her some children's books with animal pictures. Within a couple of months she had learned to imitate most of the animal sounds, and by the time she reached the tender age of fourteen months she and her books were inseparable. Her library had expanded to include books with pictures of mommies, daddies, babies, trees, and flowers, and I was often treated to the sight of her sitting by her toybox "reading" to herself. I heard mostly nonsense words, punctuated every now and then with a "Ball!" "Arf-arf!" "Meow!" "Baby!" "Duck!" or "Ribbut!"

I was amazed at how quickly her vocabulary grew because Jon and I took the time to sit down with her and her little books. She made the fascinating discovery that every time she and Mommy or Daddy opened a book, she learned something new — a new sound, a new name — and she loved it. I believe a big factor, too, in her love of books was that I am an avid reader and she often saw me with a book in hand. Often when I was reading on the couch, she would get a book, climb up, and join me.

"Zachary has his own little photo album," says Terri, "and I give him all my seconds whenever I get two prints. He's played more with pictures than with any other toy I've invested in." When Megan was fifteen months old, I got an inexpensive photo album with clear plastic pages and filled it with pictures of her grandparents, uncles, aunts, cousins, and of course, Mommy and Daddy and Megan. It rapidly became her favorite picture book. She enjoyed being able to recognize the people she loved, and it was also a good way to acquaint her with her relatives who live out of state.

Thirteen-month-old Lindsie's favorite game is for LeEtta to teach her the parts of her body. "I ask her, 'Where's Mommy's hair?'" says LeEtta, "and she thinks it's so funny to reach up and grab it. Sometimes she'll just come up to me on her own and start pointing at my nose or ears or eyes, and now she's doing it with everybody — even strangers." This game is a good way to keep your child occupied while you change her diaper.

Toddling Along

The parents in this book generally found that the best toys for holding their toddlers' attention were creative ones: toys with multiple uses, such as building blocks, dolls, and even cardboard boxes. Carol says, "Play Doh is great for a toddler who's finished teething — say, three years old. We keep some in a jar on a low shelf so our little boy can get to it, and it keeps him busy for a long time. He loves crayons and paper too — just very basic toys."

When rainy weather keeps them inside, Janice gives three-year-old Brock and his big brother, Brandt, an old catalog and a couple of pairs of round-tipped scissors. "They'll cut out pictures for hours," she says.

"Remember," says Terri, "you're not too old to get down on your child's level and play games and just be silly." Wanda's daughter, Michelle, puts in a word here: "It makes me feel important when Mommy and Daddy take time to play with me."

Nancy says, "Hannah is two. One of her favorite games is to play 'butterfly.' We usually do this while we're making the beds. We each take an appropriately sized blanket and put it over our shoulders and run around the house flapping our 'wings.' Sometimes I cover a headband in foil and use long twist ties to make antennae. She loves it, and it costs absolutely nothing! And sometimes I read her a children's book on how a caterpillar becomes a butterfly. She gets very wide-eyed and in hushed, awed tones says, 'Wow!'"

The mothers I interviewed are strong believers in the idea that the best way to persuade your toddler to let you do your housework is to let him in on the act. "Let your child help you in everything possible," says Patty. "It takes longer to get things done, but it's worth it because you're also making memories and building your toddler's confidence and sense of self-worth. At two, Jennifer helps wash dishes, fold laundry, and make beds. She loves it!"

"When I'm baking," says Terri, "my little boy is sitting on the counter and my little girl is in her high chair beside me. One gets to put in the baking powder, and the other gets to put in the flour. And I tell you, at four years old Zachary right now can probably cook better than my husband. He wants to be right there doing whatever I'm doing, and since I've taken the time to teach him to help, I've found that he doesn't have much interest in television."

"My three-year-old loves to help with all my chores," says Lisa. "Most of the time it takes me twice as long to get things done, but we have fun! I've discovered he's a great laundry sorter — he sorts my whites and darks better than my husband does. I even let him sort sometimes while I get something else done, which has been a great help. I look forward to seeing what other budding talents he has. If we never let them try, they'll never learn."

An excellent side benefit of letting your toddler participate in the housework is that it builds good work habits for the time when he'll have daily chores to do by himself. It can still be yielding benefits years later when he's married and is sharing the housework with his working wife or helping out after the children arrive.

Donna stresses the need for children to get fresh air and physical exercise by playing outside and taking walks. When Megan began walking, we got into the habit of taking a stroll around the block right before naptime when the weather was nice. She toddled along, holding onto Mommy with one hand and picking up leaves and grass with the other, constantly asking "Zat?" She especially loved it when we took along a small paper bag that she could fill with her treasures. She learned much about the world around her, met some new friends, and got tired enough to take a long nap and give Mommy a break when we got home. Virginia's children loved to play in their sandbox when they were little: "I stayed with them for a few minutes at first to give them some ideas about making little mounds and cakes," she says. "Then I sat on the back porch where I could

> An excellent side benefit of letting your toddler participate in the housework is that it builds good work habits for the time when he'll have daily chores to do by himself.

watch them while I relaxed and read. They played sometimes for hours. When they finished, I picked them up and took them straight to the bathtub, and after their bath they were usually so tired that they went right to sleep."

Out and About

Until their children were old enough to eat table food, the mothers I interviewed generally found it best to feed their babies just before they went out to dinner. This kept their babies from becoming hungry and cranky while their parents ate. It's also best to avoid going out when it's almost naptime or when your baby is obviously getting tired and grumpy.

The trick to peaceful restaurant meals is keeping your baby occupied. It's only natural that he should become bored during an evening out—after all, he's already eaten *his* dinner. Here are some possible attention keepers: a piece of waxed paper or a colorful greeting card, peeled carrots that have been kept cold in a cup of ice water, a bottle of water or juice, a special toy, or a cloth or vinyl book.

The mothers who discovered this trick thought they had done something unique until they got together with our other moms who had done the same thing: Quite a few of their babies like lemon wedges. "Ian loves them," says Julie. "It's hysterical because when we give them to him in a restaurant, people just stare. He makes the worst faces, but he won't quit. The sour taste seems to keep him coming back for more."

The Mommy and Daddy Book · A Busy Baby is a Happy Baby

Carol made the same discovery: "Kristie would be happy through the whole meal as long as we kept handing her lemons. We just made sure there were no seeds." Megan loved them too — in fact, for a while our biggest problem when we went out to eat was persuading her to give up her lemon wedge at the end of the meal. We found that squeezing the lemon wedge and then dipping it into our iced tea or water before giving it to her kept it from being too sour.

You probably shouldn't try this until your baby is at least four months old. Also, when your little one starts cutting teeth, you'll need to watch to make sure she doesn't chew off a hunk of the rind. And make this a rare treat, because constant exposure to the acid in a lemon wedge can erode your baby's tooth enamel.

The mothers who discovered this trick thought they had done something unique until they got together with our other moms who had done the same thing: Quite a few of their babies like lemon wedges.

LeEtta was surprised to find that not all restaurants provide high chairs. If you're taking your child out to eat at a new place and aren't carrying your own baby seat, she recommends that you call first.

"Unless your baby or toddler is naturally quiet and contented," says Patty, "don't take him to a formal restaurant where everyone will be made to feel tense and uncomfortable if he decides to fuss. Until he matures enough to understand what's expected of him in social settings, confine your family meals out to family restaurants, where baby noises are not out of place."

These mothers agree that it's your responsibility to supply the toys to keep your child entertained during visits to friends' homes. Carol says, "We had a little garbage pail with a lid, and we filled it with inexpensive toys, books, and a doll or two and just picked it up by the handle and took it with us whenever we went anywhere." Carol adds, "And if you accidentally go out without the toys, you can always ask your friend for a few plastic bowls and measuring cups."

When Vicky takes Lauren shopping, she takes along a bottle or cup and a packet of Gatorade. She says, "I just stop at a drinking fountain and add water, and I always have something for her to drink." For older babies, a plastic container of crackers or Cheerios can also work wonders to keep you from wishing you'd never left home.

"I always take a well-stocked diaper bag wherever I go, with snacks and toys I vary frequently," says Lisa. "On trips to the grocery store, my three-year-old and I play games like, 'Who will find the cereal first?' I let the baby hold and touch things in the basket that she can't break, squash, or choke on. I try to avoid going when the kids are tired and not likely to be at their best. But when they do cry and yell, I try to look on the bright side — I usually get extra help bagging my groceries and get my bags taken out to my car quickly. They want me and the noise out of there!"

When Terri's toddlers become restless in church, she keeps them quiet by hiding coins between the hymnal pages. Zachary and Ashley love looking for them, and this quiet game keeps them occupied for quite a while. Of course, this game shouldn't be played with a teething toddler, who might put the coins into his mouth.

"In children's church and other places where I was supervising several small children," says Glenda, "we played the 'silent game' to see who could be quiet the longest. They loved it, and it gave me a welcome rest."

Over the River and through the Woods

We took an extended car trip when Megan was four months old, and we saved our sanity and kept her entertained by stringing a one-inch-wide strip of elastic between the windows in the back seat and using it to hang toys in front of her car seat. We made sure the toys hung just low enough for her to touch, bat, and tug on, but not low enough to smack her in the face if we hit a bump. A knot tied in each end of the elastic will keep it from slipping out of the closed car window, and it's a good idea to change the toys frequently.

"We always bought small, inexpensive, safe new toys when we made a long car trip," says Glenda, "and we never gave them all to them at the same time. Just one or two would keep them occupied for quite a while." Wanda still assembles a vacation box during the weeks before a long trip even though her daughter is now ten years old. She includes inexpensive toys and games, books, coloring books, and whatever else she thinks will help the miles go by faster for Michelle. (But Stephanie warns against leaving crayons in the car during the summertime. They melt.)

> "We always bought small, inexpensive, safe new toys when we made a long car trip," says Glenda, "and we never gave them all to them at the same time."

Patty adds, "With a toddler, it's especially important to take along a favorite blanket or stuffed animal to help her go to sleep."

🦜 "As our toddlers grew older," says Glenda, "we played games while traveling, such as counting trucks or cars or cows or certain types of signs. It kept them occupied for a long time and taught them to be observant. We also sang songs together and did word games. These things were fun and educational."

🐚 Cassette tapes of children's songs and stories are also favorite occupiers for road trips. Cil says, "At our public library, they've got a huge collection of children's books on tape. They've even got some of the books we've read at home." Many library systems are countywide. If your local branch doesn't have a good selection, ask if books and tapes can be requested from other branches. Check your church library too.

🐢 Remember that your little one needs a chance to get out and stretch now and then, even if you don't. Make frequent rest stops where you can unbuckle your baby and let him crawl or toddle around and get some fresh air.

∘ ∘ ∘ ∘ ∘

IT HAS BEEN SAID that play is the business of childhood. It's one of the primary ways young children learn about the world they've so recently entered. But play is Mom and Dad's business too, because watching your child play, helping him discover the things he enjoys, and playing with him are some of the best ways to learn about your child.

They're great ways to have fun, too.

Chapter 8

Never Too Little for Jesus

The first step toward raising a child who has a vital relationship with Jesus is to have such a relationship of your own. For better or for worse, the parents in this book acknowledge that you are the first image of God your baby will see: the omnipresent giver of food, help, and solace; the omniscient being who always manages to catch him when he's about to turn the knobs on the stereo or eat the magazines, even if he was sure you weren't looking. The child whose parents shower him with love and affection and are patient with his childish mistakes, while dealing firmly with direct disobedience, probably isn't going to have too much trouble grasping the concept of a God who is also loving yet just.

"Children's perceptions of God are affected by their parents," says Marilee. "If a child's parents are very lenient, he may get the idea that he doesn't really have to obey God or anyone else. On the other hand, if his parents are overbearing, quick to punish, and never say 'I'm sorry' when they're wrong, the child may get the idea that God is just waiting around with a baseball bat to knock him on the head when he makes a mistake. We are the examples of God to our children. If we're not walking our Christianity right, they're going to get a distorted view of what he is like."

It has already been mentioned that children love to imitate — a trait that can be both delightful and scary. The first time your little prodigy says "Mama!"

is wonderful and precious; the first time you see your toddler echoing an attitude you thought was well hidden may not be. But your child's natural gift for imitation is vital to his or her spiritual training. "The Bible says we are to be imitators of Christ," says Cheryl, "and until our children reach the point where they can understand that, they are imitators of us."

"When Claire was very little," says Cil, "I was watching her play with her baby doll one day. She was hugging and kissing her, talking very sweet, singing to her. Suddenly I realized that was just how I acted with her. It dawned on me — 'Everything I do affects her!'"

Where It Begins

Now that you're thoroughly frightened, let's talk about where spiritual training starts — and these parents insist it begins long before your child is able to understand the words you use as you pray over a meal. "It starts even before you conceive the child," says Adrienne, who, with six children, is perhaps the professional mother of our group. "You tell God you want a baby, and then all through your pregnancy you pray for the child and for your wisdom as a mother." Virginia adds, "We started praying beside the crib when our children were babies. Even though they may not understand, children sense your prayers."

> "The Bible says we are to be imitators of Christ," says Cheryl, "and until our children reach the point where they can understand that, they are imitators of us."

But please don't despair if your baby is already here and you're getting a late start. Nancy was one of several mothers whose interest in spiritual things was reawakened with the birth of her child. Parents in general are more willing to do things for the sake of their little ones than for their own good, and reconciling with the Lord is no exception. But Nancy's renewed walk with God became more than a dull, dry church attendance for the sake of her family; it grew into a beautiful, vital relationship. As she puts it, "My husband and I learned right along with the children."

Many mothers in this book recommend that you pray daily, not only for your child but with him, even while he's still tiny. Aside from the blessed fact that God will hear and answer, your child's understanding will grow in time and a habit of prayer interwoven into daily life will have been formed. Also, several mothers began reading Bible stories to their children while they were still infants. Reading to a young baby may consist of nothing more than pointing to the characters and telling him their names, or telling nursery rhymes in a singsong voice while trying to wrestle the pages from his grasping little hands. Again, though, his understanding will grow with time, and if you make his story-times fun, you'll have the added benefit of a child who loves books.

Cheryl says, "When my children were tiny, I had a bedtime routine of rocking them gently and reading short Bible stories, singing praise songs, and praying." (Elizabeth does this too, and she says, "That's my extra quiet time!") Cheryl goes on, "We still do our bedtime devotion every night, although it has taken different forms as my kids have grown bigger. Someone once asked me why I insisted on doing it every day, the same way. She thought I was wasting my time because my children were so little and couldn't understand. But you know what? Their *spirits* could understand and absorb God's goodness. Also, this routine has formed a way of life. My children love to sing praise songs to Jesus."

The growth of the Christian music industry has given parents another powerful spiritual tool. "We've always been lovers of Christian music," says Tim. "We surrounded our children with it from the very beginning. It creates an environment, and it makes a difference." Most Christian bookstores carry tapes and CDs in a wide variety of musical styles.

Tim also points out that your baby's first few months are the time for husband and wife to work through any differences in your spiritual viewpoints: "If you're from different denominations, even if you're both Christians, it can really be a point of friction. You may have been able to compromise for a while, but when it comes down to the responsibility of raising your child, the differences are going to come out."

The Chef Eats First

A new mother can't expect to be the best spiritual trainer since Susanna Wesley if she's starving spiritually herself. Charles Wesley's mother had the right idea. She knew that to give her children a good spiritual foundation, she had to spend time alone with God, and if *she* could find the time, back in the days before appliances, so can we.

Society is so fast-paced today that it's easy to feel guilty just for sitting down when there is work to be done. But come to think of it, things haven't really changed that much in the past couple of thousand years. Jesus' friend Martha was the type who had to make sure the house was in order and dinner was ready to be served before she would sit down with the Lord; she probably never did sit down and really listen to him. Her mind was most likely running ahead to the meal's next course, worrying about whether the Lord would like it or whether the new servant girl would trip and spill it on his lap. Mary's room may have been a bit messy and her meals a bit late, but I'm willing to bet she rarely missed her personal devotions.

"You just have to set your priorities and do it," says Kathy. "You can't let all these other things get in the way." The parents in this chapter agree that maintaining your relationship with the Lord is vital to both your own spiritual health and that of your children. As Kathy says, "You can't live the life in front of them unless you have that special time yourself."

Carol, like most of us, learned this lesson the hard way: "I was getting off track until a dear friend came to me and said, 'Carol, you've lost your joy.' The idea that you don't have time is an attack of the enemy. If you leave that time out, Satan gets in."

A recent national fad used the catchphrase, "What would Jesus do?" People wore WWJD bracelets and put WWJD posters on their walls. It's a noble thought; after all, as Christians, we are called to be like Christ. But as I pondered the question, I realized how tempting it was to answer with my opinion of what Jesus would do in any given situation, rather than with biblical truth. The only way I can really hope to imitate Christ, as a mother or in any other aspect of my life, is to have an intimate knowledge of who he is, based on careful study of the Bible. Otherwise, I may find myself acting in ways that seem reasonable to me, but that are probably flavored more by society's values than by God's. (And if you've been a Christian for much time at all, you've discovered that God's ways and society's ways pretty much run in opposite directions.)

> The only way I can really hope to imitate Christ, as a mother or in any other aspect of my life, is to have an intimate knowledge of who he is, based on careful study of the Bible.

All right, so devotional time is important. But you're a new parent, and privacy is a thing of the past. How do you find time to keep growing in your relationship with God?

If your baby and your energy level permit, first thing in the morning is prime devotional time. Cheryl says, "I enjoy my quiet time before the kids get up. It allows me to get focused. I like to sit in the bathtub, with the water really hot, and meditate." Linking your quiet time with something pleasant or relaxing (for me, it's a good cup of hot coffee) can give you an extra incentive to get out of bed. It can help, too, to think of your quiet times as a love-gift to God, a sacrifice of the new parent's most precious commodity: time. "I prayed earnestly for time with God," says Jennifer. "He started waking me up at 4:30 A.M.! I said okay and got myself an extra cup of coffee. I complained some, but it was worth it."

If early mornings are out of the question, your best bet for uninterrupted devotional time while your baby is small is probably during his naps or while he's nursing. As he grows older and spends less time sleeping, you'll probably have to become more creative. During this season of your life, your quiet times may have to be shorter than you would like, with extended times worked in here and there. Two important things to remember: First, God knows your heart. And second: *It won't always be like this.*

Christin places flip calendars with daily devotional readings and Bible verses in several different places around her home — the bathrooms, the kitchen, the family room. As she spends time in each place, she reads them and meditates on the verses.

Julie says, "At one point I had three kids ages four and under, and they didn't take naps. I learned to 'pray without ceasing.' While putting clothes in the laundry, while doing dishes. I'd read a few Bible verses here and there throughout the day. I snatched it where I could." These "on the hoof" devotions may not be the ideal, but they're definitely better than no devotional time at all.

Support from other Christians can be invaluable too. Stephanie says, "I've found somebody who is holding me accountable, and I'm holding her accountable, that five times a week we are going to do *something*, whether it's time spent in prayer, or reading a devotional book or our Bibles, or whatever."

"I really enjoy my women's Bible study group that I attend every Tuesday morning," says Cheryl. "It's a time of encouragement, prayer, and study." Church Bible study groups can be helpful to young mothers on many levels. They're a place to interact with other Christian women and to provide a break from the constant demands of young motherhood, as well as to learn and be encouraged.

Speaking of creative devotional ideas, Stephanie keeps her devotional book in the bathroom. "It's the only place I can be alone! Sometimes Erica is in there with me. I've tried naptime, but I'm so tired then! Plus I'm distracted by the million things I need to do. So for me, potty time is the best time. Or when I take a bath. I make sure I know what the kids are doing, and I leave the door open." (Oswald Chambers' classic, *My Utmost for His Highest*, is ideal for this kind of devotional reading. His daily devotions are brief but incredibly rich and thought-provoking.)

What about Dad? If he's to be the spiritual head of the home, he has to be spending time with God too. Many of the things that work for young mothers can work for young fathers as well: accountability with friends, small-group Bible studies, a good devotional book or study Bible, devotional flip calendars for the desk or workplace, plus flexibility and alertness to watch for opportunities. It also helps to know what works best with your personality. Glenn has his devotional time in the morning, over breakfast. He says, "If I didn't do it in the morning, I'd never do it. From the time I leave the house, I'm going ninety to nothing the whole day. When I come home, I want to read the last two sections of the newspaper and play with Wendy." On the other hand, Loren says, "I'm the opposite. I do my devotions at night. If I try to have them in the morning, I've got all the stuff for the day going through my mind, and I'm distracted. At the end of the day, I seem to be able to let it go and focus better. Typically, I have my best thoughts at night."

I have yet to meet a parent for whom finding devotional time is effortless. Even those of us whose children are older still struggle with the Mary-Martha syndrome. It can be comforting to know you're not alone in the struggle, but what it all boils down to, of course, is a matter of priority. If something is important enough to you, you will find a way to do it. That sounds harsh, perhaps, but it's true.

Talking to God

Ideally, you should pray with your little one so often that prayer becomes second nature to him. "If you'll pray with your child about small things," says Connie, "he'll learn early to turn to the Lord in everything. I prayed with Lisa on one occasion for a hurt finger when she was about two years old. She said, 'How God gonna heal it? God gotta Band-Aid?' She thought Band-Aids could fix anything. But now, practically every day as she leaves for school, she says, 'Pray for me today, Mother. I have an English test (or a math test, or whatever).'"

With that in mind, here is a list of ways to build your child's prayer life:

As soon as your toddler begins putting words together into simple sentences, teach him to repeat short prayers after you. Always explain what you're doing, making sure he understands what you're asking or thanking God for.

Stay away from formula prayers. Pray simply and sincerely about the needs of the moment. "God bless Mommy, Daddy, Grandma, Grandpa, and so on" can be included but shouldn't make up the whole prayer every time.

As his understanding grows, ask your child to pray for you. "We have asked Mary, who's three, to pray for us many times," says Adrienne. "Her prayers are short and to the point—sometimes just, 'Dear Jesus, help Mommy to feel better,' but we know that Jesus hears them." Karen says, "When Randy or I don't feel well or have an 'ouchie', Josh prays for us." Teach your child to pray for his little friends too.

It can be tempting to see a child's prayers strictly as training exercises, without any real spiritual power. That's a big mistake. The power in prayer isn't based on the age or experience of the person praying but on the eternal and omnipotent God who listens and answers.

Intersperse prayer throughout the day. Shari says, "We're on a prayer chain at church, and we hear prayer requests come through on our local Christian radio station. Every time someone calls, I tell Hannah about it and we pray together right then. Prayer becomes part of everyday life, not just a mealtime and bedtime thing."

Let your child see the answers to his prayers. "Tell him when you feel better and thank him for praying," says Cheryl, "or if you were praying for money and the Lord provides, tell how he provided and then have a prayer of thanksgiving. Prayer is real. It works. Let your child see it work." Dana agrees: "Bryan had a little friend at the end of our street who had an asthma attack. When his mother told me about it on the phone, I said, 'Bryan, why don't you and I pray for Chris?' We prayed, and that night when I called Chris's mother, she told me he was much better and was playing outside. Bryan's faith grew by leaps and bounds."

"We keep a prayer journal with our kids," says Cheryl. They record not only the things they've been praying for but also the ways God has answered. "It helps them see the power of God at work."

Teach your child to give thanks. These mothers agree that by the time a toddler is two and a half or three he can answer the question, "What are you thankful to Jesus for today?" Thanking Jesus for Mommy, Daddy, grandparents, food, trees, flowers, and so on helps your little one understand that these blessings are not owed him; they are indeed gifts from a God who loves him very much.

Finally, don't force your child to pray aloud if he doesn't want to. Keep offering the opportunity, but don't push it. After all, aren't there times when you don't feel like praying? On the other hand, Rita points out that a child who

> The power in prayer isn't based on the age or experience of the person praying but on the eternal and omnipotent God who listens and answers.

declines to pray because of bashfulness may need some encouragement. "Brian never wanted to pray at the dinner table because he was shy," she says, "so when I saw him in the kitchen after dinner, I would tell him, 'Brian, that was a beautiful prayer.' That bit of encouragement really bolstered him. Now if anybody hesitates when we start to pray, Brian jumps right in."

Family Devotional Ideas That Work

While your child is small, most of the parents in this book agree it's best to simply incorporate spiritual training into daily life rather than enforcing a structured devotional time. "When a child is hungry," says Marilee, "that's when you feed him. When his mind is off somewhere else is not the time to force him to sit down and listen to a Bible story. It won't sink in then anyway.

"Capitalize on the times when he asks about things during the day. Sometimes, all of a sudden, my little boy will ask something like, 'Mommy, why does that man smoke?' Then I tell him very simply about habits. I tell him how sometimes when you start something, it's hard to stop and that smoking hurts our bodies, and Jesus gave us very special bodies and he wants us to take care of them. Just about any question he asks during the day can be turned into a simple spiritual lesson."

"Christianity is not a part of your life; it *is* your life. Spiritual training is not so much what you say but what you're living."

"I think that's more what 'training a child up' is all about rather than sitting down and trying to teach," says Cheryl. "Christianity is not a part of your life; it *is* your life. Spiritual training is not so much what you say but what you're living."

A bedtime Bible story and prayer is a good way to get Daddy involved. Marilee says, "Jeff always makes sure he goes in right before our little boy goes to bed. He tells him a story about Moses and Pharaoh or David and Goliath, since those are the things we want him to go to bed thinking about. At the end of the story, Jeff always turns it around and tries to apply it to our lives." For instance, you could use David and Goliath to teach that even when we are small, God can use us to do big things for him.

"Bedtime is a very teachable time," says Jeff. "Not only to read and talk about the Bible story but to pray with Hannah and to let her pray. It's really cute to see the different things she prays for. I think it's important for daddies to be part of that. I can see where, if they weren't, when a son grew up he might think he would outgrow that devotional time because Dad wasn't involved. I have friends who grew up going to church with their moms, but when they got to a certain age, since Dad didn't go, all of a sudden church was for women, and spiritual things were for Mom."

"I don't think you can substitute anything for those precious moments you have together just before they go to bed," says Nathaniel's dad, Loren. "It's important to take time to talk to them, because they'll tell you things then that they won't tell you at any other time during the day. It's hard, because a lot of times you just want to put them to bed because you've got other things to do. But I learn the most about Nathaniel during that time. I've developed the habit of asking him almost every night what his favorite thing today was and what his hardest thing was. I know I'd never find out if I didn't do that. It just opens up the communication, hopefully preparing a foundation for future years."

These bedtime sessions are probably the best "formal" devotional times for young children. The best devotional setting may be with everyone cuddled together in Mom and Dad's bed, or sitting on the floor in the children's room. Don't assume that your family devotions have to look like some preconceived notion from your own youth. Think about what you're trying to accomplish: to develop an awareness of God's unconditional love and holiness, to spark your child's interest in spiritual things, to develop godly character traits, to develop your child's faith through prayer, and to establish yourself firmly as your child's spiritual teacher and role model. Once you have your goals in mind, you can consider the most effective way to teach those things at your child's current age and level of understanding.

> The most influential devotional book your child will ever read — and he's already reading it — is your life.

Many of these young parents have found children's devotional books helpful. The books usually have a picture, a short Bible story, and a couple of questions on each page. But remember, the most influential devotional book your child will ever read — and he's already reading it — is your life.

Gadgets for Your Spiritual Toolbox

Bible stories are great to use throughout the day as well. "My boys would much rather hear about Noah or David and Goliath than something like Hansel and Gretel," says Cheryl. "I just keep the books on hand, and when they want a story I say, 'Okay, here's a story about Noah,' rather than telling them,

'Sit down. It's time for Bible study.'" She recommends reading only as long as your toddler's attention holds, since forcing a child to sit still while you plow through to the end is one good way to make him dread Bible story time. "Start skipping pages when you feel yourself losing him," advises Adrienne. "He won't notice if you come to the end sooner than usual."

Virginia made hand puppets from paper bags and used them to populate her stories. "Even when my children were only one or two years old, those puppets got their attention," she says. "As they grow older, they like to help make the puppets too," adds Wanda.

In the absence of puppets, pictures are necessary when telling stories to a young child. "They need the pictures," says Adrienne. "The things they picture in their minds are not always in the story. A friend of mine was reading a story to her little boy, and she came to a part where it said, 'Suddenly his eyes dropped to the floor.' The little boy got very upset and didn't want to hear any more. When she finally got him calmed down and asked what was wrong, she realized that he thought the character's eyes had really fallen onto the floor!" Fortunately, there are many good illustrated Bible story books, children's Bibles, Christian storybooks, and devotional books for children on the market. Your local Christian bookstore and church library should be good resources for these materials.

Children learn best and have the most fun when they can get involved, whether the involvement is asking and answering questions about a Bible story, praying for Mommy and Daddy, or something a little more active. Virginia began teaching her children Bible story songs with hand motions before they were a year old. At first all they could do was copy Mommy's gestures and babble along, which they loved, but they gradually learned more and more of the words. "It was something happy and joyful that they could do," she says. "They learned a lot that way." Your church nursery should be a good source for these songs.

For older toddlers, Scripture songs are a wonderful way to learn Bible verses, but these mothers have other ways of teaching their children God's Word as well. "When Ashley was born," says Christine, "a friend gave me a pillow with her name and a Bible verse for each letter of her name embroidered on it. When she was about fourteen months old, I started reading it to her every morning while I made her bed. At eighteen months she could say the last word of most of the verses, and at two years old she could say almost all of every one of them — not by herself but with just a little help."

Terri's four-year-old son Zachary has a set of twenty-six cards with a Bible verse for each letter of the alphabet. Terri says, "Zachary loves to memorize those cards. He has a wallet-sized set he takes almost everywhere he goes and a big set at home. I wish I had gotten them sooner—he was already four when we started, and he had no trouble at all learning one a day." Of course, be sure you don't push your child to learn too much too quickly. Let him proceed at his own pace—after all, you want this to be a good experience. Terri recommends offering lots of encouragement and praise as each verse is learned. Making Scripture memorization fun for your child will pay off, not only in spiritual benefits as you explain the verses to him but in self-discipline and the self-esteem that comes from accomplishment.

These mothers make no apologies for using flash cards and pillows to help their children memorize Scripture. "Call it a gimmick, call it what you will," says Dana. "It's a learning tool, and it works." Adrienne, who was the friend who made Ashley's pillow, adds, "When you use the child's name, you give her Scriptures to grow up with. Those become her special Scriptures. I didn't just put those verses down at random for Christine's little girl. I really thought them over and tried to pick ones a small child could grow up with. I wanted her to be able to say, 'God meant that verse for me.'"

Answering the Great Questions of Life (in Twenty-five Words or Less)

Children have a matter-of-fact way of asking questions that have stumped wise men since Creation. "Where did God come from, anyway?" demanded Kristy's little girl Jennifer. "Did he crack out of an egg, or what?"

Janet's three-year-old son, Derek, had just been acquainted by his babysitter with the term "Jesus' house" for church, and as they prepared to go to services that Sunday, Derek was very excited and kept telling his mommy that he was going to see Jesus at his house and sing him a song. On the way there, Janet asked Derek, "Do you want to practice the song you're going to sing for Jesus?" "No," he answered, "I'll just wait till I get to his house."

Later as they were leaving church, Derek had a troubled look on his face. "Mommy," he said, "I didn't see him. I didn't see Jesus." At that point Janet knew it was time for Derek's spiritual training to go a step further. "Jesus is everywhere, Derek," she told him. "He's in the car with us." Derek was fascinated by this bit of news. "And on motorcycles?" he asked. "And in the sky? Up there in those clouds?" He accepted Mommy's answer without hesitation, which small children do most of the time, to the great relief of their parents.

The most important thing about answering a small child's questions, according to Nancy, is not to overexplain. "Give a child only what he asks for," she says. "I found that worked so well with my four little ones. When you've satisfied the child's curiosity, stop right there." For example, if your child asks where God came from, keep it as simple as possible: "Well, God has always been here. Nobody made him, but he made us."

As a child grows older, his questions may not be so easily resolved. Shannon says Nathaniel, age four, is still struggling with the idea that God is always with him: "He says, 'But I can't feel him, Mommy!'" It's hard not to panic at such times, but your calm reassurance will go a long way. Just tell him, "Even though you can't feel him, he's still there, sweetheart. I promise." Then pray that God will help him see the truth in that promise. Much as we would like to be able to turn the lights on in our children's hearts and minds, God's hand is the only one that can reach the switch.

Many of these first spiritual issues seem to surface around age four. One night during her bedtime Bible story, Hannah shocked her parents Jeff and Shari with, "I don't want to go to heaven!" Jeff says, "She doesn't understand what heaven is, and she likes it here." Shari adds, "In her mind, it's a separation. 'I'm going there, and I won't be home.' She asks lots of questions — 'When do I have to go? Do I get to come back? When do I come back?' She doesn't want to go away."

> Many of these first spiritual issues seem to surface around age four. One night during her bedtime Bible story, Hannah shocked her parents Jeff and Shari with, "I don't want to go to heaven!"

When asked how they're handling the issue, Shari sighs. "We haven't really found an answer. She still talks about it." Jeff adds, "We've had a couple of deaths in our Sunday school class, of women who were very young and left children behind who are our kids' ages. I think that might have a lot to do with the questioning, because some of her friends have lost their mommies. I've told her it's not something she needs to think about right now." Shari says, "But I'm afraid to tell her that, because we never know when someone might die, or when the Lord is coming back. I just keep reassuring her, 'It will be more wonderful than we can imagine.'"

Here's an analogy that might help: "Before you were born, you were in Mommy's womb. [You might want to show your child pictures of yourself when you were pregnant.] I bet you liked it in there. You were warm and cozy and safe. If we could have told you that you'd be born soon, you probably would have said, 'No! I want to stay here!' because you didn't know what being born would be like. But now that you're here with Mommy and Daddy, you're glad. Dying and going to heaven is like that. It seems scary because we've never done it, and we're comfortable here. But the Bible tells us that it's even more wonderful than living here and that we'll be with all the people we love who love Jesus. I'm excited that we can be together in heaven forever."

Guiding your children through these issues will keep you on your toes — and on your knees. It will also force you to think through your beliefs in ways you may not have done for years. It may even reveal gaps in your own understanding of spiritual issues. That can be a wonderful thing, for both you and your child, if it makes you hunt for the answers. Once again, your Christian bookstore and church library can be helpful resources. There are several books available with simple answers to common childhood spiritual questions. And don't forget your pastor, children's pastor, or children's ministry leaders.

"If all else fails," says Adrienne, "it's not bad to say, 'I don't understand it either. I choose to believe it, though, because the Bible teaches us that it's true.'" Pointing to the Bible is not a cop-out. In a world where millions of things are unexplainable, it teaches your child to have faith in the ultimate authority of God's Word.

Loren adds, "It's important to ask your children questions that reveal what they understand about God and what they're thinking about him. The other day I was talking to Nathaniel, who's four. A situation came up where we thought he had done something wrong but then realized he hadn't. He asked me, 'Does that mean Jesus doesn't have to die on the cross again for me?' He was thinking Jesus died on the cross every time he did something wrong." Another common misconception among these parents' children was that they needed to ask Jesus into their hearts again every time they sinned.

"The best thing my mom ever did for me," says Lisa, " — and there were many very good things she did — was pray for me daily and commit me daily to the Lord."

There's probably no way to avoid occasional confusion as your child's little mind and heart try to absorb spiritual lessons. Your best defense is to talk simply and often about spiritual things, asking God for a child's-eye view and making yourself very approachable for questions (which means treating every question with respect and trying never to look shocked, even when you are). The single most important thing you can do as your child's spiritual mentor is to develop an active prayer life. Pray for wisdom and integrity as a parent, as well as for your child to have an understanding heart and a desire to know and love God. "The best thing my mom ever did for me," says Lisa, " — and there were many very good things she did — was pray for me daily and commit me daily to the Lord."

As you teach your child to pray, he'll inevitably come up with requests — unreasonable requests or requests for unnecessary miracles — that you know God won't grant. Those are the times when Mommy and Daddy have to do a little fast thinking. "My little boy Bryan had some mosquito bites the other night," says Dana, "and he was scratching and scratching. So when Bridget prayed that night, she prayed that God would take away all the mosquitoes so Bryan wouldn't get bitten anymore. How do you explain it when he comes up with another bite?" Actually, this might be a good time for a little biology lesson about how God has a purpose for every creature and that mosquitoes lay eggs in the water for the fish to eat. I can't think of any other purpose for mosquitoes.

"We've had bad situations happen because of carelessness," says Carol, "and our daughter Kristie will pray and pray and not see an answer. That's when we share that sometimes God uses these situations to help us grow and learn to be good stewards of what we have."

Sometimes, though, God chooses not to grant a child's valid request without giving a clear explanation. A composite answer these parents use at such times goes something like this: "Jesus hears you when you pray, just as Mommy hears you when you ask for something. But sometimes Jesus has to tell you no, just like Mommy sometimes has to say no. We don't always understand why he says no, but we do know that he loves us and always does what's best for us."

Visiting Jesus' House

While your child is an infant, these parents agree that church is primarily for you, not the baby. They're divided on the issue of using the church nursery, though. As a first-time mother, I hesitated to leave Megan in the nursery. I was sure she would be traumatized by my departure, and I just knew the other babies would beat her up. Also, Megan ended up with a cold several times after being left in the nursery with all those runny-nosed kids.

By the time she was a year old, I was desperate enough to risk an occasional cold. Worship services had become ordeals, with Jon and me juggling Megan between us, alternately stuffing Cheerios into her mouth and half-drowning her with bottles of water. She seldom cried, but being a friendly child, she had the habit of peeking over the back of the pew and saying, "Hi!" and, "Oooo, whazzat?" making it hard for the people behind us to pay attention to the sermon. Jon always ended up taking her out of church before the service was half over.

"It comes to the point where you have to say, 'What am I going to church for?'" says Dana. "Sometimes you have to put your child into the nursery so you can get some spiritual food from the sermon to take home with you."

Of course, in some churches, whether to use the nursery isn't an issue simply because there isn't a nursery. Several mothers found themselves in that situation, and they learned to make the best of it. Taking along an infant seat kept them from having to juggle the baby quite so much; and quiet toys, Cheerios, and a bottle went a long way toward leaving them free to hear what was going on. Also, they found that their child's personality was a big factor in determining whether he did well in worship services. Cheryl says, "Jason would work up to a cry, so I could see it coming and slip out. Brian didn't. It was just 'Yaaa!' and there he was for the whole congregation to hear. Our church had a nursery, and as soon as he was a couple of months old, that's where he went."

Trading off take-out duty with your husband or a kindhearted friend or relative can help a new mother get more out of the service. Or you can try the solution Marilee and her husband, Jeff, found: During David's first few weeks, they traded off going to services alone — one week Marilee went to Sunday morning service while Jeff stayed home with the baby, then she stayed home while Jeff went to the Sunday evening and Wednesday night services. The next week they switched. True, this isn't a good long-term solution, but it can help you stay spiritually fed while waiting for your baby to grow old enough to go into the nursery, or when your baby is sick.

Even after your child reaches the toddler stage, the spiritual training he receives at church isn't going to affect him a fraction as much as the training, negative or positive, he receives at home. His in-church time will be three or four hours a week at most — and that's counting Sunday morning, Sunday night, and Wednesday night. You've got him the rest of the time. As Lois says, "If you neglect the training at home, I don't care where you take them — they're not going to get it. They'll think, 'Well, that's good enough for the preacher, but it's not good enough for Mommy and Daddy.'"

Church is important, though, and needs to be seen in its proper role as a special place where we meet with other people to worship the God we live with every day at home. Stephanie adds, "Sunday school and church teach so much more than parents can in terms of socialization and the idea that others share our values. In your family circle, you can't teach that very well beyond, 'This is who we are as a family.' Church brings a whole new dynamic in." In the best situations, church and home work in harmony, each reinforcing the lessons the other is teaching. All of this puts a big responsibility on the church to be a loving place for children, where both the curriculum and the teachers are carefully chosen. It also puts a big responsibility on parents to choose their church wisely.

The mothers I interviewed feel that during worship service a child should be allowed her little occupiers — dolls, Bible story coloring books, and other quiet toys — until she reaches kindergarten or her first grade year at least. "By then children are in a more regimented schedule at school," says Dana. "That carries over to help them sit still and listen in church. Bryan is eight now, and he doesn't write in church anymore. With him it was a gradual thing, a transition from childish things to, 'I don't do that anymore. I'm grown up now.'"

"When Ryan and Jason were younger," says Luellen, "we attended a church that offered children's chapel at the same time the adult service was going on. It was wonderful! They were learning the same truths we were, but much more on their level."

Making the Decision

Stella encouraged Shauna to accept Jesus as her Savior when Shauna began asking questions about the lessons she was learning in Sunday school. Stella says, "I know she'll come to have a deeper realization of what sin is and why she needs the Lord as she grows older, but that doesn't mean these early decisions aren't valid and important." Christine agrees. She bought Ashley a Christian storybook in which the child protagonist learned the gospel story and asked Jesus to come into her heart. "When we finished reading, I asked her, 'Would you like for Jesus to come into your heart too?' She said yes, and we prayed together right then."

It's important to realize that your job as spiritual trainer is not finished when your child makes a decision for Jesus; it has only begun. A solid Christian walk is built one step at a time, day by day, year after year, as you and your child live, love, pray, laugh, read, worship, and learn together.

> It's important to realize that your job as spiritual trainer is not finished when your child makes a decision for Jesus; it has only begun.

Spiritual Lessons from Strangers

A hundred years ago, a child's main sources of spiritual and moral input were his parents and their friends (including the people at church), his extended family, his teachers, and his peers. Today, another primary source of spiritual and moral input for many children is the black box in the family room. The stereo and the computer contribute their share too. The frightening thing is, it seems as if many parents — even sincere Christian parents — are unaware of how effectively the media are shaping our children's hearts and minds. Think about it this way: In most American homes, the television is on for several hours every day. How many parents spend that much time interacting daily with their children?

When you turn on the TV or sign on to the internet, you're inviting strangers into your home. The same is true when you watch a movie, open a book or magazine, or listen to the radio or a CD. You wouldn't allow just anyone to come in off the street and give moral and spiritual lessons to your family. Use the same caution and discernment in your media choices.

> When you turn on the TV or sign on to the internet, you're inviting strangers into your home. The same is true when you watch a movie, open a book or magazine, or listen to the radio or a CD.

As the parents in this book monitored the available children's programming, they were horrified to realize that Saturday morning cartoons are often very little more than a combination of advertisements, violence, and occultism. Lois recommends, though, that if you decide to make certain shows off-limits to your child, you make sure he understands why. "Don't make arbitrary rules," she says. "If he's at a friend's house and a forbidden show comes on, he needs to be able to say, 'Uh-oh, that's about witchcraft. I'm not supposed to watch it.' He may not like the rule, but at least he'll know why it's there."

The consensus among these parents is that the least painful way to keep your child away from programs you don't want him to watch is simply never to introduce them to him in the first place. Terri says, "Zachary doesn't know about any of the popular TV shows, with maybe a couple of exceptions, and I want to keep it that way. Since we've never had these shows on in the first place, he just doesn't realize he's missing anything."

Of course, your child probably isn't the only person in the house who likes the TV. "My husband says watching TV is the one place where he can just 'veg out,'" says one mom. "But he's so immune to it that sometimes he doesn't realize when a program is inappropriate for the children. I'll be cleaning the kitchen and he'll be in there with the kids, and I'll look in and say, 'Helloooooo. . .' One Saturday I went somewhere and came home, and he had both boys in his lap, and our daughter was right there, watching *Jaws*."

Jeff says, "TV was my babysitter when I was growing up. I still watch too much, although Shari has helped me cut back. But TV today is not the same as it was when I was a kid. Network TV is disgusting—the language, the content, the commercials." Shari adds, "I saw things I never should have seen as a child. Those pictures have never left my head. You can't wipe them away. And you can't always turn the TV off fast enough for the children not to see or hear something that will take away some of their innocence. I know they're going to run into it at school and in other places, but I don't want to take away Hannah's innocence in our own home. I've become very sensitive to that. When she does see things, we do explain to her why it was wrong and what was wrong about it. But the memory is still there. And that concerns me."

"It's so dumb that there should be such a struggle to turn it off!" says Jeff. "We have some of our best and funnest nights listening to the radio, dancing with the kids. Our kids need to see us able to turn off the TV, as opposed to just changing the channel. They need to see that we have control over it, and it's not something that's an every night, 'Now it's TV time.'"

This is yet another issue to be talked through between you and your spouse. How much TV is appropriate and healthy, for both you and your child? What limits should be set? (The consensus among the parents I interviewed was that an hour a day of TV is plenty for a young child.) What kinds of programs should be avoided while your child is watching?

This is also the time for an "integrity check" regarding the programs you watch while your child is asleep. Ask yourself: *How are this program's values affecting me? If my child were to ask me, 'Why do you watch that program?' how would I answer?* Here's the kicker: *Is this a program Jesus might watch?* Some programs—news, for instance—are appropriate and helpful for adults, but not for children. Others may represent spiritual compromises we don't even realize we've made until our children bring them to light.

We'll talk more about television in chapter 10, but for now let me leave you with this: "Above all else, guard your heart, for it is the wellspring of life" (Prov. 4:23).

When Mommy and Daddy Blow It

There are probably few people who wouldn't like to be thought of as perfect—or at least almost perfect. And it's tempting to allow our children to put us on pedestals and look at us as gods instead of as just grown-up people who were once little, like themselves, and who make a mistake every now and then. The problem is, your child is bound to discover the truth sooner or later, and these parents insist that letting her in on the secret from the beginning can prevent emotional scars for everyone involved.

"It's important for your kids to see how you handle it when you make mistakes," says Adrienne. "So many people grow up thinking a Christian has to be a perfect person. If your child grows up thinking you're a Christian and you're perfect, when *he* makes a mistake, he's liable to feel as if it's not worth it to try anymore. If he sees that you make mistakes along the way and sees how you handle it with God, he learns that it's okay to make mistakes. God forgives you."

Another of our moms shares, "I can't remember my parents ever admitting to me that they had made a mistake. I grew up thinking they were perfect. One of the biggest problems I had when I was growing up was condemning myself because I couldn't be like Mom and Dad, yet somehow I never saw the areas in their lives where they were inconsistent. I've often thought that my kids will never grow up with the mistaken idea that their mother is perfect. I've let them know time and time again that there are ways I've failed, and yet that God still loves me and is willing to take my heart and wash it clean. My children are so open now to saying at night when they pray, 'Lord, I blew it.' It's a protection against the feeling of condemnation that comes when a child does wrong and thinks, 'Mom never makes a mistake. I must not be a Christian.'"

"Let them hear you pray, 'Lord, help me to be a good mother. Give me wisdom,'" says Kristy. "I pray that in front of my children every day." As your child sees you leaning on Jesus, she learns that he is strong enough to hold her up as well.

It's also important to ask your child to forgive you when the situation calls for it. "If you've done something that has hurt your child," says Wanda, "even if it was unintentional, you need to ask her forgiveness." Not only does seeking your child's forgiveness heal your relationship and prevent resentment from creeping in, it also teaches her that it's okay to apologize and that it's important to be sensitive to the feelings of others. "Sometimes it's hard," says Lisa, "because I don't want my children to see me as weak. But actually, I've found the opposite to be true. When I confess a shortcoming and discuss why it was wrong and pray for forgiveness and healing with my children, I feel strengthened, with a closer bond with my children that I know only the Lord can provide."

Jeff and Shari are actively teaching forgiveness in their home. Not only do they ask forgiveness when they've done something to hurt Hannah, Jeff says, "We even 'forgive' Hannah for Zachary, who's less than a year old. When we've caught her doing something to him, she'll ask, 'Will you forgive me for him?' because he's not old enough to give her the forgiveness she needs." Shari adds,

"When he gets old enough to say yes, he'll say that himself. But for now, we require her to apologize specifically and to ask forgiveness. That's something I didn't grow up with, and to this day I have a hard time saying I'm sorry. It's important that they see repentance. That's so important to model, as a parent. You can talk to them about it forever, but they have to see it. Hannah's only four, and she probably doesn't really understand it yet, but she's getting into the habit, and as she grows older, she'll start to understand. It's a building process."

What about disagreements between Mommy and Daddy? These parents feel it's best not to inflict your more serious arguments on your child. "But if she sees the disagreement," says Cheryl, "she should see the forgiveness and reconciliation too. All of that is a part of her spiritual training." Several mothers also point out that a child who has witnessed a parental argument should be reassured that although Mommy and Daddy disagree sometimes, they love each other very much. If there are serious marital problems, a child will need frequent calm reassurance that the trouble is not her fault.

> Your mistakes can be turned to good in your child's life if you use them to model confession and repentance.

Helen, whose children are now grown and serving the Lord, feels it's not a bad thing for children to witness minor parental differences of opinion as long as you and your husband can disagree agreeably and not let it get out of hand: "It's good for them to know that their parents have separate ideas about some things. That gives the child an opening to say eventually, 'I'm an individual too, and I can have my own thoughts.'"

Every parent makes mistakes. To expect that you will somehow be exempt from that truth is to hold yourself to an impossible standard. There is only one perfect Parent (and even he has trouble with his children). As we've already seen, your mistakes can be turned to good in your child's life if you use them to model confession and repentance. But true repentance means to turn away from wrong behavior. For you and your child to reap the greatest and most immediate benefit from your mistakes, it's vital to learn from them and to commit, with God's help, to change.

A child's first decade can be a highly effective "integrity boot camp" for his parents, giving them the chance to establish the moral consistency and authority they'll need badly during their child's teen years. The reason for this is that children — especially strong-willed children — are excellent hypocrisy alarms.

Even the best of us have blind spots. Doug says, "After a while, your kids begin to point out the chinks in your armor. They'll say, 'You're telling me to do this, but that isn't what *you* do.'" He paused. "I would imagine that only increases as they get older." As the parent of a wonderful, strong-willed teenager, let me tell you: Either it increases or you learn to live with integrity. The wise parent, when confronted with evidence of his or her inconsistency, will say, "You know what? You're right. I didn't realize that, and I'm going to try to do better. I want to be a good example for you, so I hope you'll let me know — politely — if you see any other areas where I'm saying one thing and doing something else." Dan says, "I'm changing. I'm spending more time working on myself right now, changing *me* to better help *them*."

Sometimes, though, children will detect hypocrisy that isn't there. I know one indignant young lady who asked, "How come you get to tell me what to do, but I don't get to tell *you* what to do?" Such questions are great opportunities to explain the reason behind your parental authority: God has given you the job of teaching your child right behavior, while the reverse isn't true.

For all of us flawed human parents, there will be times when we need to take comfort in the fact that the final authority and ultimate control in our children's lives does not belong to us. Lisa says, "I didn't do as well as I would have liked with my eldest daughter when she was little. I did the best I could with what I knew at the time. All I can do now is strive to do better as I learn and grow as a mother. Bottom line — God has it all under control. Clinging daily to this confidence in the Lord gives me great peace of mind about the spiritual well-being of all my children. I continually commit them to the Lord. He can and will work wonders in them, in spite of my failings."

"Mommy, Why Won't Daddy Go to Church?"

It's sad but true in many families that while one spouse is trying to train the children, the other is undoing the lessons — passively at least. But as hard as it is, the mothers I've interviewed caution against making your child's spiritual training a marital battleground. "Be as submissive to your husband as you can," says Cheryl, "and ask the Lord to open doors during the time when you're alone with your child."

A mother who is home all day can still read her child Bible stories, pray with him, and sing little songs. A mother with a full-time job has more difficulty. Chapter 12 shares ways a working mother can make the most of her time with her child. Also, a Christian day care center or babysitter can help, and few husbands are sufficiently anti-Christian to keep their wives and children from attending church.

"Children understand more than we give them credit for," says one of our moms, whose husband played the Christian role for a while but eventually left her for another woman. "My kids love their daddy, but they know he needs Jesus in his heart. He may not support prayer at bedtime or meals when they're with him, but they know about the things of God because I've taught them."

According to Adrienne, the bottom line in one-parent spiritual training is this: "You do the best you can, whenever you can, and trust God to take care of your child." After all, that's all any Christian parent or set of parents can do.

"I used to worry about how we could be sure we were doing the right things with our girls," says Connie. "How could we make sure they would turn out right? I finally decided to do the very best I could and leave the rest to God."

Where the Final Responsibility Lies

Your child's spiritual training is a serious responsibility. At times it may feel overwhelming, especially if your child doesn't seem to "get it." But you need to know this: Every child will encounter countless anti-Christian influences as he grows, and his ultimate spiritual welfare is between him and God. "God doesn't say, 'Okay, here's your child. You have to make him love me,'" says Adrienne. "That child has a choice, just as you do. You have to teach him that he has that choice, and that your choice for God has been good for you, and that you know it will be good for him too. You can't say, 'You must be a Christian.' Pray that he will choose to love God, but don't force it down his throat. Forcing him is the best way to turn him off."

> The same God who has drawn you into a relationship with him is at work in your child's life.

Remember, you're not doing this alone. The same God who has drawn you into a relationship with him is at work in your child's life. He answers prayer, and he can be trusted.

"For the Lord is good and his love endures forever; his faithfulness continues through all generations" (Ps. 100:5).

Chapter 9

Who's in Charge Here, Anyway?

A Loving Foundation for Discipline

Have you ever noticed how dogmatic people are about the way other people's children should be raised — especially before they've had children of their own? Few are so virtuous that they can see a toddler running amok in a department store without forgetting all about Jesus' guidelines for throwing stones and saying in their hearts, *If that were* my *kid* . . . Chances are you've done it yourself. I know I have.

Our pomposity comes home to roost, though, because even rarer than an understanding bystander is the toddler, however well disciplined, who has never embarrassed the daylights out of his parents — or at least tried to. The older I grow as a mother, the more convinced I become that our children are God's favorite teaching tools in our lives and that humility is his favorite lesson.

No parent makes it her aim to raise an out-of-control child. If you were to take the aforementioned toddler's harried mom aside, she'd say without hesitation that she wants him to be well disciplined. She has one of two problems, though: Either (1) she doesn't know how to go about disciplining him or (2) she knows how but is having a bad day.

In this chapter, it is our intention to deprive you of excuse number one.

An Up-Front Word about Spanking

Spanking is a controversial method of discipline that is often misunderstood and just as often misused. For that reason, we need to take a minute right away to clarify our stance on the subject.

The parents in this chapter were chosen because their children are thriving and well adjusted, yet every one of them advocates the judicious use of spanking, when appropriate, as a disciplinary tool. The reason is not because we enjoy hitting our children or even because we believe spanking is always the best way to discipline a child. Some children, frankly, don't need it. Also, we recognize that there are some children, particularly hyperactive children, adopted children who have previously been abused, and other children with special needs, for whom spanking may not be a good idea. We also recognize that as a child grows older there are other disciplinary methods that work as well, or better, depending on the situation. We'll elaborate on that subject later in this chapter.

When and if it becomes necessary to spank your child, it's vital that you do it right.

The reason we feel so strongly about spanking as a valid disciplinary option (we include such mild, early corporal punishment as hand and leg swats in this category) is that it is one of only three measures that work with older babies and young toddlers, the other two being distraction (offering an alternative for the forbidden object) and physical removal from the tempting situation. Mommy's no carries no clout unless it is followed by one of the above three measures when the transgression is repeated, which it most likely will be.

In recent years, some psychologists have made the claim that a parent who spanks her child is teaching him to use violence to solve his problems. Perhaps this is true with the parent who lashes out in anger at her child, but it is purely false when the spanking is done thoughtfully and lovingly, with the child's best interest at heart.

When and if it becomes necessary to spank your child, it's vital that you do it right. Because of this, a fair amount of space in this chapter is devoted not only to the physical mechanics of spanking and other disciplinary methods but to the parental attitude involved as well.

An interesting sideline: I noticed that the mothers in this chapter have a tendency to be assertive, at least where their children are concerned. It's not that they're domineering; they just know what kind of behavior is appropriate for their children and how to go about teaching it. They respect their children and expect their children to respect them in return — and they're not mealy-mouthed about enforcing established rules.

They also tend to have a strong sense of fair play and to be very affectionate — traits that probably help prevent them from becoming overly strict.

And now, on with the chapter.

Cardinal Rules

Discipline of a small child is fairly simple, but its effects, positive or negative, snowball in a way that makes your child and the people around him feel its repercussions all his life. Do it well, and you establish in him a loving respect for your parental authority that will make it easier to discipline him in later years. Do it poorly or don't do it at all, and you set up a host of people for heartache: your child, his future teachers, employers, friends, spouse — and yourself most of all.

These parents believe there are certain unshakable tenets in the great art of childrearing that can be followed from the time you give your baby his first no until the day he goes off to college, although of course other factors will come into play as he grows older. (For example, spanking a teenager is a definite no-no.) These cardinal rules are:

> **It's important to ingrain in your child, right from the start, the knowledge that although you may not love certain types of behavior, you always love *him* — a variation on God's policy of hating the sin, not the sinner.**

 Hug your child often. "Be sure to administer *way* more hugs than spankings," says Dana. It's important to ingrain in your child, right from the start, the knowledge that although you may not love certain types of behavior, you always love *him* — a variation on God's policy of hating the sin, not the sinner. Even before he begins to walk, make a habit of taking your baby in your arms and kissing him after you discipline him, saying, "Mommy loves you very much, but when she says no, she means no."

Of course, it's important to express affection at other times, too. As we'll see in chapter 11, hugs and "I love you's" are hard to overdo.

 Plot disciplinary strategy with your spouse. As the time to start disciplining draws near, it's important to communicate with your spouse about what the no-no's will be in your home. "Come to an understanding with each other about acceptable and unacceptable behavior," says Patty. "Do it privately, and never argue about it in front of your child." Discuss which disciplinary methods you'll use and when you'll use them. Discuss, too, how each of you should handle it if you disagree with the way your spouse is disciplining your child.

Remember, a thriving family is a team. On an effective team, the coaches communicate with each other to keep from sending the players mixed messages — and they never second-guess each other in front of the players.

This sounds easier than it is, and many of the young parents I've interviewed confess that they struggle in this area. One reason is that the differences in your personalities and backgrounds may make you and your spouse want to handle disciplinary issues in different ways. Another reason is that new disciplinary issues will continually arise, often before you've had a chance to discuss them. Chris says, "There are things I let Natalie do, and Kim doesn't. Kim will ask, 'Why are you letting her do that?' And I'm like, 'What? She's not hurting anything.' I'm sure that's confusing to Natalie. We're still working those things out."

Doug and Julie find it helpful to touch base through a phone call during the day. Julie says, "If I'm having a difficult time, I'll fill him in and let him know what's going on." Doug adds, "That way, even before I come in the door, I know what's up."

Christine has gotten into the habit of handling Ashley's discipline while her husband, David, is at work, but turning it over to him when he comes home. She says, "When he's there, I don't reprimand her at all unless she's doing something dangerous. She's learned now that when Daddy is home, he's the authority. I'm in charge while he's gone." This practice keeps Christine from becoming the heavy in Ashley's eyes.

It's vital that children not see one parent as the disciplinarian and the other as "safe." Glenda says: "I may not quit disciplining entirely when Joe comes home, but my kids know that if their dad is home, he's the authority. What he says goes."

Look for the reasons behind the behavior. Kids act up for many reasons — when they're tired, sick, teething, hungry, scared, frazzled from too much time at the mall, or simply lonely and needing some attention. Sometimes the best disciplinary tactic you can use is to feed them, put them to bed, or take them into a quiet room and hold and comfort them. Reserve punishment for times when your child's misbehavior is a matter of choice.

"With Michelle," says Tim, "when she's irritable and giving us a hard time, it helps just to sit down and give her a hug and talk to her." Doug agrees: "I've tried that, and it works. When Michael's acting like a pest, I'll bring him over and put my arm around him and tell him I love him and ask how his day was. It's not a cure-all, and not always appropriate, but it does help."

Don't discipline for behavior you've never made clearly off-limits. Believe it or not, children aren't born knowing not to stick their fingers into electrical sockets, hit their playmates, climb up onto the kitchen counter via the dining-room chairs, or run through the pile of leaves Daddy just spent two hours raking. Karin says, "One day Matthew climbed up onto our boat, and Wayne just took him down and spanked him. Matthew was heartbroken. He kept crying and asking, 'Why?' That was when I realized children need to understand the rules before they're spanked for breaking them. We should have taken him down and warned him, 'Don't climb up on the boat, because you could fall down and hurt yourself.'"

It's important also to make sure your instructions or warnings have been heard and understood. "Tell your child clearly what you expect," says Patty, "and then watch until it's carried through."

With a baby who is just entering the wonderful world of discipline, it's a good practice to go over to her, touch the object, look her in the eyes, give her a firm no and move her away. No smiles, please! You know she's gotten the message if she starts to touch a forbidden object, then glances over to see if you're watching.

It's sometimes hard to know whether your child has understood you, but Glenda says, "Even at a year old, you can explain, 'When Mommy says "Come here," you must come here.' Just get right in front of her, lock eyes with her, and explain it so that she's listening intently to what you're saying. Then in the future, if you're sure you called loud enough to hear, immediately go and get her. She has to know you mean business."

> To discipline a child is to make him a disciple. To do that, he has to understand, as much as possible, the reasons why.

Christine adds, "When you get a child to look into your eyes, you break her concentration. The older they get, the easier it is to tell when they're deliberately tuning you out."

Communicate, communicate, communicate. This topic will be covered more thoroughly in the next chapter. The important thing to remember is that to discipline a child is to make him a disciple. To do that, he has to understand, as much as possible, the reasons why. And he has to see that you're not trying to spoil his fun — you're on *his* side, working toward what is best for him.

Encourage good behavior. This is much more effective than simply punishing bad behavior, and tangible rewards usually aren't necessary. A smile and a sincere thank-you or "Very good!" when your child obeys, together with a hug, can work wonders.

Scott and Jennifer are practicing the fine art of "catching" their child doing something right. Scott says, "Wes wouldn't take his medicine. He'd try to spit it out or just let it dribble all over the place. When he actually did drink it, we'd say, 'Yay, Wes!' and clap our hands. Now we'll give it to him, and as soon as he finishes he goes, 'Yay, Wes!' and claps his hands. He doesn't have a problem with it at all now." Jennifer says, "Praise really works well with him." She laughs. "He's learned, *Mommy and Daddy really like it when I keep all my food on the table.*"

Lisa agrees: "It's amazing how children respond to attention and praise," she says. "I find that my children misbehave the most when I'm busy. If I consciously give them attention and praise at the beginning of the day as soon as I spot something good they're doing (and sometimes I have to look hard), and do it again periodically through the day, they're less likely to act out and test me. Praising and encouraging your children becomes a habit, just like nagging at your children can become a habit. Get into the habit of encouraging and you'll spend a lot less time having to reprimand them."

> As you discipline yourself to "look for the good and praise it," you learn to see your child in a positive light, full of unique qualities and wonderful possibilities straight from the hand of a loving God.

Sincere praise and encouragement are among a parent's most powerful tools. Not only do they help your child *want* to behave better, they enable your relationship with your child to thrive in a way no other disciplinary method can. The reason: Sincere praise and encouragement affect the way you and your child view each other. As you discipline yourself to "look for the good and praise it," you learn to see your child in a positive light, full of unique qualities and wonderful possibilities straight from the hand of a loving God. As you prove yourself to be a consistent source of encouragement and support through the years, your child learns to trust you. And you *must* have his trust if you're to guide him effectively as he grows older.

Protect your child's dignity. Nancy says, "This means never to belittle or yell; it also means you should discipline in private instead of in front of family and friends." Once your child is old enough not to be confused by a momentary delay between transgression and discipline, it's good to get into the habit of removing him to a private place. This is true even when the discipline being used is a time-out or, when he's older, the infamous parental lecture.

Remember the relationship. It's easy for busy parents these days to become all business — to take care of their children's physical and intellectual needs but shortchange the emotional ones. "I had that realization about a month ago," says

Elizabeth. "I wanted the house to be clean and straight, and I wouldn't let Stewart pull the cushions off the couch in the TV room. He wanted to make a tent. Finally I asked myself, *Elizabeth, which is more important, the house being straight or your child having fun?* I finally realized it's okay if the house isn't totally picked up if we're having fun together. And if he wants me to get inside and play with him, that's the most important thing."

Remember: As you discipline and train your child, you're building a relationship that will last forever. With Megan and Anna, I've found that the more I nurture our relationship by taking time for us to have fun and laugh and talk together, and the more I hug them and express my love to them, the more they want to please me. Discipline becomes much, much easier when your child actively wants to please you. Besides, a good relationship brings joy to everyone involved.

> Discipline becomes much, much easier when your child actively wants to please you. Besides, a good relationship brings joy to everyone involved.

I try hard to filter everything I do through the question, "How, in the long-term, will this affect our relationship?" I work to stay sensitive to my daughters' perception of the attitudes I'm showing, the words I'm saying, and the discipline I'm using. That doesn't mean Megan and Anna don't sometimes become angry with me when they're disciplined. But am I communicating my love and respect for them through whatever method of discipline I've chosen? Can they sense that my greatest desire is to do what is best for them?

The effects of nurturing your relationship will last well beyond your child's early years. Kim says, "Because I received that nurturing from my parents, my respect for them grew. And that carried over through high school and college. Even when I wasn't with them, there were a lot of things I wouldn't do because I thought, *This is not something my parents would approve of.*"

As Megan and Anna have grown, I've tried to operate by the philosophy that I'm raising my future best friends. Now, as Megan looks around for the right college and Anna enters her adolescent years, they show every sign of becoming exactly that—and I am grateful and thrilled.

Don't phrase as a request what you mean as a command. "This was such a subtle mistake that I didn't realize I was doing it until it started causing problems," says Lisa. "I was simply trying to tell my child what I wanted her to do in a nice way. Often that sounded like, 'Would you like to clear the table?' When she headed the other way, I had no right to punish her, because I had given her a choice. I should have simply said, 'Please clear the table,' with a smile. That would have been plenty nice, while making it clear who was in charge."

As a parent, you have every right to give your child reasonable commands and expect them to be obeyed. God gave you that authority in the Bible so you could teach your little one how to get along in the world. Denying a parental command is disobedience, but the freedom to deny a request is one that should be allowed the youngest of human beings. The ability to say no to nonessentials, such as, "Would you like some more bananas?" or "Would you like to kiss Uncle Fred?" encourages independent thought without encouraging rebellion. Teach your child the difference right away.

Don't cry wolf. The parent who says no, gives a command, or threatens to discipline without being prepared to follow through is asking for trouble. "Don't say no unless you mean it," says Connie, "and whatever you say you'll do, keep your word." Dana says, "Lots of no's or wordy explanations or threats to discipline will only confuse your child and teach him that he can get away with his disobedience a little longer. Follow through after one warning, and he'll learn that you will not allow his disobedience." Karen adds, "Always follow through with your promises—whether for discipline reasons or for fun things. Your child will learn quickly whether you keep your word."

> Firmness lets your child know you mean business; sternness warns about impending consequences. Anger vents frustration.

Teaching your baby to heed your no the first time you say it does more than save you from the exasperation of having a child who doesn't listen. It may keep him from pulling the iron down on his head or running out into a busy street someday.

Discipline in love, not anger. There's a big difference between firmness—or even sternness—and anger. Firmness lets your child know you mean business; sternness warns about impending consequences. Anger vents frustration.

For parents intent on building a thriving family, anger is an enemy to be resisted. It doesn't make disciples. It frightens children into submission and hurts your relationship because it makes you unsafe in your child's eyes. It also teaches your child that anger is an appropriate response when things don't go his way. Don't let the fact that anger gets short-term results trick you into considering it a valid disciplinary tool.

"When it becomes necessary to spank your child," says Stella, "you have to keep in mind why you're spanking." Try to remember, when your child pulls a whole row of books out of the bookcase, or when he hits the off switch on the TV two seconds after you tell him no, or when he runs away when you tell him to come, that he's not doing it to insult you. He's testing his limits to see how far they stretch, and it's up to you to calmly but firmly give him the answer.

Stella says, "Your attitude has to be, 'I still love you, but you're going to be spanked because you disobeyed and brought this upon yourself.' You'll find that when you spank with that attitude, you hate to do it because you're not angry or upset, and it's hard to spank when you're not angry and upset. But you know you're doing it for your child's good, out of love, and he feels that love."

Remember, too, that discipline and spanking are not necessarily synonymous, and that this rule applies to other methods of discipline as well. When your toddler is old enough to be given a time-out for rambunctiousness or deprived of privileges for shirking his responsibilities, those means should be employed to help him learn appropriate, responsible behavior, not to torture him for irritating you.

An excellent reason for following through with discipline after one warning — aside from the fact that it teaches your child to obey right away — is that it doesn't give you time to become upset and exasperated. The parent who finds herself losing control while spanking, gaining satisfaction from hitting her child, or inflicting physical injuries on her child should seek out a qualified Christian counselor, who can help her bring her emotions under control while still recognizing the importance of discipline. It's better to just put your baby or toddler into his crib and walk away for a few minutes than to risk taking your anger out on him.

Let the punishment fit the crime — and the child. "There are no cookie-cutter kids," says Dana. Some of these parents' little ones were so tenderhearted that a firm no was enough to bring them into line. Others required several spankings for the same transgression before realizing Mommy and Daddy meant what they said, and a few seemed to take spankings as a personal challenge, their little eyes flashing as if to say, "I bet I can last longer than you can!"

We'll cover alternative methods of discipline in the section on older toddlers, since, as we've said, the only disciplinary methods that work with a baby or young toddler are distraction, spanking, and being physically removed from the tempting situation. The basic idea is to make sure you are never guilty of trying to swat a fly with a sledgehammer. Don't use a harsher form of punishment than needed, but at the same time make sure the form of discipline you choose is one that will motivate your child to obey. "Every child in a family has a different personality," says Glenda, "and you have to use the measures that work best for him as an individual."

Also, keep in mind that the goal of discipline is not to control your child or to change his personality — both of which are impossible anyway — but to train him and help him reach his full potential as the unique person God created him to be.

Be consistent. This is probably the hardest rule to follow, but it's also the most important. One reason consistency is such a challenge is that there are so many areas where it is vital: the objects and behaviors that are off-limits, your own attitude, your methods for dealing with disobedience, and the hugs, kisses, and talks that follow after.

"Children seem to want you to parent them correctly," says Lisa. "When you do your job right, it makes them feel safe and loved. They don't really want to be able to do whatever they want. They want the security of knowing what the rules are and that you will follow through fairly and consistently in enforcing them. It seems to comfort them to know what to expect."

> One reason consistency is such a challenge is that there are so many areas where it is vital.

Good discipline is predictable. Discipline that is dished out arbitrarily is worse than none at all. Your child must always know, beyond a doubt, what the results of his actions will be. Otherwise he'll never learn to avoid misbehaving in order to avoid the consequences. "Set specific boundaries and hold to them," says Patty. "What's not okay today must remain not okay tomorrow."

"Your consistency in discipline lays the foundation for self-discipline," says Marilee. "Younger children learn to catch themselves before they do something unacceptable because they don't want to be disciplined; in later years they become able to keep from doing unacceptable things, or to make themselves do necessary things, simply because of the sense of right and wrong that has been ingrained in them."

Consistency means following through at Grandma's house and in public too. Glenda says, "Many times in a new place the child will completely ignore you, thinking, *Maybe if I keep going she won't say anything.* Even if he knows something isn't permitted at home, he'll test you in public to see if you follow through." "Every kid has tried that," adds Virginia.

In the struggle for consistency, it can help to pick your battles carefully. Trying to keep track of a zillion rules is just about impossible; besides, your child needs the freedom to be a child. Resist the temptation to "knee-jerk" discipline out of irritation. Doug says, "I'm the type who could very easily micromanage my kids. I have to stop myself and think, *Is it really important that they not shuffle through the leaves while they're walking up to the house?* If you're the kind of parent who's always harping at your kids, it seems like that's a pretty good recipe for problems later on."

🐦 *Don't yell.* In view of what we've already said, this rule may seem a bit redundant. It would seem only logical that discipline without anger would be discipline without yelling, but with some parents yelling seems to be the standard way of communicating with their children. The problem is, when you try to discipline your child by turning up the volume on your vocal cords, you show him that you don't mean what you're saying unless you're yelling. Cheryl says, "I don't like to yell, because it puts me in the position — in front of my child — of losing both my dignity and the battle."

Even when it gets results, yelling tends to backfire. "My husband and I are dealing with a two-and-a-half-year-old who likes to raise his voice after he feels he's been unheard or his requests are refused," says Lisa. "We realized very quickly where he learned this — from us, of course! When we thought it through, we realized we tended to repeat ourselves more loudly a second time when we needed him to do something or stop doing something and our hands were full of something else, like a dirty diaper and the baby. Our son logically assumed that if we thought it would work on him, it might work on us! Needless to say, we're trying very hard not to raise our voices now."

Besides, yelling does a poor job of conveying love. "Show your love in everything," says Dana. "Even when you say, 'Pick up your toys,' the tone of your voice will convey an emotion to your child. Let your voice say, 'I love you lots!' even when you're having to discipline him. I heard a speaker once who put it like this: 'In everything my mother said to me, her *attitude* said, "I wish I had a hundred little boys just like you!"'"

When I began to discipline Megan, my goal — and I reached it when she was about a year old — was to be able to say, "No, honey," in a loving, gentle tone and have her obey me. The reason she learned to obey me, though, is because I started out by saying it in a no-nonsense tone of voice and following through consistently with the appropriate disciplinary measures. Yes, I had to continually reinforce this lesson as she approached two years old. (And yes, during that phase I blew it and lost my temper more often than I care to admit.)

🐾 *Model the behavior you want to see in your child.* "We were feeling as if Nathaniel wasn't thankful," says Loren. (Shannon laughs: "He had a birthday.") "Reflecting on it, I realized that rather than trying to force him to have the right attitude, Shannon and I need to model what thankfulness is all about. He'll catch those values."

Unfortunately, modeling alone isn't enough; discipline would be a lot simpler if it were. You'll need to let your child know that the behavior you're modeling is expected of him too. He'll need reminders, and sometimes consequences, to hold him accountable. But trying to teach positive attitudes and actions without modeling them is doomed.

Off to a Good Start

Now that we've gone over the basic rules, let's look at how they apply to the very beginning of a child's disciplinary training.

The purpose of discipline for an older baby or young toddler is to protect him from his environment (and in some cases, his environment from him) while at the same time establishing respect for your authority. Tender though this age may seem, the parents in this book began seeing the light of understanding in their little ones' eyes during the second half of their first year, which, interestingly enough, was also the age when their babies began crawling around and getting into mischief. A baby that young can't yet understand the word no, of course, but he gets the general idea by your facial expression and the tone of your voice.

> The purpose of discipline for an older baby or young toddler is to protect him from his environment (and in some cases, his environment from him) while at the same time establishing respect for your authority.

👶 *Babyproof your home as thoroughly as you can.* There will inevitably be a few things left down that you can use to teach your child the meaning of the word no, such as the TV controls, a bookcase, a magazine rack, or piles of folded laundry on laundry day. "If something is pretty and is going to catch a baby's eye," says Cheryl, "natural curiosity is going to make him want to touch it. If it's going to break, it should be put away." "A baby needs plenty of room to explore," says Patty. "Try not to frustrate him."

These parents want their children to be curious. "How else can they learn?" asks Donna. Whenever possible, close the doors to all the rooms you don't want your little one to enter, and let him roam — keeping a sharp eye on him, of course, because babies can get themselves into predicaments that would never occur to their parents. Several mothers even found a way to let their children explore the no-no's by allowing them to sit on Mommy's lap and handle, taste, and touch each item before Mommy put it back up out of reach. "I find that the 'one finger rule' works for Hannah's curious little hands," says Nancy. "It allows her to explore without grabbing or crumpling. It also keeps her from constantly having to hear no."

Most of us have been guilty, at least a few times, of reacting with a knee-jerk no when our babies touched something they hadn't played with before. "Think about what you're saying," says Marilee, "and only come down on your baby for the things that are important. If it can't hurt him and he can't hurt it, let him play with it. It's a learning experience for him to taste, feel, and touch."

Offer alternatives for no-no's whenever possible. Megan knew that the magazines under the coffee table were forbidden, but she had plenty of opportunities to explore the fascinating properties of paper because I gave her my daily junk mail before I threw it out. Christine does the same thing, and she says, "Even a nine-month-old baby can be made to understand that she can have only the magazines Mommy gives her." Adrienne suggests giving your baby her very own little magazine rack or box filled with outdated catalogs, pamphlets, and colorful flyers. (Watch your baby carefully when she plays with paper, though, to make sure she doesn't put it in her mouth.) As your baby grows a little older, she can learn that it's okay to crumple and tear junk mail, but not her little storybooks because those are special. Along the same lines, Megan knew she couldn't play with my piles of folded laundry, but she was welcome to wade through the heap and drag clothes through the family room before I folded them. It gave me an incentive to do my folding quickly!

Plan ahead to avoid discipline problems. If you know that a given circumstance tends to cause your child problems, try to plan a game or distraction to help him through it. For instance, a number of parents reported that as their children approached toddlerhood they began to resist having their diapers and clothes changed. For some of these parents, it helped to give their child a toy to distract him at the changing table, or to talk or sing to him while he was being changed. (The "Where's Mommy's nose?" game can come in handy here.)

If your child's changing times do become wrestling matches, though, it's important that you win. Kim has found it helpful to lean gently over Natalie on the changing table and hold her in place, talking to her softly until she calms down, or in extreme cases, to pick her up and hold her until she stops crying.

Then she proceeds to change her. For safety's sake, while Stephanie's children were going through this stage, she changed them on the floor.

🐘 *Be consistent, even in the very first weeks of your baby's discipline.* A nine-month-old is usually too young to exhibit much rebellion, but parents who aren't consistent to discipline for disobedience from the very beginning arm a time bomb that will go off in their faces when their baby reaches full-fledged toddlerhood at one and a half or two years old.

If your baby starts reaching for the pretty breakables at a friend's home, get to him quickly and distract him with a safe alternative. If it works, you're home free. If not, give him a firm no and follow through if he disobeys. At home, though, your baby has to be made to understand in no uncertain terms which permanent fixtures are off-limits. If you do it right the first few times, you won't have to be constantly nagging him, eroding the love between you and your child. If saying no and turning your child away from a forbidden object several times is enough to make him leave it alone, that's great. But if not, don't be afraid to administer a mild swat to emphasize your point.

"It's good to begin early with enforcing obedience," says Dana. "When he starts touching things he's not supposed to touch, make him look you in the eye and give him a firm no. If he goes right back to it, proceed to physically discipline him by turning him away or giving him a swat on the hand. That way he'll learn quickly to obey."

Before their babies began to toddle, most of the mothers I interviewed just smacked their child's hand lightly with their own when he touched an item that he had been warned was a no-no, or did the same with the back of their baby's leg when he tried to climb over the couch or stand up in the high chair after having been told no. Babies' memories are very short. For a swat to be effective, it needs to catch your little one in the act if at all possible, since a delay of even a few seconds can make your child wonder why you're spanking him.

Dana objects to the fact that many children mind their fathers better than they do their mothers: "That shows a lack of consistency," she says. True, Daddy is bigger than Mommy and has a deeper voice and he's not home as much. But several mothers I interviewed believe the real reason that children often mind their fathers better is because they've learned that Mommy doesn't always follow through, whereas they haven't made that discovery about Daddy. Familiarity unfortunately *does* breed contempt unless your child knows you unerringly mean what you say. "Saying, 'No, don't do that' over and over again is nagging," says Marilee, "and your child will just ignore you after a while because he knows you don't mean it. Mean it when you say it and take care of it right away. If you do, and you make your child feel the consequences of his disobedience, you won't have to nag all the time."

🐣 *Show affection after you discipline.* Karin has strong feelings about the need to pick up your baby after a spanking to reassure him of your love. She says, "I've heard people say you shouldn't pick a child up while he's still crying — that you should let him cry it out first — but I disagree." I do too, and I agree with Karin that the child whose parent spanks him and then walks away is going to feel that he's not only been disciplined; he's been rejected as well. When Megan reached the age when discipline became necessary, I made it a practice always to pick her up and console her after a spanking, saying gently, "Mommy loves you very much, but when she says no, she means no." She rapidly got to the point where the first thing she did after a spanking was hold out her little arms for me to pick her up. (By the way, don't be thrown if your child doesn't cry when you swat his hand or leg. Your aim isn't to make him cry; it's to get his attention and correct the behavior. If he stops doing whatever it was he wasn't supposed to do, you've accomplished your mission. But still, after he stops, give him a hug.)

Familiarity unfortunately **does** *breed contempt unless your child knows you unerringly mean what you say.*

According to Dana, an unaffectionate family background gives you no excuse to be an unaffectionate parent: "You've got to learn to be affectionate, that's all," she says. Several parents in this book came from undemonstrative families and have felt a lifelong yearning for the physical closeness they missed with their own parents. One mother says, "It's important to hug your kids, and it's important for your kids to see you and your husband hug. I never saw affection between my mother and my father, and now my husband says I'm a cold person. It's funny — I'm affectionate with my children because I really want to make up for what I lost with my parents. My husband says I give them more intimacy than I do him."

👶 *Teach your baby to share.* You can begin teaching a child to share as soon as he's old enough to crawl around and appropriate other children's toys — which is a good reason to get together regularly with your friends who have babies his age. Your child will be well into toddlerhood before he really understands what sharing is about, but that doesn't mean you can't start ingraining good habits early. "Sharing is a learned skill," says Cheryl, "and children don't learn it just by watching. It's something the parents have to take an active part in teaching. Now, at four years old, Jason understands when I tell him, 'You need to share that toy.' But between nine and eighteen months is the time to begin to actively teach sharing when they're with other children."

Cheryl recommends calm mediation — after all, it's silly to reproach your one-year-old for not sharing when he's never been taught how — and says it's best to actually help your child hand over a toy: "Let's let Brian play with the truck for a while. Thank you! It's good to share our toys. Now, what can we find for you to play with?" Make sure each child has ample time to play with a favorite toy and give lots of short explanations, all variations on, "You played with this for a while; it's Brian's turn now." She adds, "Be sure to hug your child when he does share. It should definitely be rewarded, so he can see some benefit from sharing. He needs to learn that it's not just a chore but a nice thing to do, and you're pleased with him for doing it." Don't be disheartened if your little one sends up wails of protest at first. It's only natural.

Glenda says it's possible to acquaint a first child or an only child with the idea of sharing by teaching her to share with Mommy and Daddy. "Even small children can learn to share their cookies, or whatever," she says, "but be sure to use the word *share* while you're doing it." When Megan began eating finger foods at around eight months, I began teaching her to share her Cheerios, asking, "Will you share with Mommy? Will you give Mommy some?" At first she leaned toward me with a piece of cereal in her little fingers but jerked back as I was about to take it. Then once, probably by accident, she let go and it dropped into my hand. I said "Thank you!" and popped it into my mouth with a funny noise, and it was clear sailing from there on out. Little did I know I was creating a monster — soon not only did she want to put the Cheerio into my mouth herself but she wanted me to stick out my tongue so she could make sure it was in there.

Teach your child to play on her own. Several mothers in this book taught their older babies and young toddlers to play by themselves for short periods (with emphasis on the word *short*), breaking them of the habit of constantly wanting Mommy's attention. But it wasn't easy. Christine says, "You have to just sit the child down and say, 'Mommy has to work, and you have to play with your toys. Mommy can't hold you right now.' Then give her a hug and put her down with her toys. Ashley cried a lot for the first couple of days, but after a while she got the idea and became interested in other things besides Mommy. We finally got to where after breakfast she would get her toys and play by herself, checking up on me from time to time."

A word of caution: Small children need a lot of love and attention, so make sure you don't abuse this method to get out of the time you need to spend with your baby. Glenda says, "Your child needs to know how to play by herself when you really have to get something done, but you also must realize when you're overdoing it and need to stop and spend time with her." Virginia believes too much disciplining is done on a selfish basis—what Mommy or Daddy is really saying is, "Go away, kid; ya bother me." "I see it in so many families I know," she says, "and it tears my heart out. The mother will say, 'I have something I want to do, so you have to get out of the way.'" Jennifer says, "I was frantically cleaning house, not realizing how much time had passed, when Jessica wistfully said, 'I wish Daddy would come home. *He'll* play with me.' Ouch!"

Much misbehavior, with children of all ages, is a bid for attention that occurs because the child is left at loose ends, with nothing to occupy her mind or her hands. Dana recommends taking some creative toys to each area of the house where you work to give your child the security of being able to play in the same room with you rather than being stuck in a playpen in the living room while you're working in the bedroom.

> Much misbehavior, with children of all ages, is a bid for attention that occurs because the child is left at loose ends, with nothing to occupy her mind or her hands.

Lisa agrees: "I have a basket of toys behind my bedroom door for the kids to play with when I shower or work in my room. The basket moves with us to the other upstairs rooms as we do our chores. There are other toys in other areas of the house, tucked away for when they're needed. As we leave each area, we clean up what we've gotten out so that there aren't messes all over the house. This way, my kids don't feel alone, I know they're safe, and they get used to playing some on their own. Everybody's happy—well, most of the time!"

As soon as your child is old enough, let her "help" with whatever you're doing.

An Encouraging Word

Finally, here's a word of reassurance to young parents who may be afraid of losing their child's affection through consistent discipline: You won't.

"You're not going to lose that child's affection if you do it wisely," says Glenda, "because you're not always going to say no. You'll give him hugs and kisses, and you'll compliment him when he does things right. It's not all no-no's, although some days it feels like it!" Children go through cycles of testing their limits and then resting within them, and these parents generally found that if they stuck to their guns during the times of testing, the times of resting became longer and longer.

Love is not weak and conciliating; it's strong and persevering. Parents who enforce loving discipline give their child a happy legacy that will stay with him all his life — a legacy that is far too rare. People today are losing jobs and breaking laws because they never learned to yield cheerfully to authority, and marriages are crumbling because the partners never learned to give as well as take.

Wanda says, "Small children learn that Mommy and Daddy love them and discipline them because they've done something wrong and must learn to obey. And that's a lesson they have to learn, because people in the real world won't be as understanding as Mommy and Daddy. They won't discipline; they'll punish."

Love is not weak and conciliating; it's strong and persevering.

When you're tempted to let a transgression slide by to keep from upsetting your child, remember the scriptural teaching that God disciplines us out of love, because we are his children. He's not afraid to let us get mad at him, and we must show the same loving courage with our own children. "A nine-month-old baby can't understand that yet," says Cheryl, "but you need to know it for yourself. Know for yourself that you're doing the right thing and that you're not going to lose your child's love. You're going to gain his respect."

Chapter 10

Still in Charge?

Loving Discipline for Toddlers

Once your child passes the baby stage, discipline becomes more than just a choice between distracting him, changing his geographical location, or spanking him, since toddlers are capable of doing much more than touching something Mommy said no about. They can also run through the house or be otherwise undesirably rowdy; they can take toys away from other children; they can be openly defiant; they can neglect to do assigned tasks — the list goes on and on, and it grows as time goes by. But don't panic — toddlers can also hug and kiss and say "I love you, Mommy," and the intellectual, emotional, and spiritual growth that takes place during toddlerhood is nothing short of amazing.

It's important to note that the disciplinary tips in this chapter are based on the cardinal rules at the beginning of chapter 9. Whenever I feel as if my daughters are responding badly to my parental discipline, even now during their adolescent years, it usually turns out to be because I've forgotten one of those rules. Because of this, I strongly encourage you to review them frequently.

Communication Is Crucial

Remember the Recipe for a Thriving Family we shared in chapter 2? Its basic elements are respect, communication, time, and teamwork. In chapters 8 and 9, we laid the groundwork for establishing those elements in your relationship with your children. We'll continue doing that for the rest of the book.

In chapter 11, especially, we'll talk about the role of respect and encouragement in giving your child a healthy sense of self-esteem. But now is the time to talk about the most important skill you will need to develop as you seek to guide your child: communication.

The older your children grow, the more crucial communication will become in all areas, but especially in the area of discipline. This is because, as they grow older and begin to reason, children do a fair amount of "projecting." If you don't carefully explain your motives to them and reassure them of your love, they'll try to work out in their little minds what your motives might be. Since the only frame of reference they have is their own very limited experience, the thought process goes something like this: *If I were doing this to someone, here's what I would be feeling and why I would be doing it. Therefore, that must be what Mommy is feeling and why she is doing it.* It's frighteningly easy for our children to mistake our motives and see us as bullies instead of as parents who love them very much and who are working toward their best interests.

> **If you don't carefully explain your motives to them and reassure them of your love, they'll try to work out in their little minds what your motives might be.**

A toddler deserves an explanation when an object or a behavior is made off-limits. Karin says, "My little girl, Meagin, is not quite a year old, and I already explain things to her. If you just say, 'Don't touch the stove,' a toddler is going to reach over and touch it to try to figure out why it's forbidden." Even a young toddler can usually understand a simple explanation, although she may need to hear it several times. Keep it short and to the point, but with lots of emphasis. ("Don't touch — hot! Ouch!")

Explanations are just as important after your child has committed an offense as they are before. He needs to know he's being spanked, or made to sit still, or whatever, to help him learn right behavior — and not because he pushed Mommy past her limit. Again, though, keep your explanations short and to the point to avoid confusing him. "I always explain before I discipline," says Cheryl, "because my boys have to know what they've done wrong."

Karin says Matthew clearly understood her explanations when he was about eighteen months old. "That may seem awfully young," she says, "but I think children understand more than we give them credit for." She adds that giving a reason for saying no, rather than just dictating to him, has made Matthew act more responsibly: "It makes him feel good that we trust him with the information."

Lisa says, "At two and a half, my son can even verbalize what he's done that isn't right. I'll say, 'Honey, you aren't allowed to jump off the couch. Do you know why? It's because . . .' and he'll finish, 'Get hurt.' This helps me be sure he's heard me and understands the rules." Elizabeth agrees: "Stewart is two and a half, and he can tell me, in some form of gibberish, what he's done. 'Stewart hit Hallie' or something. So we've been trying to encourage him to say he's sorry and 'Please forgive me.' And I'll forgive him for Hallie — 'Hallie forgives you.'"

Stephanie says, "Kristen's a little over three now, and Rachel's four and a half. We usually don't have to tell them what they did wrong anymore — we let them tell us."

An especially important cardinal rule to remember is the need to show affection and restore your relationship after you discipline your child. "As my children grow older," says Dana, "I've observed that what they convey after being punished for disobedience is often the exact opposite of their real desires.

"Bryan, for instance, will try to pull away from me. So I take him by the hand and make him come and sit down with me. Then I pull him onto my lap and hug him to me tightly. He resists for a matter of seconds, as if that's the last thing in the world he wants, but then suddenly he clutches me with all his strength. Then we cry together and talk it out. He's so much more content when he knows he's been disciplined for wrong actions and then the slate is wiped clean. We may have to repeat the process over and over for the same type of disobedience, but it's important always to follow through."

Along with the hugs and talks, Patty recommends praying with your child after he has been disciplined. She says, "It teaches him what repentance and forgiveness mean, early on." Lisa adds, "It also teaches our children that the reason they should obey us is because there is a great big God who also wants what's best for them. Mommy and Daddy's desire for them to grow into capable, responsible adults is intertwined with what their heavenly Father wants for them. I try to point out to my children that they belong to God first and have a responsibility to obey us because that is what he requires."

"Something I find myself falling into," says Jeff, "is not being really clear with Hannah. For instance, I like to kid around and play with her, and it's very important to say, 'Okay, we're finished playing. Now you need to focus on what I asked you to do.' I've really been working on that, because sometimes play-time's over just because I've had enough. 'Okay, Hannah, leave me alone. Okay, now you're in trouble. You stepped over the line. I didn't tell you where the line was, but you stepped over it.'"

In Choosing the Method, Remember the Goal

As the variety of possible behavior issues increases during your child's toddler years, so does the variety of possible methods of dealing with them. Your toddler's personality plays a big part in the method of discipline you should choose, as does the nature of his transgression. Don't fall into the rut of spanking your child every time he does something you don't like. There are times when other methods are more effective.

Your toddler's personality plays a big part in the method of discipline you should choose, as does the nature of his transgression.

The goal of discipline for toddlers and preschoolers is no longer simply to protect them and their environment from each other, although that's still part of it. Your goal during these years is also to teach self-control and guide your child toward right behavior while protecting and nurturing your relationship. Using any disciplinary method that harms your relationship will also harm your future chances of serving as your child's spiritual and moral guide. As always, your attitude in disciplining your child should be loving, patient, kind, and firm. Remember: Anger is an enemy and is never a valid disciplinary tool.

The parents in this book generally agree with Dr. James Dobson's recommendation that spanking be used only for direct disobedience and rebellion — the felonies of the juvenile world — and that more creative methods be employed to handle rambunctiousness, grumpiness, irresponsibility, and other misdemeanors.

Typical Toddler Behaviors

As unique as every child is, toddlers have an amazing number of common behavioral issues. In this section, we'll look at some of the problems the parents in this book ran into and show how they've handled them.

ROWDINESS AND GRUMPINESS

Marilee says, "If my kids are chasing each other around and starting to hit and can't seem to settle down, we'll sit one down on one end of the couch and the other on the other end and make them stay there for a few minutes." "I think a lot of times having to sit still and be quiet is more punishment for a toddler than a spanking is," adds Cheryl. "When Jason is being too rough with his friends outside, it's a real punishment for me to bring him in and make him sit still while

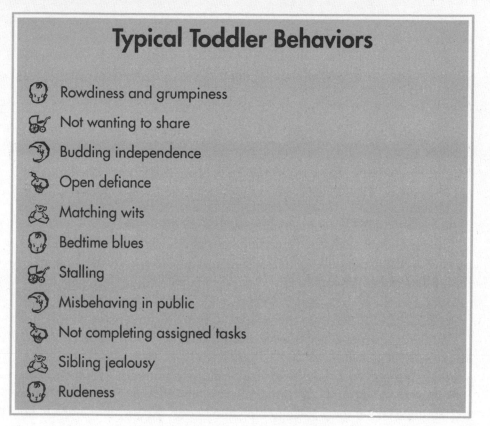

Typical Toddler Behaviors

- Rowdiness and grumpiness
- Not wanting to share
- Budding independence
- Open defiance
- Matching wits
- Bedtime blues
- Stalling
- Misbehaving in public
- Not completing assigned tasks
- Sibling jealousy
- Rudeness

Brian is out there having fun. That's a much more effective way to discipline him than just giving him a quick spanking and sending him back out to play."

A kitchen timer is an essential piece of equipment to have when your child enters toddlerhood. After you sit him down and explain to him why he's going to have to sit still, say, "Mommy is going to set this timer so that it will ring when three minutes are up. When the bell goes off, you may get up." Then set the timer and put it up out of reach. Luellen says, "I tell Benjamin the clock starts *after* he quits crying and protesting. Time-out must be *quiet* time!" (A good rule of thumb is to use one minute of time-out for each year of your child's age.)

Christine and Michele both cured their little girls of the early-morning and midafternoon grumps by letting them discover that their whining got the exact opposite results from the ones desired. Instead of giving Ashley more attention when she started whining, Christine says, "I told her she was acting like she was still sleepy, so she'd have to go back to bed for five minutes — which was an eternity for her. It's amazing how well that worked." When Sarah became grumpy and unmanageable, Michele told her, "Go into your room until you can be sweet." At first Sarah stayed in her room and pouted for a while, but she quickly caught on and before long would run into her room, make a sharp U-turn, then race back out with a big smile, exclaiming, "I s'eet girl, Mommy!"

NOT WANTING TO SHARE

The kitchen timer comes in handy again when kids don't want to share. Marilee makes use of it when both of her children want to play with a one-child toy. When the timer goes off after five minutes or so, it's the other child's turn.

When her two boys fight over a favorite toy, Cheryl disciplines by confiscating it. She says, "There have been times when I've said, 'This toy is not worth fighting about. Let's put it up and play with something else.'"

Remember, though, that "catching your child doing something right" is a powerful character-building tool. When your child does share, be quick to notice and praise him for it.

BUDDING INDEPENDENCE

Budding independence is not the same thing as rebellion, but it can look suspiciously like it at times.

My darling older daughter's first complete sentence, at age eighteen months, was, "Megan do it!" Suddenly she wanted to do everything herself, from putting on her shoes and climbing into her car seat, to not wanting to hold my hand while we walked through crowded stores.

It was comforting to talk with other parents involved in this project and learn that their experiences as their children approached age two had been almost identical to mine. As I did further research I found that our children's you-say-yes-I-say-no behavior was a well-documented toddler phase called negativism. This, I discovered, was where the infamous Terrible Twos got their name.

> My darling older daughter's first complete sentence, at age eighteen months, was, "Megan do it!"

After a few major clashes, I sat down and analyzed the situation. I realized upon reflection that Megan wasn't so much rebelling against my authority as she was simply trying to become more independent. I decided to allow her to do everything for herself that she was capable of, as long as no danger was involved. I even allowed her occasionally to try things she wasn't capable of, such as tying her shoes, to help her learn her limitations.

I stood behind her to make sure she didn't fall while she climbed into her car seat, and I found that it worked well to offer her alternatives in potentially dangerous situations, such as the aforementioned crowded store: "Megan, you may ride in the cart if you like. Otherwise, either Mommy must hold you or you must hold Mommy's hand. Which do you want to do?"

I asked her to "be a big girl" and help me with small fetch-and-carry tasks, and encouraged her sincerely when she did. She was so eager to grow up that she willingly took on all the "big girl" tasks I would give her. She often surprised me with the number of things she could do, and our relationship improved dramatically.

For some reason, we mothers tend to think that the more we do for our family the better we are at our job, and we feel guilty when we begin to cut the apron strings. But the general attitude among the mothers in this book is that you do your child a big favor when you teach him to take on responsibility as soon as he is able.

I heard songwriter and author Gloria Gaither say once, while speaking to a group of women, that a mother's primary goal should be to work herself out of a job. That's hard to accept, because it means gradually making yourself physically, although not emotionally, dispensable to your child. But it's the only way to raise capable, responsible, emotionally healthy children.

OPEN DEFIANCE

Open defiance is another nearly universal toddler phenomenon and a natural result of the push for independence. Even so, it's hard to take. Probably the most crushing thing a toddler can do to his loving parents is answer their instructions with a rebellious no. And probably the most difficult thing for the toddler's parents to do is deal with their child's rebellion in love, without giving up on the command(which would give the toddler a sense of power and guarantee a repeat performance)or losing their tempers and becoming authoritarian.

Remember, your child isn't really attacking you personally when he first tries this — although he soon will be if you show him that it pays off. He's testing his limits, and whether he becomes chronically rebellious depends on how you handle these first few experiments. "When my children said no to me," says Glenda, "I asked, 'What did you say?' If they repeated it, I explained to them, 'You don't tell Mother no,' and spanked them for it after that. If you let that sort of thing go, even at that very young age, your child will lose respect for you and your authority because he knows you'll just take whatever he dishes out." Dana adds, "It's strange how children have a certain age where you can start to see the rebellion.

My sister used to not believe in original sin — the idea that we're born with sinful natures because of Adam's fall. Then she had kids of her own!"

At four years old, Donna's little girl came out with an even more disturbing statement than no — "I hate you!" But hard as it was, Donna kept her cool. She knew that April was feeling threatened because her baby brother had just arrived, and she responded to April's anger with, "But I sure do love *you*."

Cheryl says, "At ages two, three, and four, my boys began sometimes to equate discipline with levels of affection. They'd say, 'I like Daddy better than you, because he didn't spank me today.' Don't let that discourage you." Children begin early to test the effectiveness of words as weapons, and if you want to nip this type of behavior in the bud, it's vital not to let on even if something your child says does hurt. "But never let them say that and get away with it," says Glenda. Such times are good opportunities to deliver the well-known lecture, "Mommy disciplines you because she loves you and wants you to learn to behave." You might also want to point out that Daddy has a habit of disciplining too.

When their children became old enough to be spanked for disobedience, as opposed to simply having their hand or leg swatted, most of the parents in this book warned their children the first time they caught them in a transgression, then spanked the second time around. (This transition usually happened around two years of age.) And most of these parents opted to use a paddle. They gave several reasons — not the least of which is that Mommy's hand didn't always produce the desired effect on her toddler's sturdy behind. Cheryl found herself with that problem when Jason was three, and it was Jason himself who offered the solution: "He told me one day, 'You need a paddle.' Evidently they had one in the nursery he attended. So we went to the store and he showed me what to buy. I'm sure he thought his brother was going to get it more often than he was!"

The most popular paddle among the parents in this book is a lightweight wooden spoon, although Elizabeth has found a flexible plastic spatula (the type used to spread frosting) effective. These parents recommend the buttocks or the back of the leg as your primary target, since both locations have plenty of natural padding and no protruding bones. Remember, a spanking is just to remind your child who's in charge. It's supposed to sting, but it should never injure your child or leave welts or bruises. Try out your technique a few times on the back of your own leg to make sure you're not too heavy-handed before using it on your toddler, and have your husband do the same. (On *his* leg, not yours. There are limits to motherly sacrifice.)

A paddle offers more advantages than simply being more effective than a hand. "The nice thing about a paddle," says Cheryl, "is that you have to actually go and get it — you don't just haul off and smack the child when you've reached the point of anger. And now that Jason's four, sometimes I'll tell him to go and get the paddle. That gives me a minute to cool down and gives him a little time to contemplate his sins."

Karin agrees: "I try always to do my disciplining in a set way so that Matthew will always know how he's going to be disciplined. He doesn't have to worry whether he's going to be slapped across the face. He knows he's been warned and it's time to be spanked with the paddle."

As with any other kind of discipline, spanking for rebellion and defiance must be preceded by an explanation and followed with a big hug and kiss — and then forgotten about. It's essential that you and your little one not harbor resentment toward each other.

> **As with any other kind of discipline, spanking for rebellion and defiance must be preceded by an explanation and followed with a big hug and kiss — and then forgotten about.**

A final comment about spankings: With my older daughter, Megan, corporal punishment became counterproductive by the time she was around eight. By then, even when done in love, spankings simply made her angry and risked setting up a Megan-against-Mom (or Dad) relationship. Since she was then old enough to reason with, I found the most effective disciplinary tools (in addition to encouragement and working toward a strong, loving relationship) to be heartfelt communication, with occasional time-outs and loss of privileges. She's now in her late teens, and communication is still a crucial part of our relationship, but I can't remember the last time it was necessary to punish her. I said all that to say this: Your child's disciplinary needs will change as time goes by. If something is no longer working or is damaging your relationship, it's time to reevaluate.

A *word about tantrums:* Many of the parents I interviewed never had to deal with them, but whether your child tries them will most likely have more to do with his personality than with your childrearing methods. But just because your child tries them probably doesn't mean you have to live with them. As with other unacceptable behavior, the way you deal with tantrums will usually determine whether they continue. It's important to note, however, that our advice on dealing with tantrums doesn't necessarily apply to children with special emotional or mental needs. For one of these children, consult your pediatrician or a child psychologist.

Not all tantrums are alike. Because of this, they can't all be dealt with in the same way. My daughter Megan was blessed to inherit a strong personality from both sides of the family, and she tried her hand at two different kinds of tantrums before discovering they didn't work. The first kind, a minor fit involving an exasperated yell and maybe a kick or two when her purposes were thwarted by Mommy, could usually be stopped by my telling her calmly, "No. If you throw a fit, Mommy will spank," and then following through if she disobeyed. But there were times when, either because she had become overtired or for some other reason, she completely lost control of herself, and at those times spanking simply made the matter worse. I, along with many of our other parents, found that a full-fledged tantrum is best left alone — in fact, Megan's tantrums halted abruptly when I began to put her into her bedroom and close the door, with me on the outside, as soon as one started.

Tantrums are a way of venting frustration. And when you're frustrated, it helps to know there's someone on your side. "When Stewart is throwing a tantrum or crying," says Elizabeth, "I'll get right in his face and say, 'Mommy wants to help you. But you have to stop crying to tell me what you need.' He'll usually stop after that." If he doesn't, she removes his audience — that is, herself.

What about tantrums in public? Elizabeth says, "Stewart has done that. I just pick him up and we walk out. If you get flustered or angry, it's probably going to make things worse." I believe Elizabeth's answer is the best one for public tantrums: Pick up your screaming child. If you can, give the adults around you an apologetic smile. Go out to the car and hold him until he calms down, or go home and give him a time-out. When he's calm, explain as much as he can understand about what went wrong and reassure him of your love. It can help, too, to head these things off at the pass. If mall trips invariably end in tantrums, try to do your shopping when your husband or a friend can watch your child.

"Nathaniel would try to throw those fits when I was grocery shopping," says Shannon. "He hated to stop. We always had to be moving. As soon as I'd stop to try to pick something up, he'd start having a fit. Well, I would just stand there until he was ready to calm down. And I would talk to him as calmly as I could while he was screaming. He would eventually give in."

None of the parents in this book had to deal with self-destructive behavior during tantrums. If your child is inclined to use head-banging or other such ways of venting his frustration, check with a qualified family counselor for ways to deal with the behavior without allowing your child to injure himself. The parents I interviewed feel that under no circumstances should you give in to your child when he or she throws a tantrum — unless of course you like tantrums and want them to continue.

It's easy to become alarmed when you see signs of defiance in your child — especially if he's extremely strong-willed. Just remember, the same strong will that's giving you headaches now can help him accomplish wonderful things someday! It's crucial to see a good and godly future for your child and to communicate that vision to him. Tell yourself: *My child's character is not terminally flawed. He can and will learn this lesson. God has wonderful plans for him. I will continue to guide and correct and love him for as long as it takes, and to forgive seventy times seven.*

"[Love] . . . always hopes, always perseveres" (1 Cor. 13:7).

It's crucial to see a good and godly future for your child and to communicate that vision to him.

MATCHING WITS

The drawback to helping your child reach his full intellectual potential is that sooner or later he'll use that blossoming intellect to outwit you. "Children are smart," says Marilee. "The times when they pull things are the times when they know you don't want to deal with it — when you've worked hard all day and have just fallen into your chair exhausted, or when a phone call comes, or when you're kneading bread and your hands are covered with flour."

The parents in this book agree that a lot of poor discipline happens because Mommy and Daddy just don't want to drop what they're doing and take care of the situation. "But then they end up with the problems and the headaches," says Glenda. The parents who won't spend time, effort, prayer, and emotional energy making sure their children are reared with fair, loving discipline will pay for that mistake the rest of their child's life — and tragically, so will their child.

One of the most important things you can do in this area is take care of yourself physically, spiritually, and emotionally so you can give your children the time and loving discipline they deserve. Make sure you get enough rest (or at least as much as possible), and avoid wearing yourself out with nonfamily commitments. Lisa says, "I'm currently reconsidering my obligations to church, family, and friends, because although I'm doing many 'important and valuable' things, I'm left with limited energy to parent my children the way they deserve to be parented. It's easy to get caught up in too many good activities and forget there is a *best* place you're called to be. My children need to be given the best of my energy, not just what is left over."

BEDTIME BLUES

"Be firm about bedtime," says Patty. "Nearly all children resist their naps." Enforcing bedtime isn't too hard with a young toddler. When he becomes tired and cranky, it's a fairly simple matter just to rock him for a few minutes, tell him a story or do whatever bedtime ritual you've established, and then gently but firmly put him into his crib. Even if he protests, his only option is to grump himself to sleep. But as he grows older, sooner or later he's going to have a regular bed and you'll have to make sure he stays in it. (Some of these parents' toddlers even learned to climb out of their cribs.)

Cheryl says it helps to have an established routine that includes a rule about getting out of bed. She says, "In our family, once you're in bed, you're in bed. Unless you're sick or going to wet the bed, you stay there." Disobedience in this area should be treated the same as disobedience in any other: First, look for the reasons behind the behavior. Is your child sick or frightened or feeling insecure for some reason? If so, some extra cuddle time may be in order. If not, give one warning, then follow through with consequences if he gets up again.

These parents aren't bedtime ogres. Most of them read their children stories, cuddle, and pray together before saying good night. Christine bought Ashley some storytime tapes and let her listen to them while she fell asleep. And all of the parents in this book allow their little ones to have their favorite animals, dolls, and blankets in bed with them. But as in any other area of discipline, consistency at the start will prevent headaches later on.

STALLING

Rarer than the proverbial hen's tooth is the toddler who has never tried to ignore Mommy when she told him to do something he wasn't in the mood to do. "When Ashley first started toddling," says Christine, "I went on a trip with my dad, who's a psychologist, and while we were riding I asked him how he thought I was doing as a mother. He said, 'Great, except for one thing. You don't make Ashley do what you say the first time you say it.'

"At the time, I wasn't even sure she understood me when I told her to do something, but now I wish I had taken his advice, because I'm having to repeat myself over and over. And it's not fair to her for me to tell her again and again to do something, then all of a sudden swat her. Believe me, you're better off to do the best you can to make sure your toddler understands, and then discipline if she doesn't obey."

No one likes to be rudely interrupted. Try using Dr. Dobson's suggestion to give your child the courtesy of a few minutes' warning rather than telling him out of the blue, "Put your toys away. It's time to take a bath." Set the kitchen timer for five or ten minutes and say, "It's almost time to take a bath. When the bell rings, you must put your toys away." Then be prepared to see that your instructions are followed when the timer goes off. Marilee says, "If you wait to discipline your child until you've called several times and finally become upset, you're teaching him that he doesn't have to respond until you get upset."

Also, Cheryl says, "Make sure they hear and understand you. Have them repeat what you told them if you're unsure."

MISBEHAVING IN PUBLIC

If you've taught your child from infancy not to grab things off the store shelves or play with Grandpa's stereo knobs, chances are he won't turn into a little monster now. But he will probably challenge you, so following through is still vital.

Several mothers stress the importance of telling your toddler just before you enter a public place exactly what behavior is expected and exactly what the results will be if your instructions are disobeyed: "Joshua, you must hold Mommy's hand in the store and not touch anything. If you run away or touch things, Mommy will spank." Sofie says, "I remember trips to the bathroom where pants were taken down and the children were spanked for repeatedly ignoring my warnings about their behavior. It's difficult to stop what you're doing and discipline, but it takes only a few times to let the child know you *will* follow through. It got to the point where I had only to say, 'Do you want to go to the bathroom with Mommy?'"

> Remember, encouraging your child for good behavior will give him a strong motivation to keep it up.

But don't stop only to take note of poor behavior. Remember, encouraging your child for good behavior (especially early in the shopping trip) will give him a strong motivation to keep it up. Stop in the middle of the department store, give him a big kiss, and say, "Joshua, I'm so proud of you! You're doing exactly as Mommy told you — you haven't touched anything, and you're holding Mommy's hand."

The Mommy and Daddy Book · Still in Charge?

Also, make sure you don't push your child past the point of endurance. Too much time at the mall is hard for grown men to tolerate good-naturedly, much less little children.

When grocery shopping, Jennifer says, "It helps me to put Jessica in a shopping cart and strap her in *every time* we go to a store. I let her play with sturdy fruits or vegetables. (If she plays with something she picks out, she's willing to eat it later.) I also engage her in conversation while we shop. I ask her opinion about things, and listen!"

Glenda says part of the problem with consistency in public, when both parents are there, is that the parents have never gotten together on strategy. "If one disciplines, the other objects, and if the other disciplines, the first one objects. So rather than have an argument in public, they just sit there, which is disastrous!"

Another problem is interference from well-meaning friends and grandparents. If a child senses that Grandma will shield him from Mommy's discipline, he'll run to her without hesitation. Virginia says, "I've had my in-laws get mad at me because I wouldn't allow them to do that. They did it with the other grandkids, and they thought I was just awful!" Of course, Virginia's children are now the grandkids her in-laws brag about for their good behavior.

NOT COMPLETING ASSIGNED TASKS

"Train your child to put toys away as soon as he can walk and carry things," says Patty. "Don't be his maid. It doesn't do you *or* him any favors." Donna agrees with chagrin: "April was an only child until she was four years old, and I always picked up after her; and now that we have another baby, I'm picking up his toys *and* her toys. I've got problems! And it's hard on April as well as me because I failed to teach her to pick up after herself when she was little. I can't blame her; I can only blame myself."

For many parents in this book, it was no problem to get their children to pick up their toys or perform other little tasks, the reason being that they didn't make the mistake of expecting them to do it alone. To a toddler, working with Mommy or Daddy is fun; working alone is punishment. I began teaching Megan to put her toys away when she was about fourteen months old. I sat by the toybox and told her, "Bring Mommy the doll" (or clown, or ball, or whatever). She didn't always understand what toy I was asking for, but I gave her lots of encouragement and a big kiss as she brought me each one, and I told her its name as she handed it to me. She quickly learned the names of her toys and came to look on putting them away as a game. Telling her that the toys were going "night-night" helped keep her from wanting to take them right back out.

Before long she was helping me put her toys into the box rather than just handing them to me, although it was months before she was ready to do the whole job by herself—and even then it was necessary to give her encouragement and supervision. Christine says, "If you start when your baby is a year old, she might put only one toy in the toybox, and she might not even realize she's putting the toy *away*, but if you can just help her get the idea that she's helping Mommy, you've accomplished a lot." Adrienne agrees: "You can always build from there. You've got a long time to work on it."

Using praise and hugs can work through the years, to the time when you're ready to let your little one help with such jobs as straightening her room, making her bed, helping to set the table, and putting her dirty clothes into the hamper. Even when your child graduates to the point where she's able to do these things alone, she'll need lots of encouragement. Thank her sincerely and let her know how much you appreciate and depend on her help. Children aren't born able to do work just for the pleasure of a job well done—that ability has to be cultivated by you, the parent, helping your child feel good about herself for completing an assigned task.

SIBLING JEALOUSY

A child's first four years are often the time when a little brother or sister comes along, and much has been said about the jealousy a toddler feels at having a little intruder usurp his throne. But several parents in this project found that using hugs, praise, and participation kept their toddlers from showing any noticeable jealousy.

Terri took a set of individually wrapped matchbox cars to the hospital with her and brought them home as a gift to Zachary from his new little sister. She says, "My little boy was never jealous of his baby sister. He thought she was the greatest thing ever. He said, 'Oh, boy, my new baby sister brought me a birthday party home from the hospital!'"

"It's all in how you handle it," says Glenda, "and how you let the toddler take part in the new baby's care. Our first two were only fourteen months apart, but we never experienced any jealousy with Greg, because he thought of the baby as 'his' and was allowed to go and get diapers and help in other small ways. You have to promote the idea of the new baby coming and then follow through afterward. A lot of times the mother is afraid to let the toddler be around the new baby, so she just shuts him off. That breeds resentment. You have to be very, very careful not to lose that toddler when the baby comes in." Cheryl adds, "Even if the baby's already here and the problem's already started, you can begin right where you are to involve the toddler. It may require a complete change of attitude, but it can be done."

Dana says, "When I brought Bridget home from the hospital, Bryan was the third person to hold her, after me and his daddy. I realized that a blue-eyed baby girl was going to get a lot of attention, so I made sure I gave Bryan *more* love and attention than I had before Bridget came. To this day, I honestly don't think it has ever crossed his mind that we might love her more than we do him."

Brynn has found that it helps her son Cole to see pictures of himself as an infant. The pictures show him that he was once a baby like his little sister, Kaylie, and that people made the same fuss over him back then that they're making over her now.

In the midst of all the love and reassurance you're giving your toddler, make sure you don't let up on your discipline. In Glenda's family, everyone was so concerned that Greg would feel displaced by his new sister that they overdid it. Greg decided, since he was receiving all this attention, that he might as well try getting away with a few things. "We had to put our foot down," says Glenda, "and that's difficult with grandparents around. They didn't like it when we disciplined him."

> Even if your toddler adores his new little sister, put a childproof gate across the nursery door and make sure you never leave him alone with her.

Even if your toddler adores his new little sister, put a childproof gate across the nursery door and make sure you never leave him alone with her. He doesn't yet know how to pick her up without dropping her, or what kind of hugs are okay. And there may be some jealousy you haven't yet seen. Glenda says, "To protect the baby, we put her in an infant seat in the middle of a mesh playpen. She stayed occupied watching her big brother, but he couldn't reach her. I still had to watch them, though, because he dropped toys in when she cried, trying to get her to play."

As the new baby in the house approaches toddlerhood and learns to play with her big brother or sister, there's bound to be a clash of wills every now and then. But these parents dismiss as a cop-out the idea that sibling rivalry is just a natural part of growing up. It may be natural, but it's certainly not healthy, and it can cause deep emotional scars.

Most of them require their children to kiss and make up after exchanging harsh words. Dana goes even further and doesn't allow her children to fight at all. She says, "All their lives they've got to get along with people. I decided that the best place to start is in the home. I've seen a lot of families who treat every-one else better than they treat each other, and I decided we weren't going to be that way — we were going to be examples. We were going to treat each other better than we treat our best friends."

How does she go about working this miracle? "I just don't allow them to argue. I tell them, 'You resolve it quietly; you don't fight.' If they're hateful to each other, they get disciplined, then they kiss and make up." In the event that each of them blames the other for starting it, Dana refuses to play referee: "I ask, 'Can you work it out calmly and lovingly with each other, or will Mommy have to discipline you both? Don't you think it would be much better to work it out yourselves, calmly and quietly, before I have to step in? Because if I step in, I'll discipline both of you.' That way they're motivated to compromise and give in to each other.

"Bridget and Bryan are very loving and close — Bridget wants to marry her 'Bubba' — because they've had no choice. They don't have the scars that come from fighting and ugly words because those things haven't been allowed." Dana concedes the necessity of staying within earshot of your children to learn whether one is consistently instigating the arguments or is being made always to give in, and the need to discipline separately a child who is a habitual bully. But she says that in her family Bridget, the youngest, is usually both the insti-gator and the first to yield.

RUDENESS

When Megan was about two years old she learned the magic words "I want," and she said them loudly and often. After putting up with it for a while because of her extreme youth, I decided that any child capable of saying "I want" was also capable of saying "May I please." Sure enough, she was, and within a month or so she was amazing our friends with her politeness.

I went about her training in etiquette by applying a healthy dose of what psychologist Kevin Leman calls Reality Discipline: Quite simply, when she said "I want" instead of "May I please," she didn't get what she asked for. I did a fair amount of motherly prompting ("How do we ask, dear?") and I usually allowed her to repent and ask again politely when she forgot. And I tried to reward her for asking politely by granting her request if it was reasonable and by giving her a good explanation and an alternative if it was not.

We made up funny little songs about the situation — real Grammy material, with lyrics like: "We don't say 'I want,' 'cause that's a yukky thing to say; we say 'May I please,' 'cause that's the polite thing to say."

Table manners are another major area where parents run into etiquette problems with their children. You can't expect too much in the way of decorum at the dinner table from a two- or three-year-old, but you can require that he eat with his fork or spoon — not his fingers.

Several parents found that the best way to deal with violations of this rule, after one warning, was to confiscate the child's dinner. That sounds harsh, but it shouldn't be necessary to do it more than once or twice before your child realizes you mean business. And with Megan, I found I needed to take her dinner away for only a couple of minutes for her to learn to obey.

A few warnings: Make sure your child understands and is capable of what you're asking. Give thorough explanations and demonstrations and encourage him sincerely when you see him doing a good job. Also, if you choose to have your child skip the rest of a meal because of etiquette violations, don't give snacks later. If anything, serve your child the same meal again, reheated, and confiscate it again — with no reprieve this time — if he continues to break the rules.

And don't confiscate a meal consisting entirely of foods your child hates. He'll think you're doing him a favor.

As your child grows older, he'll need to learn such niceties as putting his napkin on his lap before beginning to eat, not talking with his mouth full, keeping his left hand in his lap, and keeping his elbows off the table. Using games to teach these lessons, as Dr. James Dobson suggests, will create an awareness of good manners while at the same time making dinner a fun family time rather than an ordeal.

Here's one fun etiquette game: Establish a few simple etiquette rules and a silly penalty for breaking them, such as having the violator march around the dinner table or hop up and down while chanting five times, "I will not talk with food in my mouth." Let your children catch you breaking the rules first, just to get things rolling on a positive note. Then have each of your family members watch the others for infractions (or if your children become too aggressive with each other, have the parents watch the children and the children watch the parents).

TV ADDICTION

"TV is the hottest issue in our family right now," says Carol. "Last summer our set was hit by lightning and we didn't get it fixed. We had an old-fashioned summer — we played games, we read. It was wonderful. But when football season came, my husband got another TV, and now we have one in the bedroom and one in the family room. I've had to learn to turn the TV off, no matter what, when there's something on we don't want our children to see. It's hard — we have temper tantrums sometimes because the kids get addicted to it. The more TV they get, the more they want. This summer we may have to put it into the closet."

Kids need to be able to curl up occasionally and do nothing, just as adults do. And there really is a fair amount of good, wholesome children's programming available, especially on the cable networks — some of it even Christian — but it's just another variation of Murphy's Law that whenever you or your child want to sit down and unwind in front of the TV set, the airwaves are bound to be cluttered with junk. For families who can afford them, videotape recorders offer a way out. Terri says, "I record the shows I want Zachary to see. He's at the age where he wants to do things over and over, and he's even started reading a little bit from watching *Sesame Street* again and again." Wonderful video series such as *Adventures in Odyssey* and *VeggieTales* teach Christian values while they entertain.

Lois interjects this point: "It's important to have a balanced life. TV can be an easy babysitter, and to allow a child to sit there for six to eight hours a day, even when all the shows are good shows, teaches him no balance at all. He doesn't learn to appreciate reading, he doesn't go out to play, and he doesn't learn how to occupy himself. The TV monopolizes all his time." For a young child, an hour a day of TV watching is probably more than enough.

It makes sense that if you limit your child's television viewing, the time that would have been taken by the TV set has to be filled with something else. Many of the mothers I interviewed have a strong desire to instill a love of reading in their children, but they've found it takes self-discipline to sit down and read with them when there is housework that needs doing. "You have to make yourself do it," says Carol. "You have to take the time. The dishes won't go anywhere." Check your church library and the public library for good read-aloud books appropriate to your child's age. Public libraries often have lists of award-winning or popular books in various categories. (For other nontelevision ways to occupy toddlers, see chapter 7.)

Finally, the young parents I've interviewed who are connected with the internet are applying roughly the same rules to their computers as they are to their television sets: Supervise carefully, and set time limits. Scott says, "Wes is super-familiar with the computer. He could play on that all the time. But it doesn't develop values or teach him how to interact with people. I let him spend twenty or thirty minutes playing with the computer, teaching him how to learn things on there — his colors and numbers and stuff. But after a while it's time to say, 'Okay, Wes, we're going to do something else. Let's go play with toys.'"

PEER INFLUENCE

The parental struggle against the negative effects of peer pressure starts early, mainly because children show just as much talent for imitating each other as they do for imitating adults. "Jason is four," says Cheryl, "and we never had trouble with rebellion until just recently. I know that our main problem is a couple of kids in the neighborhood, so I'm having to decide whether I'm going to let him play with them. It's hard to know where to draw the line — I want him to have friends."

Wanda says, "You can't pick your children's friends for them, but you can help them cultivate good friendships. Michelle is an only child, and there aren't a lot of kids in the neighborhood for her to play with, but I can take an active part in her friendships by having the children I approve of over often. And it's good to point out the things you like about your child's behavior and the behavior of her friends."

Even though these parents know it's impossible to shield a child from all negative friendships, most of them have chosen to at least partially screen their children's friends. But don't make certain friends off-limits without explaining why. Even a two- or three-year-old can understand when you tell him, "No, I'm sorry, but Johnny can't come over because he runs in the house and doesn't obey Mommy."

The parents in this book are also cautious about the homes where they allow their children to play. "Get to know their friends' parents," says Wanda. "Just because your child met a friend at day care or Sunday school doesn't always protect him from wrong influences." They're also adamantly against letting a young child spend the night in the home of a child whose parents are not trusted friends.

Even if his only public exposure *sans* Mommy and Daddy is Sunday school or a good Christian day-care center, your toddler will probably bring home a bad word or two and try it out on you to see your reaction. When he does, Debby says, "Try not to blow your top. He probably won't know what it means, so just explain very simply that it's not a nice word and he's not to use it again." The same goes for bad attitudes and behaviors that are transferred from day care to home. Explain that they're not allowed (and if possible, why not), and be prepared to discipline if you're disobeyed.

"When the neighbor kids come over," says Marilee, "I make sure I can listen to their conversation with my children. Sometimes it takes me and my husband two weeks to finish explaining things the neighbor kids spent five minutes talking about!" "You have to explain those things, though," says Glenda, "because you can't shelter your children from what they're going to face outside, from the influence of other children. You have to teach them. Pretty soon you'll hear your little one telling the other kids, 'But my mommy says . . .'"

The best protection you can give your child against negative peer influence is to keep an open, honest, loving relationship with him, making yourself an example of good behavior and educating him as to why bad behavior is bad. And try to help him cultivate friendships that will reinforce the values you're trying to teach. Marilee says, "I've told David, 'It's important for you to choose friends who act right, because the people you're around all the time are the people you're going to start acting like.' Even though he may not completely understand that right now, it's laying the groundwork for his friendships when he grows older."

> The best protection you can give your child against negative peer influence is to keep an open, honest, loving relationship with him, making yourself an example of good behavior and educating him as to why bad behavior is bad.

LYING

Cheryl says, "It seems as if our culture teaches us that it's okay to lie if it gets you out of trouble, or it's okay to tell stories if it's not going to hurt anyone. As soon as Jason and Brian were old enough, we began teaching them Bible verses about not lying and about loving one another and being kind to one another.

"We've had a problem, though, with Jason's being confused when he hears an adult say something untrue, then laugh and say, 'Oh, I'm just kidding.' I've tried to explain it to him, but for the life of me I can't come up with a good explanation of the difference between teasing and telling a lie. I told Rodger, my husband, 'We're really going to have to listen to what we say and what other people say, because right now Jason can't understand the difference.' I finally told him that sometimes even adults tell stories, but it's never the right thing to do." Glenda points out that children see morality in black and white, not shades of gray: "A child can't understand. All he sees is that you're allowed to tell lies because you're kidding, but he's not."

When starting to educate your child about honesty, it's important to realize that a very young child has no concept of the moral ramifications of lying. He doesn't even know what lying is, and he certainly doesn't realize it's wrong.

With that in mind, here are some steps to raising an honest child

Avoid asking your child questions in a manner that will tempt him to lie. When you snap, "Josh, did you break this lamp?" little Josh will probably answer no out of pure self-preservation. He can tell from your tone of voice and the look in your eyes what the consequences will be if he confesses. Besides, breaking a lamp isn't a punishable offense unless it's the result of disobedience.

> When starting to educate your child about honesty, it's important to realize that a very young child has no concept of the moral ramifications of lying.

Patiently and calmly teach your child what it means to be truthful. "Josh, when I ask you to pick up your toys, don't tell me you already did it if you really didn't. That's called lying, and we don't do that." It also helps to find a storybook where the protagonist learns to tell the truth, even if it gets him into trouble. There are many good storybooks on the market dealing with kindness, honesty, unselfishness, and other virtues. Check your Christian bookstore for them. They can be invaluable teaching tools.

Be an example of honesty to your child. Don't ask him to lie for you on the telephone or at the front door. And if you slip and tell a lie, apologize to your child: "What I just said wasn't true, and I shouldn't have said it. Let's pray and ask the Lord to forgive me and help me be a good example for you."

Don't include harmless childhood fantasies in the same category as lies. When Megan came up with tall tales such as, "Today I flew in a big balloon on *Sesame Street,*" I generally answered, with a smile, "Oh, really? Was it fun?" It might be a good idea to add, "I like pretending about things like that, don't you?"

Be cautious when you discipline for lying. As their children grew older and began to understand why lying is wrong, several parents adopted the policy of disciplining their children twice if they misbehaved and then lied about it—once for the transgression and once for the lie. Be sure you're right before you follow that course, though, because children have an acute sense of fairness, and an unjust punishment will stick in your child's mind for years to come.

One mother says, "I remember that when I was little my dad wouldn't even let me tell my side of the story. If he accused me of something and I said, 'No, I didn't,' I got spanked for backtalking. I want to keep my relationship with my kids open so they'll feel free to confide in me. I want them to be able to look back and say, 'My parents were always fair when they disciplined me.'"

Luellen has used the method of double punishment if her children misbehaved and then lied about it, but she adds a twist: "If my children do something wrong and tell me about it *before* I find out, the punishment is much lighter. This has really kept the doors open for honest communication. Even now, as teenagers, they are still truthful about their actions."

Dana says, "This didn't happen with my children until they were older, but there have been times when I had to tell one of them, 'I'm not sure that what you've told me is the truth. But you know that sooner or later I'll probably find out. And even if I don't, God knows, and you know. If what you've told me isn't true, why don't you come clean and tell me the truth and ask Jesus to forgive you, and we'll go on from there.' It got to the point where I was able to tell. There was a certain indignation about them when they were lying that gave them away."

Finally, be quick to apologize if you discipline your child for lying, then discover later that he told the truth. Cheryl says, "All you can do is go to him and tell him you've asked Jesus to forgive you, and now you need his forgiveness too."

A Reassuring Word

Well, we have just spent two chapters talking about early childhood discipline, and we've only hit the high spots in this huge and complicated subject. For new parents, the challenge to "get it right" can feel overwhelming. So here's a word of encouragement: You won't.

As we said in chapter 8, all parents make mistakes. Nobody, least of all God, expects you to be a perfect parent. Your job as a mother or father is to care deeply about your child, pay attention to the lessons God is teaching you, recognize and learn from your mistakes, and depend on God as the only true source for the wisdom you need.

"I often pray for God's wisdom and strength regarding parenting issues," says Lisa. "I feel like I mess up a lot in the area of consistent discipline. God redeems those shortcomings when I let him, though. Sometimes he seems to help my children and me grow and learn together through the parenting process. Whenever I've noticed that I've messed up as a parent, and explained whatever was not working with my children, then redrawn clear boundaries or rules and consistently tried to enforce them, my children have certainly been adaptable to the change. So if you mess up, there is hope!"

As you pay close attention to the lessons God is teaching you within your family, it's important to keep educating yourself with books and courses by older, more experienced Christian parents. Most of the young parents I interviewed are devoted Dobson readers. They recommend Dr. James Dobson's books *Dare to Discipline* and *The Strong-Willed Child* for advice on ways to discipline as your child grows older, as well as ways to handle special problems. Another excellent book on disciplining children over age four is Kevin Leman's *Making Children Mind without Losing Yours.* Check with your church or local Christian bookstore for other resources.

Proverbs 19:27 says, "Stop listening to instruction, my son, and you will stray from the words of knowledge." Godly wisdom in any area, including parenting, is a lifelong pursuit. But there is no pursuit more fascinating, nor with more joyful results for you and the people you love.

Chapter 11

Someone Special, That's Me!

*I love you not for who you are, but for who I am when
I am with you.*

— UNKNOWN

People like to be with those who make them feel valued and valuable, liked and likable, loved and lovable. Helping your child develop a healthy sense of his worth will not only give him the courage and confidence to become all God created him to be; it will also have a huge impact on your future relationship.

The children of the parents I've interviewed are fairly typical in that they're all different. Some of them demonstrate the happy ability to shed peer rebuffs with little effort, while others, more sensitive, seem to have been struggling with a deficit in the self-worth department from birth. But their parents agree that home should be a sanctuary from which a naturally confident child can sally forth to win the world, or where a naturally shy child can remain for a while to build up his courage, secure in the knowledge that he's loved and accepted just as he is.

Personality differences aside, a child's development of healthy self-esteem does seem to require at least three basic ingredients: unconditional love, a sense of competence, and social acceptance. Of the three, you can give your child only the first one — and even there, what you have to offer will not be enough. (We'll talk more about that later.) The other two ingredients your child will have to learn to provide for himself. You can help, though, by providing instructions, opportunity, encouragement — and sometimes consequences — and, hardest of all, by getting out of the way.

Even knowing the ingredients, it's impossible in one chapter to give a step-by-step formula for producing a happy, confident child. (The formula wouldn't be valid anyway, given the differences among children.) Nearly every chapter in this book makes some reference to building a child's self-esteem, and you'll need to finish reading it to get a true picture of how these parents are trying to encourage their children. This chapter will be dedicated to sharing some simple do's and don'ts that we have found to be true and to reinforcing some vital points already mentioned.

No Strings Attached: Communicating Unconditional Love

Probably the most delicate balancing act we face as parents is the challenge to show our children we love them just the way they are without giving them the mistaken impression that the way they are is just fine — especially when that means yelling "Mine!" or hitting their baby sister or grabbing things off the grocery store shelves.

> A child's development of healthy self-esteem does seem to require at least three basic ingredients: unconditional love, a sense of competence, and social acceptance.

The only way we can learn to give our children true unconditional love is to ask God to help us see them from his point of view. God's attitude toward his children — and the attitude he calls us to have toward ours — is this: "I love you just the way you are. Even more than that, I love you too much to leave you the way you are." The patience, wisdom, and strength to maintain that point of view, in the face of toddler behavior (and later, preteen and teen behavior, and all the behaviors in between), can only come from him. That's why effective Christian parents tend to have calluses on their knees.

That said, here are some basic tips on communicating unconditional love:

Do tell your child *daily* how much she's loved. She won't just know; she has to be told. One of our moms says, "Not until I was married did I hear my parents say 'I love you,' even though they always showed it by their actions. The first time I said it to them over the phone, there was total silence. They didn't know how to react. Now I'm struggling to go beyond just showing it and thinking it with my children. I want to *say* it." It's very hard to overdo telling a child how special she is, how much you love her, and how very glad you are that she's yours.

Do use language your child understands. Elizabeth says, "I tell my children, 'Mommy loves Stewart' and 'Mommy loves Hallie,' 'Jesus loves Stewart'

and 'Jesus loves Hallie.' They're too little to understand what *I* and *you* mean."
Jennifer laughs about the pronoun issue: "Wes is still confused by that. He'll
say, 'Hold you?' because he's heard me ask, 'Do you want me to hold you?' Now
he's starting to get it — he'll sometimes say, 'Hold me,' and I'll answer, 'Oh, do
you want Mommy to hold you?' Then he'll think, *I said it wrong!* He'll correct
himself and say, 'Hold you?' It's confusing for him."

Do show physical affection. Luellen says, "I can tell my kids 'I love you,'
but if I forget the physical hug or playful way of twirling their hair, I haven't
reinforced the verbal statement." "We give a good-night kiss *and* a good-morn-
ing kiss in our house," says Terri. "It started as a joke when Zachary was tiny,
but now it's really important to both our children. When things get really hec-
tic, like on a Sunday when we're all running out the door for church, Zachary
will stop and say, 'We can't go to Sunday school — we haven't had a good-
morning kiss!'"

Don't wait until you feel affectionate to hug your child (or your
spouse!). The adage "Attitude follows action" is true. Show affection, and soon
you'll begin to feel it.

Do express approval of your child often. If you withhold approval until
your child "earns" it, chances are that will never (or rarely) happen. Christine
says, "If you're constantly negative, your child won't be accustomed to having
any sense of your approval anyway, so he won't work to gain it." Instead of
expecting your child to work for your approval, give so much approval that he'll
work not to lose it.

Don't be afraid to show strong disapproval of unacceptable behavior, but a
parent's resting attitude toward his or her child should be one of love and strong,
often-expressed approval rather than neutrality or indifference while waiting for
good or bad behavior to tip the scales.

And don't ever fall into the fantasy that approval can take the place of
discipline.

Do operate by the Golden Rule as much as possible. Your role as parent will dictate that you enforce unpopular rules at times, but give your child
the courtesy due him as a fellow human being made in the image of God, a fellow traveler on the road to eternity. Several parents brought out the point that
any treatment you'd hate will probably bother your child just as much.

Don't force your child to go to someone she's afraid of. "It's cruel," says
Adrienne, "and it doesn't work." Many babies go through phases when they
cling to Mommy, and it's important to keep offering social opportunities without pushing them. If a person behaves in a friendly manner while keeping his

distance, your baby will probably decide to trust him eventually after repeated nonthreatening exposure. But your child needs to know you'll never betray her by handing her over to someone she fears.

This situation can be embarrassing, especially if the feared person is a family member. Megan was terrified of my father's deep voice when she was about four months old. Every time he came near her, she began to cry. So Granddaddy stayed in the background for a while, smiling at her and playing with her — when she allowed it — as my mother or I held her. It didn't take long at all for him to win her over and become one of her favorite people.

Do watch your nonverbal communication. "I could always tell my mother was upset with me just by how she breathed," says Terri. "Now sometimes I'll hear myself doing that. Zachary will ask, 'What's wrong?' and I'll say, 'Nothing,' but I'll know he could tell I was upset because I breathed just like my mother. I've learned to say, 'Mommy's upset right now, but she'll be okay in a minute,' because a lot of times we tear our children down by our attitudes. They get the idea, 'Boy, she wishes I weren't here.'" Kathy agrees: "My four-year-old knows I'm upset just by the way I'm doing dishes. He'll come up and ask, 'Mama, are you happy?'"

> A little sigh of disgust or a roll of the eyes can speak volumes to a young child — or a spouse, for that matter.

A little sigh of disgust or a roll of the eyes can speak volumes to a young child — or a spouse, for that matter. Ask the Lord to make you hypersensitive to your negative attitudes and actions.

Do treat your child like a welcome addition to the family. Christine says, "I think it's important to take your child with you, even to restaurants if you can. I never want Ashley to have the feeling that she's more of a pain than a blessing." Wanda adds, "Be sure your child can be up high enough to see in stores and in crowds."

Do be careful not to play favorites. Most of the parents I interviewed say they have no trouble with this, but if you do have a favorite, you must try to cure yourself of it for all of your children's sakes. "Ask God to help you see what he wants to develop in your children and what's special from him in each child," says Patti.

Children are sensitive to favoritism, and there are times when an unsuspecting parent will find herself accused of it when it isn't even in her thoughts. Cheryl says, "If Jason knows he would be disciplined for doing something, then

I had better discipline Brian for the same thing. Otherwise it looks as if I'm playing favorites — and he'll tell me it does too." Rita found it helpful when she disciplined her older son to tell him that she wasn't just picking on him because he was older: "When I reprimanded Billy for the way he was treating Brian, I assured him that I wouldn't allow Brian to do that to him either. I felt that idea was really from the Lord, because I saw his whole attitude change."

Do be careful not to discuss your child's problems while he's in the room. "Remember that children are people," says Rosemary. "Don't converse with another adult in front of your child as if he were an inanimate object or deaf. Children have the same emotions adults do." New parents fall into this nasty habit while their child is a baby. They figure, "He can't understand what I'm saying, so I'm not hurting him." The problem is, they never bother to get out of the habit when their child learns to talk. "And I believe even a young baby can recognize his name and tell by your tone that you're complaining about him," says Terri.

Many of these unintentional insults are self-fulfilling. Not long ago, on a visit to a friend's house, my friend and I began to discuss her two-year-old daughter, who was playing in the same room. "Boy, Shelley's strong-willed," said my friend. "She tests me every time I turn around." I glanced over at her little daughter, who was listening, and I could practically see on her face the thought, *Boy, I'm strong-willed. I test Mommy every time she turns around.*

How much better it would have been for my friend to say, "Shelley has a very strong will, and I know it's hard for her to obey Mommy sometimes, so I'm very proud of her when she does!" I would have understood exactly what she meant, but her words would have reinforced obedience rather than disobedience. Instead of complaining, express hope to others about difficult areas: "Maybe she'll come to you next time."

All of this may sound as if we're quibbling about semantics — and we are — but if you're under the impression that your words aren't important, I urge you to take a look in your Bible at the book of James, chapter 3. Many of the points in this chapter have to do with controlling your words, which can be done only through prayer, commitment, and self-discipline. But it can be done. More than that — it *must* be done. Lisa says, "We work long and hard to help our children feel cherished. It's important to keep in mind that even one careless statement can send a child's self-esteem tumbling." That's especially true when the careless statement comes from one of the two most important people in your child's life.

Most important, these parents say you should never criticize your child, either to her face or behind her back, for something over which she has no control, such as the arrangement of her facial features, her hair color or texture, her build, or — worse yet — her sex. Christine says, "What worse thing could you say in front of a child than that she should have been something she can't do anything about?"

🦽 *Don't* resort to insults and harsh words to modify your child's behavior. Unlike the sting from a spanking, the sting of harsh words never goes away. Included in the insult category are self-fulfilling labels such as "bad boy," "bad girl," and age labeling: "the terrible twos."

"There are so many times when it would be easy to say, 'That was a stupid thing to do,'" says Terri. "And that does get the message across, but it also gets across another message: 'You're stupid.' And a lot of times we take it for granted that they know they shouldn't have done something when they don't."

🐦 *Do* apologize when you're wrong. Many parents mentioned the importance of apologizing if you lose your temper and say something to hurt your child. That goes for the little digs as well as the big ones. Cheryl says, "There are times when I'm tired or have a headache, and those are the times when I usually ask the boys to come and pray for me. I say, 'Mommy's very tired, and I don't want to get upset or yell tonight, but my head hurts. Would you please pray for Mommy?' Not only is their faith working as they pray for me, but they're also made aware that I'm not feeling well and they try to be more quiet. Or if I say something I regret I can apologize and tell them, 'Remember that Mommy told you she was very tired? I didn't mean what I just said, and I'm sorry.'"

🐛 *Do* make degrading nicknames and sarcastic humor off-limits in your home. "Ever since Ryan was born," says Kathy, "we called him Weasel, because he was so funny-looking when he was a baby — his ears stuck out. But when he was about two years old he told Hugh, 'Daddy, I'm not a weasel.' He had started feeling hurt about it, so we dropped it."

"Rodger and I don't allow sarcastic, cutting teasing between us," says Cheryl, "because not only is it bad for us but also the children will pick it up and use it against each other."

🐿 *Do* give your child some space of his own. Humans are territorial creatures — and before you deny that, try sitting in your husband's seat at dinner tonight or taking your best friend's spot at aerobics class. If you have two toddlers who must share a room, make the dividing line clear. "Every child needs a special place where he can hide his treasures," says Patti. And beyond that, give your child a special corner of the family room, a special chair — anything that says, "I belong here. I'm an important part of this family." The mother who keeps her house perfect and never allows her toddler to encroach on her decor sends him a clear message: "I'm important. You're not." Of course, several mothers laughed when I brought up this subject and said, "The whole house belongs to my kids. I'm the one who needs some space!"

 *Do* allow your child a sense of ownership. Marilee suggests allowing your child to have a few toys that need not be shared with others — especially toys that have to do with his sense of security, such as a special stuffed animal, pillow, or blanket. "A child needs freedom from the feeling that anything he has is fair game for any kid who comes into the house and wants it," she says.

Do spend time talking with and listening to your child. Cheryl says, "So often, when children reach the toddler stage and they're talking all the time, we tend to tune them out. And it's bad to ignore them or just come back with an automatic no. I've had to pray for help to think before I speak and to give my boys the courtesy of listening to what they're saying, even if I've heard it a hundred times and they're taking ten times too long to say it." Virginia adds, "It's so easy to respect other people, then come home, relax, and treat our children as if they aren't as important as the people 'out there.' They start feeling as if they really aren't. I've had to ask the Lord to help me respect each one of them as an individual."

Connie says, "When your child shares things with you, listen. Give him eye-to-eye contact. My parents were never too busy to listen, and to this day I love to share things with them. They make me feel as if they really care."

Of course, as in all other areas, you need to maintain balance. Your child shouldn't be allowed to monopolize the conversation in a group of adults simply because you're afraid of stifling his personality; on the other hand, his narratives shouldn't be fair game for interruption because they're not "important."

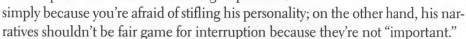

"My parents were never too busy to listen, and to this day I love to share things with them. They make me feel as if they really care."

 *Do* continue seeking to build your child's self-esteem as the years go by. This isn't hard to do, because when you seek from the time of birth to encourage your child, you develop good habits that are natural to continue. I read a lovely anonymous quote recently: "A parent's job is to keep her child's cup of self-esteem so full that the rest of the world can't poke enough holes in it to drain it dry."

Jon or I used to put a note in our children's lunchboxes every day to let them know we were thinking of them while they were in school. Elizabeth says, "My parents did things like that. I'd open up my vanity in the bathroom, and there would be a note saying they loved me. Even when I was in college, they would make banners and put them on the garage when I came home, saying, 'We missed you.' I just knew they loved me. I've always known."

🧁 *Do* give your child a strong spiritual foundation, and encourage him to accept Jesus as Savior as soon as he's able to understand what that decision means. Your love has limits, and no matter how much you love your child, you will fail him at times. God's love is limitless and never fails. Nothing reinforces a person's self-esteem more than the knowledge that Jesus died for him and that the Creator of the universe loves him enough to listen to his prayers. "That, to me, is the most important thing you can do for a child," says Terri.

🐨 *Don't* take your child for granted. "Enjoy him and treasure every minute," says Karen. "We've almost lost Josh twice, and we know God may call him home before we're ready. Children are a gift, but they're only ours to nurture for a while. They belong to God."

👶 Finally, and most important, *do* pray for and work toward consistency in your attitudes and behavior. Unconditional love doesn't evaporate when your child misbehaves or when the family finances have gone haywire or when the new baby is keeping everyone awake at night. It may seem like the impossible dream always to be patient, kind, and loving as a spouse and parent even in times of stress and conflict, but that is our calling as followers of Christ. *That's what unconditional love is: Love independent of circumstances*. It is essential to the development of trust in our family relationships, as well as to our children's self-esteem, that our loved ones see us striving, with God's help, in this direction.

We'll close this section with a poem written by a young mother, Katherine Tracy, for her daughter Morgan. If Katherine communicates her heart as clearly to her little girl through their daily life together as she does to her readers through this poem, Morgan will never have a reason to doubt her mother's love.

I Want You to Know

Dearest little one, I want you to know
that I fell in love with you
the first time I saw your face,
that I knew the moment I held you
I would fight tigers for you,
that there were days I just held you
for hours and we sat and
warmed each other.

My tiny explorer, I want you to know
the pure joy I felt watching you

drink in your bright new world,
small hands reaching, grasping
anything you saw, eyes
widening in amazement
at the wonder of everything
from teddy bears to keys.

My sleeping angel, I want you to know
that I can't rest at night until
my fingers have touched the softness
of your sleeper and waited
for the slow rise and fall
of your breathing. My hand
strokes your head and
silently I pray God's protection
on you, now and always.

My independent one, I want you to know
I applaud your efforts to try new things,
knowing that with each fresh skill
you need me less and less,
knowing my goal is for you
to leave me one day, to fly
all on your own.

Flesh of my flesh, I want you to know
that I delight in the miracle of you,
that helping you grow
into a woman, God's woman,
is my redemption, my purpose.

Dearest child, I want you to know
I would still fight tigers for you.

— KATHERINE TRACY

"I Can Do It!" — Building Your Child's Sense of Competence

Unconditional love, vital as it is, is not enough to give a growing child a secure
sense of self-worth. As she watches the world around her and sees the people func-
tioning in it, a child begins to figure out her own role. Recent medical research

has discovered that babies' brains are hardwired to identify rules and patterns. This helps them learn speech (which was the subject of the research) and also rules and patterns of behavior and how those rules apply to themselves and others.

To have a secure sense of self-worth, your child needs to know what her role is and that she can fill it well. This makes her childhood a great adventure for both of you, since her role will keep changing and growing as time goes by, as will yours.

Do give even a shy child the benefit of discipline. Parental discipline is the first step toward a child's development of self-control. It's a miserable feeling (as every yo-yo dieter has experienced) to know the rules but lack the self-discipline to follow them. It's an even worse feeling to suspect that there are no firm rules and that every protective boundary in your life will fall if you push hard enough.

Proverbs 25:28 says, "Like a city whose walls [defenses] are broken down is a man who lacks self-control." It's a paradox that our children will test and resist our rules but will feel secure when we meet their tests with answers that are firm, fair, consistent, and loving.

Don't take your child places where his behavior is important when he's tired. "If you do, you'll get negative feedback from everyone you see," says Carol. You'll also end up feeling exasperated and impatient yourself, which can hardly help but affect your behavior toward your child.

Do try to pass off your child's minor "boo-boos" as lightly as possible. When your baby falls down, pick him up and comfort him if he cries, and of course, check to see whether he has hurt himself, but don't overdo your response. If you regard every bump and bruise as a catastrophe, it won't take long for your baby to pick up that attitude. I found that most of the time when Megan fell down there was an interval of a second or two between the accident and her reaction. If I quickly smiled and said "Boom!" or made another funny noise, her crying was usually averted.

Do give your child the freedom to pass milestones at her own pace. This is a biggie, because friends, grandparents, aunts, uncles, cousins, *ad infinitum*, begin comparing your child to various standards from the moment of birth: "How much did she weigh?" "What was her Apgar rating? Oh, only eight? My Janie got a ten." After you come home from the hospital, it's a race to see whose child can crawl first, cut teeth first, say her first word first, walk first, toilet train first.

The only way to shield your child from this ridiculous contest is to refuse to take part in it. It's good to know what the average four-month-old, or nine-month-old, or one-year-old is doing, so you can tell if your child has a problem. "But you never have to express it to your child," says Cheryl. Carol says, "Don't let Satan put thoughts into your head, like, *My child isn't as good as . . .* He'll do that if he can. And the child senses it."

"Usually children catch up with each other anyway," adds Terri. "By the time they hit kindergarten they're pretty much even, so it's not as if one child is necessarily brighter than the other. It's just that some babies catch on sooner." "There are very few five-year-olds who aren't toilet trained!" says Patti.

🙂 *Do* avoid making sibling comparisons. Cheryl points out the need, if you have more than one child, to avoid comparing your children to each other and also to discourage comparisons by well-meaning friends and relatives. She says, "It has been hard, with Jason and Brian only seventeen months apart. Jason is very quick-minded, whereas Brian is more the playful, energetic type. When people say things like, 'Boy, Jason's the brain and Brian's the brawn in this family,' we just laugh it off and change the subject and try to compliment both of the boys on their strong points. Any comparison, even if you don't mean it to be bad, comes out sounding like a left-handed compliment." Ask day care workers and, later, teachers not to openly compare your children with each other.

As they grow older, children often start participating in this destructive game themselves. "We started very early telling each of our children that God has a plan for them and that because they're different, they shouldn't compare," says Carol. Virginia adds, "When one of my girls says, 'Ricky can do so-and-so, and I can't,' I answer, 'Yes, he's strong in that area, but you're strong in *this* area.'"

Stephanie adds a warning: "When you have more than one child, it's tempting to expect your second and third to grow up faster. Kristen is only a little over three, and many times I expect her to be doing what Rachel is doing at four and a half. And I have to keep reminding myself that Erica is only a year old. I've talked to my sister about it, and she says she's the same way with hers. It's easy to expect younger children to be past where they really should be. For instance, Rachel learned to tie her shoes, and Kristen said, 'I want to learn!' So I sat and worked with her and was thinking, *Why can't you get this?* Then I realized, *Well, duh! She's only three.*"

🍼 *Do* make sure the puzzles and toys you give your child are at his age and developmental level, and don't move on until he shows a need for more challenge. "Give your children realistic challenges," says Lisa. "If the bulk of their day consists of successes, confidence builds."

> "Give your children realistic challenges," says Lisa. "If the bulk of their day consists of successes, confidence builds."

The Mommy and Daddy Book · Someone Special, That's Me!

Do get excited about your child's achievements — even the little ones, like fitting a difficult puzzle piece. "Praise him for his accomplishments!" says Karen. "Clap and cheer! He'll love it, and it will encourage him to do things right." It will also give him the courage to try new things. Success really does breed success.

Do encourage your child to keep trying. Be available to help, but be careful about stepping in too often. "I didn't want Wes to be frustrated," says Jennifer. "I've had to learn, when he's doing a new puzzle and can't get a piece to go in, to say, 'Wes, you can do it!' At first, he was like, 'No, Mommy do it!' and I thought, *Okay, I've helped you a few too many times.* Now he'll just keep struggling until he figures it out. I've had to teach myself to step back and let him do it. Otherwise he won't gain the confidence to keep trying."

Do praise or criticize the action, not the child. It's good to tell your baby how adorable she is, but as she grows older, it's better to devote your most enthusiastic praise to your child's good actions rather than to things she can take no credit for, such as having a pretty face. Praising your child's inherited looks can lead to problems — especially if you have two children, one of whom is a natural beauty while the other isn't. Cheryl says, "We compliment our boys on how they look if they've made an extra effort to dress nicely — 'Hey, you're a sharp dresser!'"

Give credit where credit is due. For healthy bodies, bright minds, and cute faces, the credit belongs to the Lord. Credit goes to your child for being kind to her friends, for working to master tasks with her healthy body and bright mind, and for doing a good job of brushing the hair surrounding that cute face.

Give specific praise or criticism. Rather than saying, "You sure were a good girl today," tell your child, "I'm so proud of you! You helped Mommy put away the clothes, and you obeyed when Mommy told you to come inside." When your child knows exactly what she did right, she's more liable to repeat it. Christine is a great believer in "I" messages: "I like the way you . . ." And Kathy recommends telling your child when he is being disciplined for a transgression, "'It was wrong to do thus-and-so.' Not, 'You were bad,'" she says, "but the action itself was wrong."

Do recognize that different children have different abilities, even within the same family. Carol, who has four children, believes every child has strong points that need to be brought out. But she says, "It's important for the parent to recognize them early. God has given us gifts, and we need to know what they are."

Knowing where her strengths lie can give your child a sense of identity and confidence, so look for her strong points and reinforce them. If she loves to help, praise her for being helpful and give her as much opportunity as possible to do it. If she's bright and loves to read, praise her for mastering new books and expand her library. If she's active and good at games, praise her for working hard at them. If she's gentle with other children and shares her toys, praise her for being kind. Of course, you'll need to help your child develop a balanced lifestyle that includes all of these areas. It's also important to make sure that your own wishful thinking doesn't assign your child a strong point different from the ones she really has.

Do focus on your child's strengths rather than his weaknesses. Virginia says, "If you don't feel well or are in a bad mood, it's easy to see everything your child does wrong that day instead of seeing the good and thanking God for it."

Do praise honest effort wherever you find it. Try to see your child's world from his point of view. "We expect too much of our toddlers," says Cheryl. "It's important not to jump in and do things for them that they should be learning to do for themselves, or to expect them to do things as quickly as we would. Instead of pushing and nagging, we should be saying, 'You're really doing well!'"

Rather than constantly correcting your toddler's speech, make yourself an example of good language and praise your child when he does use a new word in the right way. Adopt a child's-eye view of the things your toddler does for you. Wear the nasty-smelling perfume he gave you for Christmas at least a few times — maybe on days when you don't have to leave the house. Accept gifts of dubious artwork with joy. Instead of asking, "What on earth is it?" say, "How beautiful! Tell me about it," and find a way to display his pictures for at least a few days. When the time comes to throw pictures away, Virginia suggests that you don't let your child see you tossing her masterpiece into the wastebasket. No artist enjoys seeing her work thrown out, especially by someone she loves.

Do give commands and instructions in a positive tone. Terri says, "With my little boy, I can say, 'Zachary, pick up the toy right now and take it into your room,' and he'll do it. But my little girl became very stubborn when I tried that with her, even at eighteen months old. I discovered that it worked much better when I said, 'Ashley, show Mommy what a big girl you can be and take the toy into your room.' Now, with that approach, she cleans circles around her older brother. She wants to please me."

Do remember that childish hands and feet are awkward and that spilled milk and broken vases are bound to happen occasionally. Don't discipline your child for them unless they're the result of direct disobedience. And that means don't yell.

Do forgive and forget. "After you've disciplined, drop it and don't bring it up again," says Rita. "I had a tendency to think of past things every time my boys made a mistake, and I had to stop it. My husband, Marvin, set a good example for me. He showed me how just to drop it and go on." Lisa adds, "How can our children learn to know their heavenly Father as the Forgiver and Forgetter of sins if we never forget their transgressions? We have to encourage them to move on, forgiven, with a new start."

🚼 Do encourage your child to make decisions and think independently. Even a two- or three-year-old can decide between eating a banana or an apple, or whether he wants a story about David and Goliath or Zacchaeus up in the tree. Allowing your child to make decisions whenever possible teaches him to make right choices and gives him confidence in his decision-making ability as well. "Teach him to live with his decisions too," says Cheryl. "If you ask, 'Would you like a toasted cheese sandwich, or peanut butter and jelly?' and he says peanut butter and then changes his mind when you're halfway through making it, he learns that every decision has a consequence — even at two years old."

"How can our children learn to know their heavenly Father as the Forgiver and Forgetter of sins if we never forget their transgressions? We have to encourage them to move on, forgiven, with a new start."

🌙 Do set an example of being able to laugh at your minor mistakes. It'll probably take some time before your child will feel secure enough to do this, but it can help immensely if he sees that Mom and Dad goof up sometimes but laugh it off and move on. (Try, though, not to laugh at your child's mistakes unless he starts laughing first.)

🧁 Do teach your child to be media-wise. As soon as she's old enough to understand, teach her that not everything aired on TV or put into print is gospel truth. If you're watching a program and something contradicting your values is portrayed as good, don't let it pass. Say, "What that man just did isn't right. Can you tell Mommy why?" It's best to screen questionable shows, but if you inadvertently allow your toddler to watch one, you can always use it as a bad example.

🧸 Do give your child responsibility as he becomes able to handle it, and praise him for jobs well done. "Two weeks ago," says Cheryl, "Jason's Sunday school lesson was all about taking responsibility for helping around the house. He brought the storybook home and showed it to me and told me what he'd learned. After dinner, while Rodger and I were watching a football game on TV, Jason went into his room and picked up his clothes, picked up *Brian's* toys, and then came out and told me he'd done just what his Sunday school teacher had said. He was so proud. Brian is just two, but I try to give him responsibility even now for little things like putting his shoes into the closet and his dirty clothes into the hamper. That teaches self-discipline, but it also builds self-esteem as I praise him for it."

Do encourage your older children to allow their younger siblings to learn without constantly being guided or corrected. An older brother or sister who knows the family rules may want to impress his little sibling with his vast knowledge, or he may simply be trying to help. But an older child who is constantly pointing out every little thing that isn't done "right" can be hard to bear. Try saying, "Thank you, sweetheart, but she needs to learn to do that for herself." You may need to point out (often), "You know, when you were learning that, we didn't keep correcting you. We just let you figure it out for yourself. Let's let your little sister do that too, okay?"

"*Do* show interest in your child's activities by physical attendance," says Ruth. "It will mean more than he'll ever say." Those little nursery school pageants and T-ball games for four-year-olds are more important than they seem. "My mom was always into other things when I was small," says one mother, "and she didn't come to a lot of the things I thought were so important. I think it would have made a big difference in my self-image if she had."

Finally, *do* give your child a sense of purpose in life. "This is one of my favorite parental projects!" says Lisa. "Children need to know that *no one* is created without special gifts and a special purpose. I want my kids to see me as their foremost ally and partner in helping them discover theirs. Nothing gives a sense of identity and confidence more than finding and using your God-given gifts as they were meant to be used."

Christine says, "Since Ashley was six months old I've been telling her, 'You are a child of destiny. You're somebody special. God has a plan for you.' She'll look up at me in wonder and say, 'He does?' It's so important, even when they're tiny, for them to get the idea 'I'm special to God, and to Mommy and Daddy. I have a special place on this earth.'"

As the old Gaither song says, a child is a promise. And your child is much more likely to keep that promise if he knows you believe he can.

Learning to Be a Friend: Setting the Stage for Social Acceptance

The intended result of knowing we're loved and of developing our special gifts is the confidence to take those gifts beyond the home and put them to use in a hurting world. As Christian parents, it's our job to teach our children to fulfill Jesus' two great commandments: To love God with all their heart, soul, mind, and strength, and to love their neighbor as themselves. Only when we have a proper view of ourselves before God — that we are both loved and equipped — can we feel free to focus on the needs of others in an emotionally and spiritually healthy way.

Besides, everybody needs friends.

🐦 Do try to make sure your child has playmates of his own age and developmental level. It's devastating for a young child to be always dominated by older playmates or to be told constantly, "You can't play with us. You're too little."

The potential for hurt feelings is even greater for a small child with older siblings. Cheryl says, "There are times when Jason has a birthday party to go to and Brian isn't invited. And there are some other things he's doing, like playing softball, that Brian's just not ready for. I've tried to arrange for Rodger or me to do something special with him when he can't participate in one of his big brother's activities. We just explain to Brian, 'Jason is going to a four-year-old party, and when you're four you'll go to some four-year-old parties too. But tonight, when Mommy takes Jason, Daddy's going to take you for some ice cream.'" Whenever you can, encourage your children to play games in which older and younger alike can participate. Several parents found it beneficial to encourage their older children to take the younger ones under their wing, not to discipline or correct them — that's your job — but to defend them from the slings and arrows of older playmates.

For the shy or slowly developing child, it may be good to provide playmates on the younger side.

But again, do figure out some way to give a younger child playmates his own age, even if that means organizing a play group or cultivating some new friends of your own who have children his age and who can be invited over, with their children, for the afternoon.

For the shy or slowly developing child, it may be good to provide playmates on the younger side. Rita's second son, Brian, had a hearing problem at birth that slowed his speech development. She says, "He's more sensitive than Billy and was a little clingier when he was small. He played with younger children. They looked up to him, and that gave him the leadership role. It helped a lot to bring him out." Patti adds, "I noticed a big change in my second child when my oldest, Keva, went to school. He got to be the leader for the first time, and he really blossomed."

🐦 Do teach your child to reach out. People tend to approach friendships the way they do restaurants: They're apt to be attracted to the ones with the most "cars" out front. But the restaurant with an overflowing parking lot is already full, and there may be a long wait. Luellen says, "We've encouraged our children to seek out the child who doesn't have a lot of friends. Sometimes a very shy or insecure child just needs someone to come over and ask him or her to play."

Do teach your child to empathize. Wise mothers make frequent use of the question, "How would you feel if someone did that to you?"

Do teach your child to love her enemies. Children can be cruel at times, and when your child is the victim, it's important that you not react by encouraging her to strike back out of hate or spite. "That's hard," says Patti, "because you want to go beat 'em up!"

Observe your child during playtime to see if she's making social mistakes you can help her correct, such as being bossy or not joining in. I found that role-playing with Megan helped her learn appropriate play behavior.

When one of Michelle's friends treats her cruelly, Wanda shares with her: "Usually when someone is mean it's because she's hurting inside and is trying to make herself feel better by hurting you — it's not because you've done anything wrong. Let's pray for her." This helps your child see that the meanness of her peers isn't her problem; it's *their* problem. "It also teaches her to reach out and meet their needs," says Patti. Lisa adds, "When you and your children pray for people who are difficult to get along with, it helps erase the negative feelings you have toward that person. And it reminds you and your child that there is One who is greater than us all, who has everything in his hands. It takes the weight of the situation off your child and puts it on the Lord, where it belongs."

Do teach your child that it's okay to steer clear of certain people. It would be emotionally and spiritually unhealthy for you to spend much time with a person who is habitually unkind, selfish, and bossy. It's unhealthy for your child too. If being with a playmate is a chronically unpleasant experience, it's time to talk with the child's mom and try to work it out. If that doesn't work, it's time to find a new playmate.

Do teach your child to consider the source. Just because a playmate says something doesn't make it true.

Do teach your child to be careful whose opinion she values. Cil says, "We've tried to teach Claire, 'Our self-worth can't be based on what people think. What does *Christ* think?'" Shari agrees: "When I was younger I was constantly miserable because I was trying to please everyone. There's a big difference between serving people as a Christian and constantly being concerned about what they think of you."

The Mommy and Daddy Book · *Someone Special, That's Me!*

Real Self-Worth

Healthy self-esteem, for the Christian, simply means seeing yourself accurately; that is, the way God does. And how does God see you? He loves you so unconditionally that he sent his Son to die for you even though he knew every sin you would ever commit. He custom-designed you to have every ability you will ever need to fulfill his purpose for your life, as well as the intelligence and opportunities to develop those abilities. And he created you to be valuable to the people around you, able to reach out and meet their needs in his name.

As we grow to understand these truths about ourselves, and as we teach them to our children, together we can become the hands and feet of Jesus to a world that desperately needs to know his love.

Chapter 12

The Working Mommy

Don't skip this chapter if you have been blessed with the freedom to stay home with your baby. As Debby points out, the title "The Working Mommy" is really a misnomer. All mothers work, and anyone who thinks they don't has never been one. Besides, you may need to help supplement the family income someday, and before we talk about mothers who toil in the outside world we'll show how some of our moms have earned money while remaining at home with their children.

And do stay with us through the first section if you work outside the home. Our purpose in putting it at the beginning of the chapter is not to make you feel guilty. It's to show you some options you may not have thought of.

Working at Home

We'll have to content ourselves with giving you some ideas and general pointers in this section, since it would be a book in itself if we tried to include everything you need to know about starting a home business. For specifics consult libraries, bookstores, and newsstands—the bigger the better. It's great to learn from experience—and you will—but learning first from someone else's experience can give you a head start and save you a lot of time and aggravation. You'd be surprised at the wide range of specialty books and trade magazines available for the home entrepreneur.

The internet is another good place to find advice on home businesses. Here, according to *Gateway Magazine,* are some of the best small-business websites:

American Express Small Business Exchange
   (www.americanexpress.com/smallbusiness)
SBDC National Research Network (www.sba.gov/SBDC/)
Small- and Home-Based Business Links (www.bizoffice.com)
Small-Business Advisor (www.isquare.com)
Small-Office Computing/Home-Office Computing
   (www.smalloffice.com)

And now, before we start giving ideas, a few warnings are in order:

Warning 1. It's not uncommon to hear of a full-fledged family business that started as a way to keep Mommy at home. But a home business usually takes a while to get off the ground, so plan on having little or no income from it at first. You may even have to spend a little money in advertising and free samples to get started. And even once you've become established, your home business will most likely be a supplement to your husband's income rather than the family's sole source of support unless you invest an unusual amount of time and effort in it.

It's great to learn from experience — and you will — but learning first from someone else's experience can give you a head start and save you a lot of time and aggravation.

Warning 2. Home businesses tend to have on and off seasons. For example, the months right before Christmas are an on-season for a craftsperson, whereas spring and summer, with their weddings, are on-seasons for a dressmaker or home caterer. Summer break is an off-season for private music teachers and word processors specializing in college term papers. These on and off seasons don't have to be a drawback if you budget and plan for them. You can even offset them by diversifying and becoming a Jackie of several trades.

Warning 3. Choose work you enjoy and find fulfilling. Otherwise you'll burn out quickly.

Warning 4. Don't charge too much for your services, but don't charge too little, either. Do some market research to find out what your competition charges, and offer a comparable value. "A lot of times we tend to sell ourselves short," says Patti.

Warning 5. If you're going to do something professionally (meaning get paid), go about it in a professional manner. Wear businesslike clothes and leave your baby with a sitter when you visit local merchants to advertise your product or service, and have inexpensive business cards printed if you can afford it. Draw up a simple written agreement, to be signed by both you and your client, with copies for each, detailing what goods or services will be provided and what payment is to be given when. If you're custom-making goods for a client, get a deposit in advance. Your potential customers will take you only as seriously as you take yourself.

Warning 6. Make sure your product or service is needed. A cobbler in Florida would have a hard time making a living from fur-lined boots no matter how well they were made. Again, do a little market research.

Warning 7. Keep your priorities straight. If you provide a needed, high-quality product or service at a reasonable price, you'll soon have as much business as you can handle, and probably more. Accept only as much as you can do well and still give top priority to your baby—after all, that's why you want to stay home, isn't it? Make sure you give yourself and your baby time in the fresh air and away from home. A lot can be done in the morning before your child wakes (if he's not an early riser), during naps, and after he goes to bed. (I should know. That's when I wrote the first edition of this book.)

Keeping your priorities straight also means guarding your time with your husband. Kim says, "If Rob or Mollie starts feeling neglected, or if I feel I'm neglecting them, that's a sign I'm doing too much."

Warning 8. The life of the home entrepreneur is not for the shrinking violet. Running a home business takes the ability to promote your business with confidence and to say thank you with a smile to the potential client who tells you he doesn't need your services—which happens to all of us. It requires you to be a self-starter who can make yourself get up each morning and work whether you feel like it or not. But there's no law that says a shrinking violet—and a lazy one at that—can't turn into a top home businesswoman. It all depends on how committed you are to it.

Warning 9. Remember Uncle Sam. Save receipts and keep strict records of all income and expenditures for income tax and social security purposes. If you have a special corner of your home reserved for your business, save your home utility stubs and tell your tax person about it. It's also a good idea to save a percentage of your profits against April 15. And do check with your local government to see whether you need a permit for your type of home business.

∘ ∘ ∘ ∘ ∘

NOW THAT YOU KNOW a little more about what you're getting into, let's go down a list of home businesses some of the mothers in this book found profitable.

Word Processing Services. Even if your typing has been strictly amateur up until now, you can run a successful word processing service as long as you turn out a professional product. You'll need a computer and printer, but your computer needn't be state of the art, since word processing doesn't require a lot of memory. (On the other hand, desktop publishing — creating newsletters, ads, and flyers — requires more memory because of the graphics involved.) Word processing programs are easy to learn, and there are excellent typing trainer programs available.

Be sure your word processing program is compatible with most businesses. (At this time, Microsoft Word seems the most popular. Ask for advice on this from your computer store.) You'll need to do a little studying to learn the proper formats for business letters, term papers, and resumes. Your public library can help you there, although Microsoft Word actually has "wizards" to guide you through creating common documents.

Probably the most lucrative place to run a word processing service is a college town, but the college doesn't have to be big. Remember, community colleges and business schools assign term papers too. There were three small colleges in the city where the first edition of this book was written, and several mothers found that they got just about all the business they wanted by putting up notices on the school bulletin boards. List your price per page, your name, your phone number, and by all means, include any extras you can offer, such as grammatical corrections or graphic enhancements. (A spelling checker is expected, but list it too.)

Cheryl recommends visiting the front office as well: "Most of the work from students comes around midterm and at the end of the term, but it helps to get your name known in the office. Now when an extra project comes up, the receptionist refers people to me." Dana charges a higher fee for midterm and end-of-term papers — inspired by hotels' seasonal rates, I guess — and Patti points out that even the professors at colleges often need typing and proofreading done, so take your business card around to them as well.

Small businesses are another potential marketplace for the home word processor. Luellen says, "I went to small start-up businesses in my area and offered to do their typing at a per-page rate. I had several clients." Small businesses would also be great places to promote a desktop publishing business, since they often need ads and flyers.

Dressmaking and Alterations. This business is a natural for the woman who likes to make her own clothes. Put your business cards up on church, day care center, and business bulletin boards and leave them at floral shops catering to brides. If you do alterations, leave your card at local dry cleaners and laundromats and ask the proprietors to send business your way. You can also get your working friends in on the act by making them an outfit for the cost of the fabric and notions, stipulating that they give their office coworkers your card when they start receiving compliments — which, of course, they will.

You can charge for this service either of two ways: by the hour, plus cost of fabric and notions, or at a flat rate determined by the article of clothing being sewn, plus cost. Whichever you choose to do, give your customer a reliable estimate and let her know if you're going to run over.

Cil and a friend had great success with a line of children's clothes they designed and sold through home parties. She says, "We did mainly seasonal clothes — Easter and Christmas — and costumes, because children like to pretend. Our kids were our walking advertisements." At one point, they had several seamstresses working for them.

> The idea that craftspeople have to be naturally artistic is a common misconception. Crafts take *no talent*. What they take is the willingness to follow instructions and stick with a project until it's done right.

Crafts. The idea that craftspeople have to be naturally artistic is a common misconception. Speaking as a person who has done everything from crochet to decoupage to macrame to flower arranging to counted cross-stitch to handtwined wreaths to furniture refinishing to basketry to bead jewelry to stained glass, let me inform you that crafts take *no talent*. What they take is the willingness to follow instructions and stick with a project until it's done right. Talent comes in when you take the instructions and modify them to make something uniquely your own — and even that can be developed with time.

Visit craft shops and stores specializing in handmade gifts to find ideas for things you can make quickly and well, and with as little expense as possible. Then take samples of your wares to local gift shops and see which ones will sell them on consignment. Or camp out on the weekends at local flea markets, or look for information on craft fairs in trade publications. Or give samples to your working friends for their desks, again with the stipulation that they recommend you to their coworkers. A couple of mothers even held parties in their friends' homes, *a la* Tupperware, at which they displayed their handmade products and took orders.

🐦 *Home Babysitting Services.* Once you're accustomed to taking care of your own little one, you may be ready to take on a couple of your working friends' children. Wanda says, "When Michelle was eighteen months old and Dennis was out of college, I was able to quit work, but we still needed a supplement, so I babysat during the day. I did register with the health department, which made the parents feel a little safer."

Wanda's advertising was mostly by word of mouth among her friends: "The parents were comfortable leaving their children with someone they knew," she says. "And I didn't make any bones about the fact that I read Christian stories to the kids and that we sang Christian songs, and that if they fell down and hurt themselves I prayed with them. If anything, that helped my business increase, because I always had more calls than I could take." To simplify her bookkeeping, Wanda charged the same per-day price whether a child stayed for a full day or only a few hours.

One thing you'll need to do that a fully staffed day care facility would not is to make the parents aware of the need to have an alternate arrangement should you or your baby become sick. Also, obtain copies of local day-care center policies and use them to help you formulate your own policies, in writing, to give to each set of parents. And be sure to check with your county health department to see how many children you can babysit without becoming a licensed day-care facility. Right now, where I live, the limit is four children in addition to your own (eight children total is the maximum), but the laws are changing and vary from county to county and state to state.

Julie adds, "If you're going to babysit, you have to like children. You'll get burned out quickly if you're just doing it for the money. Also, the ages of your own children play a big role. You have to know what you can and can't handle. I tried watching a six-week-old when Stephanie was a year old. I quit after three months. It was too stressful. I was constantly torn between my motherly instincts toward my own child and the responsibility for someone else's baby." Another point Julie brings up: "How much time do you need to unwind? Right now I only babysit two days a week."

If you choose to babysit in your home, be prepared to give your charges all the love and attention you'd want your own child to receive in someone else's care. You'll need to have a fenced-in yard where the children can run and play, or at the very least, a large, open room and lots of creative toys and books. And you'll without doubt have to adopt a relaxed attitude toward your house, since handprints on the walls and accidents on the carpet are inevitable.

Three important warnings: Check with your insurance company to make sure you're covered in the event a child is injured while in your home. Keep strict tax records, since the parents whose children you babysit will most likely be claiming your fees as a childcare tax credit on their returns. And it's a good idea to get training in infant CPR, but that's really something all mothers should do anyway.

Paper Routes. If your baby does well in the car, you may want to look into this. Lois had an afternoon paper route when her children were toddlers, and she says they still remember the discussions they had as they drove along. "My daughter has told me, 'Mom, we sure got a good spiritual foundation on that paper route!'"

Home Catering. Rita's sister Janet bakes cakes for special occasions. "She worked in supermarkets and learned cake decorating a long time ago," says Rita. "She even makes wedding cakes." Even if you've never worked in a bakery or supermarket, many community colleges offer courses in cake decorating. Advertise your wares in the same places you'd advertise dressmaking: day care centers, floral shops, bridal shops, businesses, and churches. If the proprietors are reluctant to recommend you, offer them a free sample of your goods.

Patti made dinner for a working friend one night a week. She says, "I just doubled my recipe for whatever my family was eating that night, and she paid me for it." This type of home catering business can grow quickly by word of mouth. Require your customers to pick up their food at your house on their way home from work, and charge a price comparable to what they'd pay in a family-style restaurant.

Be sure to call your county health department before you embark on this kind of enterprise. In many areas, including mine, home catering as such is illegal. A caterer must do her cooking in a facility separate from her home kitchen, that facility must be inspected, and she must be licensed.

Miscellaneous. Examine the skills you've gained from school, volunteer work, or previous employment for ways they can be used in a home business. If you're quitting a clerical or secretarial job, ask your employer to consider you for extra projects that can be done at home. "Telecommuting" via modem has opened up a whole new world for mothers who want to stay home with their children. And don't neglect the contacts you've made while in school or in the working world. Pene earns a good-sized salary proofreading at home for a news service, a job that came about as a result of a contact she made before her son Aaron was born. Other ways of earning extra income include selling products through companies that specialize in home parties — toys, jewelry, books, cookware.

If you spend a little time thinking about it, you can come up with all sorts of ideas for home businesses. All it takes to put them into action is a sizable dose of perseverance and nerve — qualities which every good mother develops with time.

A Word about Part-Time Jobs

For the mothers in this book who tried it, working at a part-time job was like buying a five-pound turkey. By the time they got rid of the skin and bones — the hidden expense — there was very little meat left.

A part-time job involves most of the expense a full-time job does, with less pay to show for it. That's especially true because most of the part-time jobs these mothers found were in the sales and clerical fields and paid little, if any, more than minimum wage.

Day care is probably the biggest expense for the mother who works outside the home. But according to our working moms, there are quite a few other expenses that need to be taken into consideration when you're figuring out how much spendable income you would earn at an outside job. You may find you could earn a comparable amount with a home business.

Here's a basic job expense list for the mother of a young child: day care; withholding taxes; transportation (extra fuel and/or extra car, upkeep, insurance); working wardrobe ("Panty hose!" says Patti); baby formula and disposable diapers for your baby's time at the sitter's; more clothing for your baby, especially in cool weather ("Yes, your baby has to have a working wardrobe!" laughs Adrienne); higher doctor bills if your babysitter watches more than one child at a time (and our working moms agree that their doctor bills really did go up). Add to this basic list money spent on household help, convenience foods, and lunches out. "That depends on your working schedule," says Wanda. "A lot of times in our family it's dinners out too — not just lunches." Most of our working moms say they now spend much more on meals out than they did when they stayed home. "Going out one night a week used to be a real treat," says Cheryl. "Now it's, 'Not again! Can't we eat at home tonight?' It gets old very fast."

On the other hand, part-time work can be valuable for reasons that go beyond finances. Cheryl says, "When I worked part-time at our church, I was doing it more for myself — to spend time with my husband, who also worked there, and with other people I liked, and to have some adult conversation. But

I didn't get much money out of the deal, even though I paid only half-price for day care because I was a church employee."

For Trudy, working part-time at a day care center was less stressful and more rewarding than babysitting in her home, which she had also done. Not only did her children receive a reduced rate at the center because she worked there, but she says, "It was just a playtime for them. Darcy would wake up from her nap, and then we'd go play for four hours with kids her own age. And it was good for me to have adult conversation with the other women there. Also, having a part-time job in the afternoons helped me discipline myself to use my mornings effectively. I couldn't put off cleaning the toilet until the afternoon—I wasn't going to be there."

Part-time work can also help you maintain or develop skills and contacts you can use in the work force when your children are older. Be careful, though, about assuming you'll return to work full-time when your children are in school. For one thing, in any given school year there will be approximately sixteen weeks when your child is not in school. That's almost *four months*, including summer, Christmas and spring breaks, and teacher workdays.

> In any given school year there will be approximately sixteen weeks when your child is not in school. That's almost *four months,* including summer, Christmas and spring breaks, and teacher workdays.

Just as important, all through his school years your child will be forming ideas about the way the world around him works and deciding whose values are worth adopting and whose aren't. I've found it crucial, when Megan and Anna come home from school, to be there—not exhausted after a frantic day's work but alert and with my antennae up, ready to listen and add my perspective.

Often during snacktime after school, my children have made value statements based on something they've heard from their friends (and what they've heard from their friends is usually heavy on popular culture and light on biblical perspective). When I ask, "Have you thought about it from *this* side?" suddenly the issue doesn't seem so clear-cut, and they often end up with a different conclusion much more in line with godly values.

If I weren't there in the afternoons, they'd still be making those judgments, but there's no guarantee the opportunity would arise for my input. This year in high school, Megan has a world history teacher who has made it his mission in life to ridicule his students' faith. Often when she comes home she needs to talk and think through the challenges he's made. I'm grateful to be there to serve as her sounding board.

Planning "quality time" to talk through deep issues rarely works. Kids are most likely to talk about important issues with people who have shown they care by giving them large blocks of their time on a regular basis. Once a child transfers her allegiance from her family to her friends, it can be difficult and painful — and sometimes impossible — to get it back. I read an article recently in which teenagers were interviewed about their relationships with their parents. One boy said, "My parents never talked to me when I was little. Now that I'm a teenager, all of a sudden they want to talk to me. They haven't earned the right."

Working Full-Time

Life is not easy for the working mother of a new baby or young toddler, and it's no use pretending that it is or that it can somehow be made that way. Aside from the sheer, physical hard work of carrying on what should be the tasks of two women, all our working moms experienced at least some guilt at leaving their babies — even when they had no choice. "Working before my children came was a breeze," says Debby. "Working with a child was a different story. Sometimes there was so much stress that I felt I was being pulled in at least three pieces. My job pulled one way, my husband pulled another, and my child pulled still another. Each demanded first priority." Luellen says, "There isn't a day when I don't wish I could be at home. Benjamin is four and a half now, and I think about him constantly. It's hard to accept that, for the most part, he's being raised by the babysitter."

With all this talk about hidden expenses and how hard the life is both emotionally and physically, I realize that this chapter runs the risk of sounding like a diatribe against working full-time. The simple fact is, the overwhelming majority of our *working* moms believe that a full-time job outside the home should be the last resort for a new mother. But if you must use that last resort, as several of them had to, be comforted by the knowledge that the Lord is able to give you strength and wisdom, just as he has done and continues to do for our working moms. Their children are happy, healthy, well-adjusted tributes to the fact that he is able to help a mother compensate for a situation she can't avoid.

For the working mothers in this book, two factors determined whether combining baby with job was merely difficult or nearly impossible. The first factor was whether they were able to have confidence that their babies were in competent, loving hands while they were gone; the second was the amount of help and support they received from their husbands.

"I found a fantastic lady who babysat in her home," says Wanda. "She had raised five of her own kids and loved Michelle as if she were one of them. It made it easier for me in that I wasn't afraid to leave her, but it didn't help me want to leave her any more. I guess I probably cried for the first three days." These mothers agree that if you possibly can, it's best to have a young baby cared for by a competent individual rather than a day care center. Debby says, "I just wanted my child to have someone's personal attention. As soon as I found out I was pregnant, I started praying about who would take care of my baby."

"I found a very reliable in-home day care provider with exceptional references," says Luellen. "In-home day care really has advantages over a commercial center. There's more one-on-one interaction, and there's no turnover with workers. Benjamin has had the same sitter for three years and looks forward to being in her home. The cost tends to run a little higher, but for my peace of mind it's worth every penny."

Wanda recommends checking with your friends who are good mothers and who may want to earn some extra money while staying at home with their own little ones. "Talk with people who have the same values and way of life you do," she says. "That way, at least they'll display the same general attitudes around your child that you would." Don't be afraid to spell out exactly what kind of care you're looking for.

If you're approaching an experienced in-home babysitter, ask to see her stock of toys and storybooks and check to see where the dreaded TV figures in her decor. Is it where your child will be spending most of her playtime? Carol's experience with TV and her toddler came from a day care center, but it applies to home child care as well: "Kristie was thirteen months old when I had to go to work," she says. "I found a day care center that was clean, they served good food, and they sat my child in front of a television set for eight hours a day. At the time I didn't know what damage that could do, but 'Wow!' is all I can say."

After a child is three years old, these mothers feel better about putting him into a good day care center. Patti says, "By then they're more ready for the social atmosphere and the higher pupil-teacher ratio."

In any day care situation, ask for the names of other mothers who have children there, and call to ask whether their children seem to be happy and doing well. Make drop-in visits to see what the children do at different times of the day and ask what activities are provided for older babies and toddlers. Have a frank talk with the sitter or the proprietor of the day care center and let her know that you're checking her out, not because you don't trust her but because you want to be sure you're doing the very best for your baby. If she resents that, she's not the right person for you anyway.

Some important questions to ask before choosing a day care center: What is the turnover rate among the center's caregivers? What education and training does the center require? What kinds of background checks are done? Do they have strict guidelines regarding the language and attitudes the caregivers should display in front of the children?

More and more churches today are sponsoring Christian schools and, along with them, day care centers. Regarding them, Cheryl says, "A church day-care center may be just fine as far as having good, moral, Christian women watching the kids, but if they're just babysitting and you've got a toddler who is ready to hear stories and have some educational stimulation, that's not necessarily the way to go. When I was looking for a day care center for my boys, I spent two days calling around and then visiting and asking questions. I ended up putting them in a secular day care franchise because I was so impressed with it."

> Once you find the right caregiver, keep alert for changes in your child's behavior that could be danger signals, and as soon as your toddler can talk, encourage him to tell you all the details of his day.

Be careful that you don't put your child into a Christian day care center with the thought that they'll do his spiritual training for you. Your child's caretakers should support your beliefs and values, but the responsibility for his spiritual upbringing belongs to you and your husband.

Cheryl says it's also important to have a day care center that takes an individual interest in your child: "I really appreciated it when Miss Barbara told me last year, 'Brian's not ready for the two-year-old class yet. His attention span isn't long enough for him to sit down and listen, so let's keep him in toddlers for half a year.' She knew him well enough to know what was best for him, and she took the time to talk to me about it."

Most important in your choice of a day care center is whether you have peace of mind after having prayed and hunted and called and asked questions and visited and then prayed some more. Trust the Lord's guidance and your own instincts if you feel it isn't the place for you, even if all the other factors seem right. And once you find the right caregiver, keep alert for changes in your child's behavior that could be danger signals, and as soon as your toddler can talk, encourage him to tell you all the details of his day. Be alert for any suspicious bruises or other marks. Cheryl says, "It's my and Rodger's responsibility as our children's spiritual leaders to keep up with what's going on. The minute there's a problem or something hits me wrong, it's time to reevaluate and possibly make a change."

She adds, "Your attitude, your peace about the situation, affects your child too. Our boys attend a Christian day care center now, and each day we pray in the car on the way there that the Lord will protect them and help them learn about Jesus. It gives them a sense of anticipation about the day."

Finally, here's a tip on acquainting your baby with his new caregivers: When you're preparing to leave him on a regular basis, begin by doing it for a short length of time — say, an hour. Build up to longer periods as he becomes accustomed to the people and surroundings.

o o o o o

HOW IMPORTANT IS IT for a working mother to have a husband who helps out at home? These mothers' reactions to this question are strong and one-sided. "It's the only way," says Carol. Wanda adds, "I couldn't do it without Dennis. A helpful husband is worth his weight in gold."

Most of our working moms say their husbands are very helpful — but they also say they didn't come packaged that way. For the most part, helpful husbands are made, not born. Debby says, "Husbands have to be made to realize that it's much harder on the mother to work at a job outside the home than it is on the father. Responsibilities of a mother seem to be just taken for granted, and many times the father simply doesn't realize the pressures on her. It's a mistake for a new mother to think that surely her husband must know how hard she has to work and that he'll just pitch in and help. My husband didn't even know what needed to be done around the house, much less do anything. The only way to get help is to ask for it — communicate. Help that new daddy understand that you are helping him with *his* responsibility to provide for the family by working at a job, and he needs to help you with yours. Otherwise, no matter how hard you try, resentments creep in and serious marital problems can crop up."

Tim's wife, Trudy, does bookkeeping in a home office. He's adopted the view that what's good for her is good for him: "I want a wife who's happy and full of energy and able to talk with me, not one who's tired and worn out. I'm as responsible for the house as she is. So I'm trying to find ways to help out. I want to learn."

With a little practice, much of the housework and babywork normally done by a wife can be done by her husband: cooking, washing dishes, laundry, dusting, vacuuming, straightening, changing diapers, bathing and feeding the baby. But you'll need to adopt an understanding attitude if your husband didn't, like you, have the benefit of years of motherly training in household responsibility. For organization's sake, make up a basic chore list that spells out when each job should be done and by whom. And do rotate the more distasteful ones — like scrubbing the toilet.

You'll also need to face the fact that, no matter how helpful your husband is, the bottom-line responsibility for your baby's welfare is yours. As with the mothers in this book, you will probably be the one to say when it's feeding time or when a diaper needs changing, or to detect when your little one feels feverish. But if your husband learns to enjoy time spent playing with the baby, to help with feedings and diapers, or to get up in the middle of the night and rock her back to sleep when she wakes up crying, both he and your child will be the richer for it.

There are more benefits to having a husband who is involved at home than just the immediate ones. As your child grows, you and your husband are giving him or her an object lesson in what marriage is like. Rita's husband, Marvin, is a paragon of helpfulness, and she believes he is giving her two sons, who are now in junior high and high school, a priceless lesson that will benefit their own wives someday: "I'm so thankful! Children watch you so intently, and they pick up everything you do. Brian and Billy have really caught his spirit for helping."

A Day in the Life . . .

Our typical working mom's day begins at around six A.M., when she rises, grabs a quick breakfast, and dresses before the children are up. "My priority before they wake up is me," says Dana. "After they wake up, it's them."

When the children are awake, she feeds them, dresses them, and makes sure they have everything they need to take to the babysitter's. It seems that early mornings are the one time when these mothers' helpful husbands aren't much help; about the most they do is make sure they get themselves dressed. This unfair arrangement makes me feel fervent gratitude for my mother-in-law, a wise lady who taught her sons to help around the house long before that became popular. I didn't work outside the home when my children were small, but for times when Jon, Megan, and I all had to be somewhere at once, we worked out a more equitable system based on who had the most to do in the morning. I rose early and ate breakfast and, when Megan woke, fed her. After Jon took his shower, I handed her over to him, and after he dressed himself and her, they played together or read a story while I fixed my face and hair. They were ready before I was!

To the question of who stays home when the baby is sick, the nearly unanimous answer is, of course, Mommy. But one of our moms says, "My husband and I alternate if our daughter is sick for more than a day or so, or if I have something particularly important to do that week. My husband's employer asked him why he stayed home when that was the mother's job, and my husband answered that he feels it's as much his responsibility as it is mine and that there are times when what I have to do at work is more urgent than what he has to do that day." Whether you can do this depends on your respective employers and should probably be discussed with them beforehand.

According to Cheryl, lunch break is the working mom's big chance to catch some time alone. But she recommends that you don't do it at home. "If I go home," she says, "I feel as if I have to clean the house — and maybe I do that once or twice a week. But for the working mom, lunch hour is the ideal time to have devotions, go down to a lake or a park to eat lunch and read, or take a walk. I know there are always things I could and should be doing — I *should* go to the store, I *should* clean the house — but that's when I try to have some time to myself."

After work, it's time to pick up her child and head for home. "You'll find that on coming home your toddler will want your immediate attention," says Dana. "He may show it in different ways, such as disobedience, showing off, or even just coming up and saying, 'What are ya doin'?' as you're cooking dinner. What he really wants is for you to sit down and give him your undivided attention. It may not take long at all to satisfy him, but when you do he'll be assured of your love." With Kristie, Carol has adopted the habit of having a milk-and-cookie time immediately after arriving home to give her daughter a chance to share her day with Mom and Dad; this practice also helps tide their growling stomachs over until dinner is ready.

Speaking of dinner — who cooks? "At our house," says Wanda, "it's whoever's the least tired. We trade off." Patti says, "I'd rather have my husband take the kids outside to play while I cook dinner." Cheryl agrees: "I've always felt that's a good time for Rodger to spend some time with the boys anyway. Usually I give them

> "You'll find that on coming home your toddler will want your immediate attention," says Dana. "He may show it in different ways, such as disobedience, showing off, or even just coming up and saying, 'What are ya doin'?' as you're cooking dinner."

a snack or a piece of fruit, since they're always hungry when they get home, then Rodger uses that time to play with them and unwind a little himself."

To make your dinner situation easier, try cooking two or three big entrees on the weekends, then freezing the leftovers in meal-sized portions and eating them during the week, with maybe a variation on the accompanying salad or vegetable. Once you get a "leftover bank" built up, you can have quite a variety of meals to choose from during the week. This method worked well for me. By using recipes that serve eight to ten people, I was able to put three meals into the freezer each time I cooked. My family ate a homemade meal nearly every night, even though I actually cooked only two or three times a week. (Setting aside the portions to be frozen before dinner will help keep your family from going back for seconds or thirds. Also, I found it essential to label and date my containers, and to keep a current list of my freezer's contents.)

Getting back to our typical working mom: Her typical toddler goes to bed at around seven-thirty (although a younger baby may stay up much later), so after dinner there is just enough time for a bath, a brief story-prayer-and-cuddle time, and then bed. But even though the baby's day is over, Mommy's and Daddy's is still going strong. There are still the dinner dishes, laundry, and miscellaneous housework to do.

"My mom worked while I was growing up," says Patti, "and all my childhood, I thought the dish fairy came every night and washed the dishes, since she never did them until after we were in bed. I fully expected to have a dish fairy when I grew up — what a disappointment!" Of course, as your toddler grows older, doing dishes together can be a good chance to spend time with her or him.

After the housework is finished, there's still the next day to prepare for. "I try to do as much as possible the night before," says Cheryl, " — lay out the clothes, pack the lunches, put together the diaper bag." Dana has gone as far as pouring the breakfast cereal, covering the bowls, and putting them on the table.

Oh Where, Oh Where Has Our Family Time Gone?

As you can see from the last section, the family in which both parents work full-time has few opportunities to sit around and enjoy being together. While the stay-at-home mother has to find ways to get out of the house, the working mother's struggle is to find ways to stay home — or at least to spend as much time as possible with her family.

The most obvious family times are dinnertime, right before bedtime, and weekends, but the working mothers in this book feel you can't build a healthy family life on just a few hours a week — especially when you consider that a good portion of your at-home time will be taken up by housework. They've had to develop the ability to say no to worthy activities, such as church choir or shopping with friends, in order to be with their families, and they've learned to steal time for their children from moments that would ordinarily have been wasted.

Debby says, "Having the baby in her carrier near the ironing board or in the kitchen as I prepared dinner provided time for me to talk to her and notice all the changes she went through from day to day. And even though her 'daytime grandmother' had her clean and nice when I picked her up after work, I always took the time to bathe my baby before bedtime. We had so much fun splashing and talking and sometimes crying with each other. It was a real release emotionally for me to hold and bathe and dress that child who was a part of me. It made all the extra work worthwhile. To have a sweet-smelling, beautiful baby ready for bed and see her settle down to sleep was my reward for the day — and I believe all mothers need some type of reward, even though it may be different for each mother."

Cheryl adds, "Some of the best time Jason and Brian and I have is driving in the car to and from day care, to and from the store, to and from the laundromat; and that's some of the best time they have with their dad too. Even if Rodger is home and could watch the kids while I go shopping, I try to take one of them with me and leave the other with him. That way we both get a chance to talk with them. When they reach the age when they're talking as much as Jason and Brian are, at two and four years old, being in the car is really one of the best times to let them tell crazy stories or have theological discussions, like, 'Where does God live?' You'd be surprised at how much time you spend in the car."

Lois agrees: "We have a wonderful Christian radio station in our area, but I don't play the radio when I'm in the car with my kids, because if I do, we'll listen and not talk. I developed that habit when I had a paper route. I'd flip the radio off and say, 'Okay, let's talk.' They'd sit there for a few minutes and not say anything, but after that, boy, the in-depth questions started to come!"

Luellen adds to her time with four-and-a-half-year-old Benjamin by letting him stay up until 9:30 P.M. She says, "He still takes naps in the afternoon, so he isn't always tired before then. Plus the later bedtime allows us to play with him or just cuddle up and watch a movie together."

Wanda adds, "We enjoy our family time together, but it's also good for Michelle to have time alone with me, just the two of us. And it's very good for Dennis and Michelle to have time just for them — and that's good for me too!" Perhaps Saturday morning could be a time for your husband to take your toddler to the park or out to breakfast, giving you a couple of hours to escape the double responsibility of being a working mother. Help your child's father to understand that the bulk of responsibility for your little one's welfare rests on your shoulders, no matter how helpful he is, and that there are times when you simply need to get away — mentally, at least.

The working mother really doesn't have less time alone with her husband than the stay-at-home mother; in fact, she may have more if they work together or if she can sometimes meet him for lunch. But her priorities are often so divided that it's easy for her husband to slide to the bottom of the list. "Time with our husbands needs to be a priority too," says Cheryl. "Have date nights out; plan on babysitters every now and then. Find times other than ten-thirty at night to be alone, whether it's meeting for lunch — Rodger and I try to do that at least once a week — or when the baby is taking a nap on the weekends. If you don't make your husband a priority, there's going to be trouble, and he may even come to resent the child. Nurturing your marriage is as important as nurturing your baby." Actually, nurturing your marriage provides a secure family for your baby, thus nurturing him as well. "It's something you have to plan for," says Virginia. "It doesn't just happen."

> Nurturing your marriage provides a secure family for your baby, thus nurturing him as well. "It's something you have to plan for," says Virginia. "It doesn't just happen."

As was typical of our working moms, Dawn hesitated to leave Melody for a night out with her husband, since she also leaves her during the day while she's at work. "Until Melody was six months old, we never went out without her," she says. "Brian never complained, but it finally got to the point where it was ridiculous. I had to realize that my marriage was important and that we really needed time alone together." Jon and I found it easier to go out on dates as Megan grew older and began going to bed at seven and seven-thirty. We asked the babysitter to arrive just before bedtime and started our evening together then.

Rita recommends letting your husband know he's in your thoughts by giving him little cards and notes and by doing special little things that really don't take extra time. "Marvin grew up on lima beans and rice," she says, "and the boys hate any kind of beans. So when I cook them we make a big deal of the fact that they're Daddy's favorites. He feels that's something special I did just for him. That sort of thing goes a long way."

Finding Help

To gain more free time with their families, several mothers found a cleaning person to come in once every week or two to help with the heavy housework. Cheryl found her housecleaner by checking the bulletin board at church and asking other working mothers if they knew of someone who would do a good job at a reasonable price.

But your housecleaner doesn't have to be a professional. Pat has used college students, and Pene's sister used a high school student with good results. A responsible teenager is less apt than a professional to have set ways of doing housework and is less likely to be offended when you spell out exactly what you want done — which is something you *will* need to do. And it wouldn't hurt to walk her through it at first.

If you don't already have a responsible student in mind, try asking among parents with teenage children or putting up notices on school bulletin boards, specifying the wage you can pay (minimum wage is fair), as well as the hours you want help. Cheryl says, "Don't make it sound like a permanent job the first time. Just say, 'I need some help getting my house clean. Could you come over for a couple of hours?' If it works out well, ask her to come every week. If it doesn't, at least you haven't committed yourself.

"Even if you can't afford or find a housecleaner," she adds, "there are many laundromats that wash, dry, and fold. That may seem like a little thing, but a load of clothes a day can begin to look like a mountain. You'd be amazed at what a difference it can make just to have someone else do your laundry."

Having help with your family's physical needs (a reasonably clean home, clean clothes, and sometimes help with meals) will allow you more time and energy to focus on their emotional and spiritual needs, and on yours too.

○ ○ ○ ○ ○

IS THERE A MAGICAL answer for working mothers, some way to "have it all" and be the ideal wife, mother, and businesswoman all at the same time? Of course not. But there is a spiritual answer for everyone, mother or father, employed or not. It's been around for almost three thousand years: "Trust in the LORD with all your heart and lean not on your own understanding; in all your ways acknowledge him, and he will make your paths straight" (Prov. 3:5–6). As you trust God with every area of your life and commit yourself to listen and obey, he will be faithful to direct your steps and give you the wisdom and strength you need.

Making Memories

Think back. What's your most treasured childhood memory? Your most precious keepsake? The reason these things are spotlighted in our minds and hearts is that they speak to our sense of self-esteem. They say, "I love you. You're important to me. I care enough to talk with you, listen to you, read to you, cuddle you, work with you, play with you, make this for you, save this for you, write this down for you." They give us a sense of belonging in a world where that feeling is rare.

We have to work hard for our special memories nowadays, and that's not surprising. Special memories are active and personal in an increasingly passive, public society that spends its days shuttling its children to and from day care centers and its nights releasing the stresses of the day before the TV set.

But those special memories, and the sense of belonging they create, are worth working toward in our children's lives. Not only do they help build close, rewarding relationships, they can also help "worldproof" our children by encouraging them to identify with us and adopt our values. David says, "It's easy to be molded in the image of our culture. My memories give me an identity as the son of some great people I would be wise to emulate. Identifying with them gives me the courage to stand alone."

You probably won't have too much trouble providing special memories for your children if your own parents provided them for you, since you'll just continue your existing traditions and think of others as you go along. But it can be hard to get started if your own family belonged to the sit-around, don't-talk-to-each-other, let-the-TV-do-the-babysitting school of thought. We'll give you a push by letting you borrow our memories. Eventually you'll think of family traditions of your own.

Another quick word about memories: As I've talked with young parents, I've found that two kinds of memories tend to stick in their minds — the special, out-of-the-ordinary times and the overall sense of what life was like at home. In the best circumstances, those special, unusual memories reinforced the love and unity their parents worked toward in daily family life.

> The question isn't, "Are we making memories?" but, "What kind of memories are we making?"

The question isn't, "Are we making memories?" but, "What kind of memories are we making?" What impression are you forming in your child's mind, day by day, of yourself as a parent and a person? That's the image of you he'll carry into adulthood.

Now, on to the fun stuff.

Intangible Memories: Fleeting Moments That Last Forever

In this chapter we'll talk about two kinds of special memories: tangible and intangible. Of the two, the intangible ones are by far the most important. They're the ones you can't put into an album or up in your closet. They're fleeting — they happen and then are preserved only in your mind. They're the most durable kind of special memory, since they can't be taken away from you or destroyed by fire, flood, or time.

They're also extremely unpredictable. In families accustomed to spending real time together, they tend to sneak up as you go about your daily life alongside the people you love. They tap you on the shoulder days or months or years later and say, "Remember me?"

"I remember one time my father let me draw a picture on his back," says Terri. "I must have been about four years old. I was down on the floor, and I had a pen and I was writing, and I think I got a mark on him by mistake. We started goofing around, and I told him, 'I'm gonna draw a whole picture on you.' He lay perfectly still and I just scribbled away on his back, which was something I was, of course, never allowed to do. I'll never forget it."

Adrienne remembers the time when she was small, listening to the radio with her father, when suddenly he asked her to dance. They waltzed around the room together for a few minutes that are now preserved for a lifetime in her heart.

"I still remember my mother praying for us every morning," says Virginia, "and another thing I remember is making homemade doughnuts together and the aroma in the kitchen as they cooked. She let us help punch out the holes and eat the dough. Those were such special times."

Kathy says, "Something I'll always remember is the contentment of going to sleep hearing my parents talking in the living room. And as they went to bed too, they'd lie there and talk. I couldn't understand what they were saying, but I could hear the mumble of their voices — no arguments or anything. I always went to sleep that way. Just knowing that they were there and that they were still awake was very important to me."

THE DAILY SPECIALS

Special memories are people-oriented; they happen while you're doing things together. And as the women quoted above have shown, often the memories that stand above the crowd are ones that somehow break the daily routine. Cheryl says, "My boys started liking picnics from the first day we went on one when they were just one and two years old. Even when we don't have a car available, they like to just take their lunches outside and spread a blanket or sit on lounge chairs with a sandwich and a cup of juice. And on rainy days sometimes we spread a blanket on the floor and have a picnic in the house."

> You may not even realize you've built a tradition until you skip it and your child says, "But we always . . ."

Special memories can also be built through daily and weekly "traditions" — and a tradition doesn't have to be fancy. It's just something fun or meaningful that you do on such a regular basis that it becomes part of who you are as a family. In fact, you may not even realize you've built a tradition until you skip it and your child says, "But we always . . ."

Several of these young families have greeting rituals. Shannon says, "Nathaniel was given a choice of what Daddy would do with him when he got home. One of the main things he chose was 'tickle time.' He wanted to be tickled, or to wrestle." Brynn says, "Cole goes in and helps Tom change in the closet. I'm not allowed in. It's a male-bonding thing."

Scott and Wes have a Saturday morning breakfast tradition: "Wes and I cook pancakes on Saturday mornings. He gets to stir."

"Nancy and I like to take a long walk after dinner each night," says David. "We never plan a topic, but it's amazing how far the conversation ranges. We put Hannah in the stroller, and when she isn't squirming to get out, I imagine she listens to what we say and hope she absorbs some of it." As they grow older, children can ride tricycles and bikes with training wheels, or even be pulled in a wagon, while Mom and Dad walk.

Bedtime rituals (Megan still remembers the lullabies we sang to her as a toddler), getting-up rituals, storytimes, greeting rituals — all these things can give children a sense of security and belonging. They say, "You're important, so I take time to be with you when I come home. You're important, so I take time to cuddle and pray with you and help you feel safe and comfortable before you go to sleep. You're important, so I greet you with a hug and kiss every morning. You're important, so you can cook with me and be my helper. *You're important, so I make time for you.*"

Another way to give your child special memories and a sense of belonging, says Connie, is to create family gestures and passwords. "Our favorite number is five," she says, "since there are five in our family. When we're at the beach and Stephanie sees five pelicans in a group, she says, 'There's our family!' or when we're visiting the mountains and April sees five fish in a stream, she says, 'There's our family!' And we have what we call a five-way kiss. We get in a circle and all turn and kiss the cheek of the one on our right, and then do the same with the one on our left." Jon and I did something similar with Megan when she was small, and later, with Anna. We'd make a "Megan sandwich" — we would stand on either side of her and kiss the dickens out of her cheeks. She loved it!

Vacations, when you make a special effort to spend time together, can also yield special memories. Connie says, "When we go to the beach, we collect shells together. In my mind I can still hear the girls saying, 'Look at this one — it's purple!' and see everyone crowding around to see it. We brought the shells back and let each girl keep the ones she found in a pretty jar on her dresser."

The mothers in this book who have several children find it useful to make sure their little ones get time alone with them by allotting each child some special time during the day. Carol says, "Right after lunch is Andrew's time — he's three. We sit down and he picks out the books and we read. Then after school the older children have their time." When Glenda's children were little, her husband, Joe, started the habit of taking them for a walk around the block as soon as he came home from work. That became their special time with Daddy, and it gave Glenda a chance to relax.

Several parents plan a weekly family night where the TV is not watched unless there's something very special on, and no commitments are made unless they can be done as a family. "Friday night was always our family night," says Virginia. "Sometimes we'd go out to eat and then play miniature golf afterwards, or if there was something special on TV we'd watch it and pop popcorn." Family night doesn't have to be fancy — talk, read stories, go for a drive, cook a special meal, play simple games, work on crafts or Christmas gifts. As Virginia says, "Whatever you do, being together is fun."

Lisa remembers playing loud disco-type music and dancing with her family: "I remember just laughing and laughing at my father and mother singing and dancing away. It was great to see that carefree, fun side of them. It's amazing how unified I remember feeling as a family on those nights and how lucky I remember feeling to be part of such a fun and special family." Carol's family has a group family night: "We've opened our home for a family Bible study on Thursday nights. It's really been special. We keep it short because of the children, but the kids really love having other children there."

SPECIAL TIMES, SPECIAL SEASONS

Christmas

As might be expected, many of these parents' most treasured memories are of holidays, particularly Christmas — and that's also the time of year when they work hardest to make special memories for their own children. They feel a strong obligation to keep the focus of Christmas on Jesus without taking the fun away, and they've developed quite a few traditions to do it.

Adrienne made her children an Advent calendar in the shape of a green burlap Christmas tree on a brown background. She says, "There are twenty-four ornaments made of stiff fabric that hang around the edges until we need them. Starting December 1, we read a little piece of Scripture every day and then put an ornament on the tree." The first six days are the six days of Creation; the seventh is Isaiah 11:1, the trunk; then the next two weeks' verses deal with Jesus' forebears — Adam and Eve, Noah, Abraham, Isaac, Jacob, and others, ending with Mary. The last three days are the Christmas story from the books of Matthew and Luke, with the last decoration being the baby Jesus lying in the manger. As each day's verses are read, Adrienne tells her children a simple story about the circumstances surrounding them. "The kids love it!" she says. "It's their favorite Christmas tradition — they wouldn't miss their Advent calendar for anything."

Shannon uses an Advent calendar too. She says, "It's confusing to kids when you go through the whole month of December buying presents and going to parties, then throw Jesus in on the last day. The Advent calendar has really helped us focus on Christ and make it more meaningful." Christian bookstores can be good sources for Christ-centered Advent calendars.

Several families celebrate the four Sundays of Advent, complete with an Advent wreath and special devotions. The Advent wreath is laid on a table, with a pillar candle in the center and four taper candles around it. The first Sunday of Advent (usually the first Sunday after Thanksgiving), one outer candle is lit while the devotion is read. An additional candle is lit each Sunday afterward, and finally, on Christmas Eve, the center candle (symbolizing Jesus as the Light of the World) is lit and the Christmas story is read. Our family loves to include Christmas carols and a prayer each week.

> "It's confusing to kids when you go through the whole month of December buying presents and going to parties, then throw Jesus in on the last day. The Advent calendar has really helped us focus on Christ and make it more meaningful."

David has special memories of his family's Advent celebrations: "These little worship services always took place in near-darkness, with candles providing the only light. The feeling was so warm and close, each person shrouded in shadows, only their faces glowing in the candlelight." You can find Advent devotions in your Christian bookstore. Check your church and public libraries, too. Or you can come up with your own devotions.

Another way these parents accomplish their dual purpose of keeping the holiday season both Christ-centered and fun is to tell lots of Christmas stories. Carol says, "During the month of December, I have a big basket by the rocking chair filled with books of Christmas stories. When my children want a story, we just reach into the basket and get one." "The more wonder you put into the Christmas stories you tell your children, the better," adds Cheryl. "Tell about the star leading the wise men across a whole country, and how they brought valuable gifts, and how the shepherds and even the animals came to see the baby Jesus. Make it so full of wonder that a couple of little elves and a fat man in a red suit pale in comparison. My two boys are more excited about Jesus' birthday than the other kids in the neighborhood are about Santa Claus." Again, your library should be a good source of Christmas books.

Marilee has older toddlers, and she includes Santa in their celebration of Jesus' birthday by telling her children the story of Saint Nicholas and how, many years ago, he began the tradition of giving gifts because of his love for Jesus. Lisa says, "My favorite decoration is a sculpture of Santa kneeling with his cap off over a manger. It always gets a prime spot in the room. Every year I try to think of new and exciting ways to make Christ real at Christmastime."

Carol keeps two nativity sets: a high-quality plastic one for the older children to play with, and a safe, wooden one on a low table for the toddlers. Kathy also keeps an inexpensive nativity set and allows her little ones to act out the Christmas story with it. "It helps them visualize the story," she says. "You can put your nice, handmade nativity set up out of reach."

Another aim these parents have at Christmastime is to teach their little ones the joy of giving, rather than reinforcing the "gimme-gimme" attitude that usually mars the spirit of the season. Terri encourages Zachary and Ashley to give birthday presents to Jesus each year by helping them clean out their toyboxes and give toys that are still in good shape to charitable organizations, citing Matthew 25:40, "I tell you the truth, whatever you did for one of the least of these brothers of mine, you did for me."

She says, "The first year, I tried and tried to explain it to Zachary, but he was so little. Finally he came to me and gave me a book and said, 'Here.' I asked, 'Is that all you're going to give?' He said, 'Yeah, it's the only thing I've got two of.' But he looks forward to it now, because I've tried to teach him that there are some kids whose mommies and daddies can't buy them toys or who maybe don't even have mommies and daddies. We take the toys down to the church and unload them, and that's big time to him. He can't wait. It also helps both Zachary and Ashley to see, when they open their own gifts a week or two later, that many times when you give you also receive." Terri says this tradition is also a great way to clear some space for the new toys your child will receive during the holidays.

If you adopt this tradition, let your child choose the toys he wants to give, and don't rebuke him if he doesn't give as much as you'd like. But don't be surprised if he, like Michele's four-year-old daughter Sarah, chooses to give the very best. "Sarah's nursery school class was told to bring toys for underprivileged children," says Michele. "She went into her room that afternoon and came out carrying her tape recorder and the bear she sleeps with. She told me, 'Mommy, these are my very favorite toys, so I know those poor little boys and girls will like them.'"

"Something we've done since our kids were little," says Glenda, "and it's one of the things they remember most, is making all kinds of goodies together. Then on Christmas Eve or Christmas Day we pack them into little bundles to send to all our neighbors and friends, and the kids get to go with their daddy to deliver them." "That's the fun part!" adds Carol.

Carol and her children make simple "gingerbread houses" from graham cracker squares glued together with icing from a squirt can. She says, "They're very small and simple, but we put them on cardboard bases and decorate them with icing and gumdrops and candy, and the kids give them as presents to our neighbors. My three-year-old loves it."

Having a birthday party for Jesus, complete with cake, is a favorite tradition among these young parents, and several families even incorporate their Christmas gift-giving into the celebration. Karin says, "It was our little boy, Matthew, who brought up the idea of a birthday party. We had been trying to emphasize to him that Christmas is Jesus' birthday, and about a week before Christmas he came to me and said, 'But Mommy, Jesus doesn't have a birthday cake.' He was really torn up about it. So I made Jesus a birthday cake."

Kathy and her family take Jesus' birthday cake with them when they go to Grandma's house to celebrate: "In one day," she says, "we'll have our Christmas in the morning, then go to one grandparent's house, and then this year we'll be going to another one later on. Our relatives don't always keep the focus on Jesus the way we'd like it to be there for our children, so this is just our little way of carrying Jesus' birthday into the other homes too."

Several of these families downplay what has in our society become the primary focus of Christmas: the gift-giving itself. Karin chooses to give little gifts throughout the year rather than swamp her children with toys and clothes at Christmas. She says, "We do give Matthew and Meagin presents at Christmas, but some parents just go nuts. We want to emphasize to our children that the whole thing isn't 'What do I get? How many more presents? What else is there?' It's Jesus' birthday.

"I used to feel guilty about it, because my parents gave me tons of presents when I was a kid. I thought, *We need to get them something more*. But then I heard the Lord's still, small voice say, 'Karin, that isn't what Christmas is about.'" "Besides," adds Glenda, "later down the road, they don't remember the big Christmases where you think you went all out and gave them everything. It's the things you did, not what you gave them, that they remember."

A few more words about toys: "Kids would rather have a jar of bubble soap and you out in the yard blowing bubbles with them than a big expensive toy," says Karin. "It means a lot more to them" — that is, of course, unless they've been brainwashed by Saturday morning TV. Your child may think she wants the latest doll for Christmas. Maybe she really does, and that's okay. But in fifteen or twenty years the doll will most likely be forgotten and it'll be the handmade Christmas ornaments and the memory of long evenings spent reading Christmas stories together that count. The toys these mothers remember are the ones they spent special times with, not the ones that were the most expensive.

Christin and her husband, Jim, have found a meaningful way to impose limits on Christmas spending. She says, "It used to get out of control every year. After praying about it, Jim and I decided that, since Jesus received three special gifts from the wise men, we would give each of our children three special gifts at Christmas. That way we can put extra thought into each gift."

> "After praying about it, Jim and I decided that, since Jesus received three special gifts from the wise men, we would give each of our children three special gifts at Christmas."

When it comes to the presents your toddler gives the people he loves, try not to resort to buying his gifts for him. If you possibly can, find the time to help him make simple gifts. The hours you spend working on them together will create special memories, and he'll have a warm sense of accomplishment at being able to give something he made himself. At the very least, go shopping with him and let him pick out inexpensive gifts with a little guidance from Mommy or Daddy. And do always make sure your toddler has *something* to give on holidays or family birthdays and anniversaries, even if it's just a handmade card. Children are devastated when, like the little drummer boy, they're the only one with no gift to bring.

Most of the young parents in this book feel it's important to make time for a private family Christmas celebration. Glenda, whose children are older, agrees: "For many years we lived far away from our families and were never home at Christmas, and for the first couple of years Joe and I felt kind of lost, since we're both from large families. But you know, as the years went by it became more and more precious to have just our immediate family there, and now our kids really cherish the time we spend together as a family at Christmas. We're back now close enough to be with all the relatives, but the times the children remember most are the quiet times with just us, sharing and reading the Bible before we open our presents, thanking the Lord for his goodness, and talking and listening to Christmas music afterward."

You may have to experiment to find what works best for your family. Jennifer and Scott have their private family time with Wes on Christmas night after the extended-family celebrations; Stephanie and Roy reserve Christmas Eve for their little family. For Shelley and Glenn, Christmas morning works well.

The Great Santa Claus Debate

Whether or not you allow your child to believe in Santa Claus and other fairy tales is a very personal decision, and the parents I interviewed weren't able to come to an agreement about it. Most of them were against telling a child point-blank that Santa is real, because after all, he's not. But aside from that point, we had a wide range of opinions.

Some of their children chose to believe that Santa was real even without the encouragement of their mommies and daddies, and their parents made no effort to burst the bubble until the children were old enough to ask. "When they ask, though," says Adrienne, "tell them." Other parents were adamantly opposed to letting their children believe something that isn't true and taught them to smile indulgently when misguided store clerks and relatives asked what they wanted Santa to bring them for Christmas. Luellen says, "We taught Ryan and Jason right from the start that Santa was fun, but Jesus is real."

Cheryl decided to let Santa stay in the picture as a fun pretend character while keeping the focus on Jesus' birthday. "Since he was two or two and a half," she says, "Jason has had no problem understanding that Santa is a fun pretend person, just like a cartoon or something you see on TV. To him, Santa is just like a Smurf or a big character at Disney World."

Megan was two and a half when she began receiving the Santa messages that were coming at her from all sides. Try as I did to explain that the man in the red suit was just somebody's nice grandpa, she couldn't understand. She would smile brightly and answer, "He's coming to my house!"

After some frustration, I finally realized that fantasy and reality were still one big, happy jumble to my little girl. For Megan, Donald Duck and Mickey Mouse were real, Big Bird and Kermit were real, and so was Santa. I decided simply to smile when she talked about Santa, to explain things as she was able to comprehend them, and to keep the focus on Jesus' birthday as much as possible. (Letting her play with a molded plastic nativity set was a big help in that area.)

Even the parents who chose not to allow their children to believe in Santa Claus rejected the idea that a child whose fantasies about Santa are dashed will question whether Jesus is real. Terri says, "The Christian influence in my family was so strong that the Santa issue didn't bother me. My own little boy *knows* that Jesus is real — we live with Jesus every day. We don't live with Santa Claus.

I know that, deep down inside, Zachary knows Santa isn't real, but he's really into pretending right now." Cheryl agrees: "If Jesus is part of our everyday experience and we're talking to him and teaching our children about him every day, they have no trouble distinguishing between him and Santa Claus. Now, with families who go to church only on Christmas and Easter and don't recognize Jesus the other 363 days of the year, that could be a problem."

The real danger in the Santa issue is to your credibility in your child's eyes. Jeff says, "I got it all in first grade, from a little Jewish boy. The truth about the Easter Bunny, the Tooth Fairy—the whole nine yards. I went back looking at my parents like . . ." He cocked an eyebrow. "That really affected me." I've heard enough stories like Jeff's to convince me that pretending is fine, but actually encouraging your child to believe in a fantasy is asking for trouble.

> The real danger in the Santa issue is to your credibility in your child's eyes.

Something that hasn't yet been mentioned is the danger you run of being lynched when your little one tells a neighbor child that Santa isn't real. Wanda made Santa's pretend status an especially fun family secret that was never to be breathed outside the home walls. "I explained to Michelle that it might ruin Christmas for the other children if we told them," she says. Some of our other moms initiated fun family traditions focusing on Christ's birth that their children could tell their friends about.

Marilee makes the point that a parent who lets her child believe that Santa brings the presents is allowing him to shower love and gratitude that rightfully belong to Mommy and Daddy on a pretend person. Dana adds, "When grownups ask my kids, 'What did Santa bring you?' they say, 'Santa didn't bring me anything. My mom and dad gave me presents because they love me very much.'

"The same thing goes with other myths, like the Tooth Fairy—these occasions can be used as tools to build a relationship with our children. When Bryan or Bridget lost a tooth, the money I put under their pillows was always accompanied by a special little note just for them from me. Those notes meant more to them than the Tooth Fairy possibly could have. These are great opportunities! We need to be using them as tools to cement the love between us and our children."

"He Is Risen!"

For Christian parents, Easter ranks right up there with Christmas as a special holiday. And as with Christmas, the focus in the secular world has somehow shifted completely away from Jesus. The parents in this book find that simple Bible story books help their little ones understand the meaning behind the holiday much earlier than might be expected for such a complex subject as death and resurrection. Karin says, "Matthew was two at Easter this year, and he went around telling people, 'He's alive again! He's alive again!' And he would turn the cross on my necklace over and ask, 'Is Jesus dead on there?' When I answered, 'No, he's alive again!' he'd give a big smile and repeat, 'He's alive again!' He ministered to a lot of people just by knowing the story."

Here's a beautiful Easter tradition Elizabeth discovered on an internet source (fiveinarow.com/archives/holidays/). The author, unfortunately, is unknown. I've adapted it slightly.

This is one of those traditions that can grow with your children. For the first few years, simply explain what each step means without reading the verses. As your children grow older, read the verses, shortening them if necessary. Eventually, your children can read the verses to you. Since there are quite a few, it's helpful to look them up and put markers in your Bible ahead of time. Use numbered strips of paper to help you turn to the right verses.

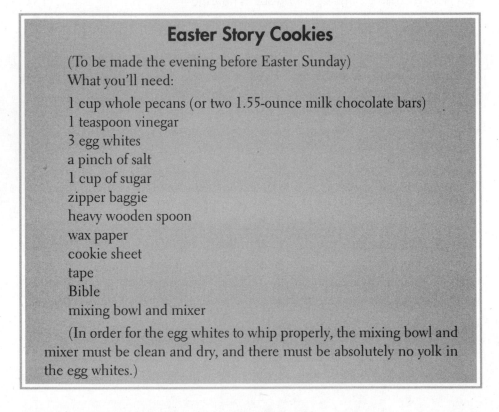

Easter Story Cookies

(To be made the evening before Easter Sunday)
What you'll need:

1 cup whole pecans (or two 1.55-ounce milk chocolate bars)
1 teaspoon vinegar
3 egg whites
a pinch of salt
1 cup of sugar
zipper baggie
heavy wooden spoon
wax paper
cookie sheet
tape
Bible
mixing bowl and mixer

(In order for the egg whites to whip properly, the mixing bowl and mixer must be clean and dry, and there must be absolutely no yolk in the egg whites.)

Preheat oven to 350 degrees.

Place the pecans in the zipper baggie and let the children beat them with the wooden spoon to break them into pieces. (Or if your family doesn't eat nuts, let them break up the chocolate bars.) Explain that after Jesus was arrested, he was beaten by the Roman soldiers. *Read John 19:1–3.*

Let each child smell the vinegar. Put it into the mixing bowl. Explain that when Jesus was thirsty on the cross, he was given vinegar to drink. *Read John 19:28–30.*

Add the egg whites to the vinegar. Eggs represent new life. Explain that Jesus gave his life to give us new life. *Read John 10:10–11.* Sprinkle a little salt into each child's hand. Let her taste it, then brush the rest into the bowl. Explain that this represents the salty tears shed by Jesus' followers and the bitterness of our sin. *Read Luke 23:26–27.*

Beat with a mixer on high speed until soft peaks begin to form. While beating, gradually add 1 cup of sugar. Sprinkle a few grains of sugar into each child's hand and let her taste it. Explain that the sweet part of the story is that Jesus died for us because he loves us. He wants us to know and belong to him. *Take a brief break and read Psalm 34:8 and John 3:16.*

Resume beating on high speed until stiff (but not dry) peaks are formed. Explain that the color white represents the purity in God's eyes of those whose sins have been washed away by Jesus. *Read Isaiah 1:18 and John 3:1–3.*

Gently fold in the broken nuts (or chocolate pieces). Drop by rounded tablespoons onto a wax-paper-covered cookie sheet. Explain that each mound represents the rocky tomb where Jesus' body was laid. *Read Matthew 27:57–60.*

Put the cookie sheet in the oven, close the door, and *turn the oven off.* Give each child a piece of tape and let him or her help seal the oven door. Explain that Jesus' tomb was sealed. *Read Matthew 27:62–66.*

Go to bed! Explain to your children that they may feel sad to leave the cookies in the oven overnight. Jesus' followers were very sad when the tomb was sealed. *Read John 16:20, 22.*

On Easter morning, open the oven and give everyone a cookie. Take a bite. The cookies are hollow! On the first Easter, Jesus' followers were amazed to find the tomb open and empty. *Read Matthew 28:1–9.* He is risen!

🐚 Virginia started a family tradition reminiscent of the Jewish Passover celebration by asking her children as soon as they awoke Easter Sunday morning, "Why is today special? What does Easter Sunday mean?" She says, "Although I had already explained it to them, I wanted to make sure they remembered. I also wanted to start them thinking about it at the beginning of the day. They told me what they thought it meant, and I explained a little more if I needed to. We just had a little storytime first thing in the morning. When you do that each year, it becomes instilled in them." Glenda's husband, Joe, is much in demand as a singer, and she believes the musicals and cantatas her children attended to hear Daddy sing helped them understand early the real meaning of Easter. Kathy adds, "The Easter Bunny and colored eggs become minor when you make Jesus major."

If you're going to be a real stickler about having only holiday symbols with their origins in the New Testament, you're going to have to give up your Christmas tree.

🐰 Speaking of the Easter Bunny and colored eggs: These parents are aware that these traditions are thought to be based on ancient pagan festivals, but most have chosen to turn the symbolism around and connect it to new life in Jesus. After all, if you're going to be a real stickler about having only holiday symbols with their origins in the New Testament, you're going to have to give up your Christmas tree. The traditional new spring clothes, too, can be worn in honor of Christ's resurrection.

🐰 Several parents hide Easter baskets filled with candy for their children to find, a tradition which is one of my most vivid childhood memories. (Another is the two live chicks my Sunday school teacher gave me and my sister one Easter. I'm sure my mom was happy with her about that.) "We put the emphasis of Easter on Jesus," says Virginia, "but we have the little fun times too." Kim says, "When I was little, on Easter morning there were always little trails of candy left, to show that the Easter Bunny had come. That way, you could tell where he'd stopped and where things were hidden. Of course, he didn't *mean* to leave the candy on the floor — it had fallen out of his basket. That was always fun." Julie says, "We have our Easter egg hunt and Easter baskets on Saturday so we can focus on Jesus Easter Sunday."

🚼 Carol chooses to forgo the Easter eggs, but she says, "We didn't want our kids to miss out on the fun, so this year I wrapped peanuts in bright foil, and after we came home from church I hid those in the yard for them — the foil catches the sunlight and makes them easier to find. Then I scooped out a water-melon and filled it with punch. I poked holes in the top, put straws through, each with a child's name on it, and put it in a red wagon in the middle of the back yard. So all the kids hunted for peanuts, then ate them and sipped punch out of the watermelon."

Other Holidays

Aside from Christmas, Halloween is probably the most publicized chil-dren's holiday — which is too bad, when you consider what the All Hallow's Eve celebration is about. In our area, though, Halloween is no longer a big problem for Christian families. Even many non-Christian parents are refusing to allow their children to trick-or-treat because of the increasingly frequent scares over poisoned candy and booby-trapped apples.

Glenda says, "Halloween was dangerous years ago in Los Angeles when my kids were little, so they weren't allowed to go trick-or-treating. We got together with our friends in the neighborhood and planned games and fixed food, and every time the kids played a game, they all got candy for their bags — not just the kid who won, although he got something special. I guess we went to about a half-dozen of our homes and did something special at each house — bobbing for apples or whatever. They loved it!"

Terri's neighborhood is one that has a safe Halloween party for the kids: "My children have never known trick-or-treating the way I did," she says. "When the reports of candy poisoning started coming in, I said, 'Forget it. We'll do something else.' It started with just a couple of families, but now a lot of them are involved. And it's a good way to get to know neighbors. When we notice a new child in the neighborhood, we go down and invite him and his parents. Kids love to dress up, and we still let them, but it's a lot safer than trick-or-treating. It's in a fenced-in yard, the parents are all there, and they know right where their children are. We don't have any unattended kids."

Joyce says, "Our church has a Fall Festival for the children on Hal-loween, and we let the kids dress up in fun things — no ghosts or demons."

∘ ∘ ∘ ∘ ∘

OTHER HOLIDAYS, AS WELL as private family celebrations, can also provide spe-cial memories for your children if you use them to start family traditions.

Our family uses Valentine's Day as an opportunity to express love to each other. Each family member makes a special card for the others — preferably with a sweet or silly poem — and we set aside time to read them and laugh over them together. (It can be great to have occasions when your children *have* to say something nice about each other!) For young children, try helping them come up with an acrostic for each family member's name. As they grow older, you can help them with their poems. ("Roses are red . . ." and its variations come in handy in case of writer's block.)

When she was growing up, Lisa says, "Valentine's Day always involved a 'red dinner' consisting of red meatballs, red Jell-O, and a heart cake (red, of course). For Saint Patrick's Day, there was, of course, green Jell-O! All of this said to us, 'You are special enough for me to go out of my way and do something different for you.'"

For Thanksgiving, our family has developed a tradition we call "passing the pumpkin." We have a clear glass pumpkin-shaped cookie jar. During the first week in November, I set it out in a prominent spot, along with some strips of orange paper and a pen. Each day, family members jot down things they're thankful for and place them in the pumpkin. (You'll need to help small children with this, of course.) On Thanksgiving Day, we set aside a special time — usually right after dinner — to take turns pulling strips out of the pumpkin and reading them. Some are serious, some are silly, but by the time the pumpkin is empty we are always filled to overflowing — not only with turkey and dressing but also with a deep sense of thankfulness.

You probably can't expect a young child to sit through this whole ceremony — the pumpkin can get pretty full — but this is another tradition that will become more meaningful for your children as time goes by. If you spend Thanksgiving at someone else's home, you could take the pumpkin with you and make filling it a one-day affair, or have your "passing the pumpkin" time privately at home.

Check craft stores for pumpkin-shaped baskets or cookie jars and orange paper.

Whenever there's a holiday — whether it's a birthday, anniversary, or Father's Day — Carol has her children help her decorate the honored person's breakfast chair with balloons and crepe paper. "Any time I can blow up a balloon and have a celebration, I do it!" she says. Elizabeth says, "We have a big, red 'You are Special' plate. I get it out for birthdays or any special day."

Carol adds, "The anticipation of birthdays is sometimes hard on children. Even if you don't overemphasize the presents, they still have the anxiety of knowing they're getting something special that day. So instead of waiting until evening for all the presents, we give them one present or something special at breakfast, along with all the balloons and decorations. That starts the day out right." (By the way, don't ever "forget" someone's birthday — child or adult — in anticipation of a surprise party at the end of the day. The joy of the surprise doesn't come near to making up for the misery of going all day thinking everyone has forgotten you.)

Kathy allows each of her toddlers to plan the menu for the evening meal on his or her birthday. Terri says, "We take ours out and let them pick the restaurant."

"We make our birthday cards," says Stephanie. "We'll use construction paper, and sometimes there's computer stuff thrown in there too."

Scott gives his son Wes the ultimate gift for his birthday each year. Jennifer says, "Scott takes the day off work to spend with him."

On the subject of the traditional birthday cake, Karin says, "Birthday cakes are more special when they're made by you. I'm not a cook, and there have been times when I've gone out and bought a cake for my children's birthdays. But last year for Matthew's second birthday, I made him a clown cake that took me three days to finish. He still takes the pictures out and says, 'Look, my mommy made me a clown cake!' It touched his little heart that I spent three days making him a cake. Now Meagin's birthday is coming up, and he's telling me, 'Mommy, Meagin needs a clown cake too.' It's important to them. And it doesn't have to be a clown cake, it can be anything — as long as they know you took the time to do it rather than just going to the store and buying it."

> "Instead of waiting until evening for all the presents, we give them one present or something special at breakfast, along with all the balloons and decorations. That starts the day out right."

Tangible Memories

As we've already said, intangible memories are without doubt the most important kind. The tangible ones are really just extras, and if you meet your child's emotional need for intangible memories, she'll probably forgive you if you don't shower her with sentimental doodads. On the other hand, tangible memories are very nice extras, and the mothers in this book cherish theirs as concrete mementos of those fleeting, intangible moments.

Again, these are just ideas to help you get started. Once you begin, you'll find ideas for tangible memories coming out of the woodwork, and your biggest problem will be figuring out where to store them all.

"HOW CAN I SAY 'CHEESE!' WHEN I CAN'T TALK YET?"

Photographs are probably the easiest and most common tangibles to collect, but these parents have come up with some creative ways to use them.

Invest in a good 35 mm camera if you can afford it. And take lots of candid shots. "You get some of your cutest pictures that way," says Terri. Several mothers follow Sofie's example: "Every now and then I take the negatives of my favorite snapshots in and have them enlarged into 5 x 7s or 8 x 10s and put them into frames. I enjoy them just as much as formal pictures—sometimes more." These enlargements are quite inexpensive and, when framed, make wonderful presents for grandparents.

Each year Kathy takes her favorite family snapshot to the photography department of a local drugstore and has it made into Christmas cards.

Several families had their favorite snapshots made into spiral-bound calendars at a local photocopying center. These make great gifts for grandparents, or for Dad's office.

Connie says, "I held April's foot in my hand and had Shelby take a picture of it and also of her hand in mine. It showed how tiny they were."

When Kathy bought Brandon his first little pair of sneakers, she took a picture of them side by side with his daddy's shoes. She says, "It's especially cute when they have identical sneakers, except one pair's big and the other is tiny."

"Take lots of pictures," says Wanda. "It's so much fun to look back at them and tell stories about the circumstances surrounding the special occasions. Kids love to hear about things they did and said when they were 'little.' They also love to hear stories of when you were small."

"One mistake we made," says Debby, "was that we took a whole bunch of pictures of Lisa, fewer of Angie, and even fewer of Marsha. Now my two younger kids are asking why I didn't take as many pictures of them as I did of Lisa."

Connie learned another lesson by hard experience: "My mother advised me to write my child's age on the back of each picture, but I ignored her, thinking, *How could I possibly forget such important memories?* But a few years and two more babies later, I did forget. I'm so glad that on some of the pictures I did jot down the names and ages, but on many of them I didn't, and I regret it." Remember, children can look similar when they're very young, and little brothers and sisters often wear hand-me-down clothes. Stephanie says, "We have to look at carpet colors to see where we were living. 'Let's see . . . the carpet's blue . . . it's an apartment . . . it's Kristen!' I'm serious! It's horrible!"

Elizabeth says, "I use my computer to print out a bunch of labels with the date and the children's ages. Then I just go through and stick them on the back. That way I don't have to write on every one."

Glenda keeps duplicate copies of her children's pictures behind the originals in the family photo album. Now that her kids are older, she says, "I've started an album for each child so that when they get married they'll have some baby pictures and some of themselves while they were growing up." Terri says, "When I got married, my mother-in-law gave me a little book of my husband's baby pictures. It was really special." It will be special to your grandchildren, too, to see the pictures you've saved of Mommy and Daddy when they were small.

Terri used her children's pictures to make Christmas ornaments: She cut a slice off one side of a styrofoam ball, which left a flat place to mount a picture that had been trimmed to fit. She then covered the rest of the ball with velvet and gold braid (although glued-on sequins and beads would do just as well), glued the picture to the ball, and trimmed around the edges with the remaining gold braid. Carol's preschooler made her a simpler ornament by gluing a trimmed picture onto a round piece of cardboard, covering the edges with gold braid, and hanging it by a ribbon. Carol says, "It really is darling, and the kids love to see their ornaments hanging on the tree year after year."

As your child grows older, your camera can help keep your attic from overflowing with art projects. Kim says, "One mom I knew took pictures of her child with her artwork. That way she didn't have to actually keep all the stuff. And it's easy to incorporate the pictures into a family scrapbook." When it's time to clean off the refrigerator for a new batch of art, have your child stand next to it and take a picture of him with his artwork. That way you have a record not only of the cute pictures your child has done but also of what he looked like when he did them.

THE BABY BOOK AND OTHER GREAT LITERARY EFFORTS

The second most common memento of babyhood is the infamous baby book, which most mothers start and few finish. These mothers had the usual amount of trouble with writing milestones down before they were forgotten, and their advice to you on this subject is, "Do as I say, not as I did."

The mothers who had the most success keeping their books up to date made a habit of jotting down events as they occurred. Patty says, "To keep track of new things Jennifer did, such as crawling, walking, and new words, I kept a calendar on the wall and quickly wrote it down when something happened. Then later on I transferred it from the calendar to my baby book." Luellen says that keeping her baby book in a prominent spot helped her remember to write in it.

Kathy kept a special baby calendar and began recording events even before Brandon was born: "I wrote down the first time I felt him move and things like, 'You kept me up all night last night. I can't wait for you to be born!'" As Zachary and Ashley make their way through toddlerhood, Terri has continued her practice of jotting down milestones on her calendar for later transfer to their baby books. She says, "It's fun to look back and see your child's progress and to read and reread all the cute things she's said. Ashley's almost two, and she's doing and saying things almost daily that need to be written down." Connie kept a separate spiral notebook of her girls' funny childhood sayings. "We laugh and laugh when we go back and read them," she says. "Be sure to put your child's name and age by each quote."

If your baby book doesn't have keepsake pockets, Terri recommends keeping a separate scrapbook for such firsts as first checkup receipts, first shoe receipts, and a lock of hair from your baby's first haircut. Adrienne's mother saved her dried-up umbilical stump!

A friend of Christine's keeps a birthday diary for her little girl. Each year on her child's birthday she takes a few minutes to record her current height and weight, things she learned to do that year, new words, special friends, and favorite dolls and toys. I'm doing something similar, except that I write in my book two or three times a year, and since I plan to give it to Megan someday, I'm addressing it to her and spreading it with a thick frosting of you're-so-special's and we're-so-blessed-to-have-you's. I hope it will be a precious keepsake for her someday.

Terri has adopted yet another variation on this tradition: Each year on her children's birthdays, she writes them a long letter on a blank greeting card. She says, "I already write to Ashley. Even though she doesn't understand right now, the letters will be there for her when she does."

To protect your written mementos from time and leaky roofs, always write on good paper with a ballpoint pen, not a pencil or water-soluble felt-tip pen.

Along with your baby's personal milestones, Kathy recommends keeping track of family history and current events in your child's diary. She says,

"Kids like to know, 'Who was president when I was born? Where did we live? What kind of car did we have?'" A couple of mothers saved the front page of the newspaper from their children's birthdays. Adrienne says, "My mother saved the newspaper from the day I was born in 1951. It shows the styles — it's incredible what they wore back then — and tells all about the things that happened. If your baby has already been born, you can buy front pages from the newspaper companies." Carol adds, "That's a neat gift too. My neighbor saved the front page of the newspaper while I was in the hospital and brought it over after I came home."

Adrienne is the most ambitious of our mothers in that she keeps a daily diary — but it's not just for keepsake reasons. She says, "It comes in handy for keeping track of immunizations and also for when one of my children isn't feeling well. It prevents me from being stuck for an answer when the doctor asks, 'How long has she been sick?' Otherwise I might answer, 'Let's see . . . two or three days,' when it's really been seven." With six children, Adrienne has learned to write in her diary during the only real time she has to sit down: in the bathroom.

Connie says, "I know you probably don't feel you have time to keep a journal, but I'm so very sorry I didn't. I keep one now, but all those daily memories I could have kept . . . gone . . ."

Adrienne adds that written records are helpful, whether they're kept daily, weekly, monthly, or yearly, because children love to hear about the things they used to do even while they're still young. "That's important to kids," she says. "They love it — they'll listen for hours. Sometimes at night my children and I get started talking. They'll ask, 'What did I do when I was two?' and I'll tell them everything I remember."

Kathy says, "I tell Ryan how he was in the breech position up until three days before he was born, and how the doctor told me that if he didn't turn around I'd have to have an operation so he could come out, and how the Lord woke me up one night and I went out and found a Scripture meant just for me and him, and at my next appointment the doctor told me, 'He turned over!' He weighed nine pounds three ounces, and I hadn't even felt it! I tell him how special he is and how even back then the Lord was with him. They love to hear that sort of thing." Dialogues like this also form a good foundation for the sex education you'll be providing for your child.

Everyone, no matter what his age, enjoys being told he's special and loved. Getting into the habit of writing to your children can produce lifelong memories. Virginia still writes to her son even though he's away at college. "Now that Rick's gone," she says, "I can think of so many things to tell him. So I write and tell him how precious he was when he was little and how much he's grown and how proud I am. He likes it even now."

Finally, several parents and grandparents are preparing "heritage books" to give their children and grandchildren a sense of family history. Elizabeth says, "I think my mom got mine at a Christian bookstore. It asks, 'What's your favorite Bible verse? What did your first house look like? What's your favorite holiday?' All kinds of memories and thoughts and feelings you can pass down to your children."

OTHER DOODADS

Christine's husband, David, is a music director, so it's not surprising that they took the first possible opportunity to put their baby's voice on tape: "We began when Ashley first started making little cooing noises," says Christine. "We just stated her age and then recorded her for maybe three minutes. We did it every three or four months, so now we have a tape of how she's sounded all along."

When Megan was two and a half, we began helping her make keepsake tapes as gifts for her grandparents' birthdays. She sang "Happy Birthday to You" and other little songs, said "I love you," and told a little story or two. Her grandparents were thrilled.

Once your baby is old enough to stand, Carol cautions of the need to buy a height chart rather than making notches on the closet door. "That way you can take it with you if you move," she says. "We moved and had to leave ours behind. It's been painted over by now." Virginia adds that children love being able to ask, "How big am I now, Mommy?" and to see how much they've grown since the last time you measured them.

"I take care of a baby girl named Monica," says Rosemary, "and her mother has used a stamp pad since her birth to sign cards with prints of her hands and feet for Father's Day, grandparents' birthdays, and other special occasions." If you do this, you might want to stamp two or three months' worth of cards at a time to keep down the number of days your baby spends with black hands and feet. And be sure to use a nontoxic ink.

"I traced Lisa's tiny feet and hands on pillowcases for Grandma and Grandpa," says Connie. "Then I wrote 'Good night, Grandma' on one pillowcase and 'Good night, Grandpa' on the other and went over it all with liquid embroidery fluid. It was a hit!"

Terri has traced her children's hands every year, starting from the very beginning. She says, "I want to make a quilt someday from all of them when

Zachary and Ashley are older, but for the time being I use the patterns to make gifts and Christmas ornaments. On Zachary's first Christmas, I traced his hand and cut it out of calico fabric, then got a plain brown hot pad and zigzagged the handprint onto it. I embroidered underneath 'Me-mom's Helping Hands' and gave it to my mother from Zachary. She has it hanging on her stove and she uses it all the time, even though it was simple to make and cost almost nothing."

Here's how Terri makes Christmas ornaments from her children's hand-prints: "I just cut two of each hand out of red and green felt, sew the two layers of felt together, maybe stuff them a little bit, and hang them on the tree." She says Zachary and Ashley love to take their ornaments off the tree and stretch their hands over them to see how much they've grown.

I made a Christmas ornament from Megan's first pair of soft white dress shoes by stitching them together near the heel and hanging them by red and green ribbons.

Carol's little girl Kristie had a beautiful wooden crib mobile that Carol couldn't bear to part with, so when the time came to take it down, she cut the figures off and hung them on the Christmas tree as ornaments.

When her children receive Christmas ornaments as gifts from grand-parents and friends, Carol marks the year and the giver's name on the back. "That way," she says, "my children can go back through their own little box of ornaments and remember who gave which to them."

"I like to do counted cross-stitch," says Terri, "so each year I make an ornament for each of my children that reflects their special interests — a train, a teddy bear, a doll — and embroider the year on it. I plan to give the completed set to them when they marry, so they'll have at least twenty or so ornaments for their first Christmas tree."

Virginia says a child old enough to help Mommy bake Christmas cook-ies is old enough to help make cookie-type ornaments from salt-and-flour dough, and Terri has yet another Christmas tradition that mixes the tangible with the intangible. She says, "I never thought I could make a gingerbread house, but on Zachary's second Christmas, he saw one and got excited when I told him it was all made out of a cookie. He said, 'Make me one!' So I bought a book of instructions for an ornate gingerbread house decorated with candy, and I've made one every year now. They're really easy to make, and the kids love to help. You can let them dry out and save them — my mother has my first one, and my mother-in-law has my second one. Some people shellac them, but my mother didn't do anything to hers and it's holding up just fine. She has a country-style house out in the woods, and she keeps it out on display year-round on an old-fashioned porcelain-topped table." This would also make an adorable decoration for a child's room. Just put it up on a shelf where your little one can't get to it without your help.

    When your child becomes old enough to start coloring pictures "just for you," try saving the special ones that are of manageable size in a notebook to keep them from wear and tear. Write your child's name and age on the back first. There are notebooks on the market that are ideal for this purpose, since they bind the pages together between two clamps rather than forcing you to poke holes in them. Hanging files and shoeboxes (which have the benefit of fitting under a bed) can also be useful for long-term storage of paper mementos. Other pictures can be matted on construction paper and used to decorate your little one's bedroom, your bathroom, your kitchen — wherever they work best.

    An often unexplored source of potential keepsakes is your child's toybox. The mothers I interviewed don't save toys indiscriminately, but the better-made ones can be kept to serve several generations. "My grandmother still has some fifty-year-old Fisher-Price toys from back when they were made of wood," says Kathy. "She saved them from her own children, and has given them now to her great-grandchildren."

> "I bought a book of instructions for an ornate gingerbread house decorated with candy, and I've made one every year now. They're really easy to make, and the kids love to help."

    Handmade wooden toys are making a comeback, although they tend to be expensive. My sister gave Megan a beautiful, handcarved wooden duck pull-toy, complete with mahogany egg. We still have it, and I hope to see my grandchildren playing with it someday. When her children receive wooden toys as gifts, Carol writes her child's name, the giver, and the date on the bottom with a woodburning kit.

    "We took Kristie's first tricycle apart and boxed it up and put it in the attic," says Carol. "When she gets married and has children, we'll give it to her again." Kathy is saving her children's cradle and bassinet, and Glenda says, "I've got six boxes of all my children's special dolls and stuffed toys, and a baby carriage that looks brand new, that I'm saving for my grandkids. It means a lot when your children can give their children toys that were theirs when they were little. When I got married I had a little stuffed teddy bear that I was given when I was four years old, and my kids played with it until it wore out. They liked it better than anything else."

These secondhand toys will have even more meaning for your child and grandchild if you have pictures of your own little one playing with them. Just make sure that all handmade toys have nontoxic finishes and meet the safety requirements we talked about in chapter 6.

🛒 Well-made clothes and baby outfits in classic styles can also be kept for future generations. Luellen says, "I've kept a box (or four!) for each of my children with their favorite outfits, toys, books, and other things they can one day pass down to their own children."

🍼 Carol says, "A friend of mine has a beautiful quilt on her family-room wall that her grandmother made, and she can point to the different squares and tell which of her baby clothes they came from." Terri has saved scraps from Ashley's clothes and plans also to make a quilt someday. It's even possible to applique a special dress—such as a christening gown—on top of a finished quilt for a real showpiece heirloom.

🍼 Save your nursery decorations! Your children may want to use them in your grandchildren's rooms someday. Again, they'll be especially meaningful if you have pictures of your baby with them.

A LASTING HERITAGE

Tangible mementos are fun to collect and will be even more fun in future years as you use them to spark those priceless intangible memories. They have a serious purpose, though.

The Bible speaks of a family and its generations as a "house." Two of my favorite verses on this subject are Proverbs 14:1, "The wise woman builds her house . . ." (the same is true of the wise man, by the way), and Proverbs 24:3–4, "By wisdom a house is built, and through understanding it is established; through knowledge its rooms are filled with rare and beautiful treasures." As you and your spouse work together to construct your family, the memories you create will be the special touches that make your "house" a joy to live in: the pictures on the walls, the carpets on the floors, the plump pillows on the overstuffed sofa, the flowers on the table and in the garden. Those special touches will reflect the wisdom God has given you and display a true knowledge of what is important in life.

A child's first years are usually full of distractions for his parents: establishing a career, getting the family finances in order, perhaps building and decorating a home, having more children, and on and on. It can be hard to keep the big picture in mind. But those years are also when the foundations for your "house" are being laid. Trying to go back and re-lay the foundation of a home that's already half constructed can be a difficult and complicated business.

And what is the foundation for your house? If a strong family is built "by wisdom," then the foundation for wisdom will be the foundation for your house's construction. Here it is: "The fear of the LORD is the beginning of wisdom; all who follow his precepts have good understanding. To him belongs eternal praise" (Ps. 111:10).

All of the tips in this book rest on the rock-solid foundation of reverence for God and for biblical truth. In these pages, we've tried to show you how we're working to fulfill Jesus' two great commandments within our families: To love God with all our heart, soul, mind, and strength, and our neighbor (including our spouse and children) as ourselves.

As I've worked toward those goals in my own family, I have found this passage in Matthew 7:24–25 to be true. I know it will be true for you as well: Jesus said, "Everyone who hears these words of mine and puts them into practice is like a wise man who built his house on the rock. The rain came down, the streams rose, and the winds blew and beat against that house; yet it did not fall, because it had its foundation on the rock."

Index

affection
  and discipline, 171, 183, 185–86
  physical, 171, 213
  verbal, 212–13
anger and discipline, 176
approval, 213
arguments, parental, 166
authority and discipline, 175–76

baby blues. *See also* depression,
    postpartum
  and ambivalence about
    motherhood, 28–29
  Christian mothers and, 24–26
  and confusion, 27–28
  and disappointment about delivery,
    31–32
  and emotional outbursts, 32–33
  and fear, 33–35
  and feelings of overwhelming
    responsibility, 26–27
  and guilt, 27–28
  and isolation, 37–40
  and lifestyle changes, 29–30
  and money issues, 36–37
  and spirituality, 30–31
  unexpected pregnancy and, 25–26
baby books, 267–70
baby food
  commercial, 106
  homemade, 106–8
babyproofing, 127–31, 180–81
babysitters. *See also* child care; day
    care
  finding, 68–69
  and home-based business, 234–35
  instructions for, 128, 130
  for working mothers, 239
baby wipes, 78
balloons, 139–40
bathing, 121–22

bathroom safety, 130
bed, graduating to, 120–21
bedtime rituals, 118–19, 252
    and devotional time, 154–55
    and rules, 198
    and weaning, 101–2
birth control, breast-feeding as, 98
birthdays, 264–65
bottle-feeding
    and burping, 100
    choosing bottles and nipples for, 99
    and cow's milk, 100
    and cuddling, 99
    and ear infections, 100
    and getting out of the house, 100
    and microwave heating, 99
    and powdered formula, 99–100
    sterilizing bottles and water for,
        99–100
    and weaning, 101–2
bouncy seats, 138
bowel training, 34. *See also* potty
        training
breast-feeding
    attitudes toward, 88–89
    and baby's weight gain, 95
    benefits, emotional, 93–94
    benefits, physical, 87–90
    as birth control, 98
    and biting, 95
    and bottles, 95–96
    and bras, 94
    and breast pads, 94
    and breast pumps, 96–97
    and colic, 115
    emotional support for, 90–92
    and engorgement, 89
    and expressing milk, 96–97
    family opposition to, 91–92

    getting started, 90–98
    and getting out of the house, 97–98
    husband's involvement in, 91–92
    and introducing solid food, 98
    and inverted nipples, 92
    and lactation consultants, 90
    and La Leche League, 90
    and leaking breasts, 94
    and nipple soreness, 93
    and nursing in public, 97–98
    premature babies, 94–95
    resources, 90, 92–93
    and weaning, 98, 101–2
    and working full-time, 97
burping, 100

car seats, 125–27
car trips, 145–46
child care. *See also* babysitters
    husband's involvement in, 63–66,
        70, 71–74, 241–42
    for working mothers, 237, 239–41
chores, 200–201
    and discipline, 224–25
Christmas, 132, 253–59
    and Advent celebrations, 253–54
    keeping Christ-centered, 254
    and Santa Claus, 254–55, 258–59
church, 145, 160–62. *See also*
        devotions; prayer; spirituality
    and parental differences, 167–168
cloth diapers, 77–78. *See also* diapers
clothing
    caring for, 133
    shopping for, 133–34
colic, 15
    and breast-feeding, 115
    and infant swings, 115
    soothing, 114–15

commitment, 74
communication
  and conveying unconditional love,
    212–19
  between husband and wife, 53–62,
    69, 171–72
  of needs and expectations, 55–57
  nonverbal, 213, 214
  between parent and child, 173,
    187–89
  and working through conflict, 57–62
comparing siblings, dangers of, 221
competence, children's sense of, 219–
    25
  and discipline, 220
computers, 205–6
  and spirituality, 163–64
conflict
  between husband and wife, 57–62
confusion
  and new mothers, 27–28
consistency and discipline, 171–73,
    176, 178–79, 182
cribs
  double-making, 118
  outgrowing, 120–21
  temporary, 118
  toys for, 138
crying
  and colic, 114–15
  due to teething, 124
  reasons for, 115–16
  remedies for, 116–17

day care, 237, 239–41. See also
    babysitters
defiance, 193–97
depression, postpartum, 20, 24–35.
    See also emotions, mother's
    postpartum

and ambivalence about
    motherhood, 28–29
and baby blues, 24–35
and confusion, 27–28
and guilt, 27–28
and isolation, 37–40
and lifestyle changes, 29–30
unexpected pregnancy and, 25–26
devotions. See also church; prayer;
    spirituality
  activities for children, 155–57
  family, 154–55
  parents' personal, 150–52
diapers
  and baby wipes, 78
  cloth, 77–78
  and diaper bags, 78–80
  and diaper rash, 78
  disposable, 75–77
dignity and discipline, 174
discipline
  and affection, 171, 183, 185–86,
    189
  and appropriate punishments,
    177–78
  for babies and young toddlers,
    180–85
  cardinal rules of, 171–80
  and children's sense of
    competence, 220
  and communication between
    husband and wife, 171–72
  and communication between
    parent and child, 187–89
  and consistency, 171–73, 176,
    178–79, 182
  and continuing parental
    education, 209–10

and defiance, 193–97
and dignity, 174
and encouraging good behavior,
    173–74
and establishing authority, 175–76
and expectations, 172–73
and grumpiness, 190–92
and independence, 184–85, 192–93
and lying, 207–9
and misbehaving in public, 196–
    97, 199–200
and modeling positive behavior, 180
and nagging, 182–83
and offering alternatives, 181
and paddling, 194–95
and parental anger, 176
and parent and child relationship,
    174–75
and peer influence, 206–7
and planning ahead, 181–82
purpose of, 180
and rowdiness, 190–92
and rudeness, 203–4
and sharing, 183–84, 192
and sibling jealousy, 201–3
and spanking, 169–70, 177
and stalling, 198–99
and table manners, 203
and tantrums, 195–97
and time-out, 191
for toddlers, 187–210
and yelling, 179–80
discipline, self
and chores, 200–201
and computers, 205–6
and enforcing bedtime, 198
and peer influence, 206–7
and playing alone, 184–85

and sharing, 183–84, 192
and television, 204–6
disposable diapers, 75–77. *See also*
    diapers
doctors, 135–36

ear infections
and bottle-feeding, 100
Easter, 259–63
Easter Bunny, 259, 262
education, importance of
and breast-feeding, 90
for children, 221–23
for parents, 47–48, 54
and spirituality, 154–57
emotions, mother's postpartum, 16–
    19, 20. *See also* depression,
    postpartum
and ambivalence about
    motherhood, 28–29
and baby blues, 24–35
and disappointment about delivery,
    31–32
and fear, 33–35
and lifestyle changes, 29–30
and outbursts, 32–33
and postpartum spirituality, 30–31
emotions, new father's, 43–46, 47–
    48, 55–57, 63–69
encouragement
    and children's self-esteem, 222–23
    and good behavior, 173–74
engorgement of breasts, 89–90
Exersaucers, 138
expectations
    and discipline, 172–73
    of new fathers, 73–74
    of new mothers, 14–16, 20–24,
    73–74

families
  characteristics of thriving and
    happy, 49–50
  and common effort, 69–74
  and common goals, 69
  and communication, 53–62
  devotional time, 154–55
  and respect, 50–53, 60
  and teamwork, 69
  and time together, 62–69
fatherhood
  adjusting to, 43–46, 47–48, 55–57,
    63–69
  benefits of, 44–46
fathers
  and devotional time, 152
  involvement in child care, 63–66,
    241–42
  role of, 39–40, 46–49
fatigue, 16–19
favoritism, 214–15
fear
  and baby blues, 33–35
  fathers and, 44, 70
feeding technique, 103–6
finger food, 108–9. *See also* food;
  solid food
finicky eaters, 109–11
food
  and avoiding sugar, 111
  commercial baby, 106
  and feeding technique, 104–6
  finger, 108–9
  and finicky eaters, 109–11
  homemade, 106–8
  introducing solid, 98, 103–6
  and vitamins, 104–5
forgiveness
  and children's self-esteem, 223–24

  and forgetting, 223–24
  and parental mistakes, 165–66
formula. *See* bottle-feeding

goals, 20–24
grandparents, 39
grooming, mother's, 23–24
Growing Kids God's Way, 48–49
grumpiness, 190–92
guilt, 27–28

Halloween, 263
happy families, principles of, 49–50
home-based businesses
  babysitting services, 234–35
  craft-related, 233–34
  dressmaking and alterations, 233
  guidelines for starting and running,
    229–32
  home catering, 235
  paper routes, 235
  and telecommuting, 235–36
  word processing, 232
household help
  finding, 16–18
  postpartum, 16–18
  and working mothers, 247
housework, 40–41
  children's involvement in, 142–43
  husband's involvement in, 17–18
  new mothers and, 20–24
  and working mothers, 244
humor, 224

independence, 184–85, 192–93
  and discipline, 224
intangible memories, 250–65
integrity
  and children, 166–67
  parental, 164

isolation, 37–40

jealousy
  in husbands, 63
  sibling, 201–3

kitchen safety, 131

lactation consultants, 90
La Leche League, 90
love, unconditional
  and children's self-esteem, 211
  communicating, 212–19
  demonstrating, 171
lying, 207–9

marriage
  Christian, 70–72
  and communication, 53–62
  and conflict, 57–62
  and respect, 50–53
  and teamwork, 69–74
  and working mothers, 244–47
mementos, 270–74
memories
  and baby books, 267–70
  and birthdays, 264–65
  and Christmas, 253–59
  creating, 249–50
  and Easter, 259–63
  and Halloween, 263
  intangible, 250–65
  and mementos, 270–74
  and photographs, 266–67
  tangible, 265–74
  and Thanksgiving, 264
  and traditions, 251–53
  and vacations, 252
  and Valentine's Day, 263–64
mistakes, parental, 164–67, 209–10
modeling positive behavior, 180

money issues, 36–37
mothers. *See also* working mothers
  and ambivalence about
    motherhood, 28–29
  and baby blues, 24–35
  and devotional time, 150–52
  and disappointment about delivery,
    31–32
  expectations of new, 14–16, 20–24
  goals for new, 20–24
  grooming for new, 23–24
  and isolation, 37–40
  and money issues, 36–37
  personal appearance, 23–24
  and postpartum emotions, 16–19,
    20–41
  and postpartum spirituality, 30–31
  and self-esteem, 35–41
  and sleep, 16–19
  work at home, 229–36

naps, 119
nighttime wetting, 84–85, 118
nursing. *See* breast-feeding

outings
  in cars, 145–46
  to church, 145
  to restaurants, 143–44
  shopping, 144–45

pacifiers, 127
paddling, 194–95
parenting resources
  finding, 48–49
pediatricians, 135–36
peer influence, 206–7
personal appearance, mother's, 23–24
  and self-esteem, 35–36
photographs, 266–67

picky eaters, 109–11
playpens, 129, 138
playtime. *See also* toys
    alone, 184–85
    and bouncy seats, 138
    and devotions, 155–57
    and Exersaucers, 138
    ideas for, 137–46
    and infant swings, 137
    for older infants, 139–41
    for toddlers, 141–43
    for young infants, 137–39
poisoning, 129–30
postpartum depression, 20, 24–35.
        See also emotions, mother's
        postpartum
    and ambivalence about
        motherhood, 28–29
    and baby blues, 24–35
    and confusion, 27–28
    and guilt, 27–28
    and isolation, 37–40
    and lifestyle changes, 29–30
    unexpected pregnancy and, 25–26
potty training, 80–85
    and bowel training, 34
praise
    and children's self-esteem, 223
    and good behavior, 173–74
prayer, 55. *See also* church;
        devotions; spirituality
    in resolving conflict, 60
    teaching, 148, 152–154, 162
pregnancy, unexpected, 25–26
premature babies and breast-feeding,
        94–95
priorities and work, 63–66
Promise Keepers, 48–49
punishments. *See* discipline

quality time
    after-school, 238
    with children, 137–46
    between husband and wife, 62–69
    and working mothers, 244–47
questions, children's spiritual, 157–60
quiet time, parental, 150–52

relationship, parent and child, 174–75
respect
    between husband and wife, 50–53
    in resolving conflict, 60
restaurants, 143–44
role models
    finding, 50
    male, 46–49
rowdiness, 190–92
rudeness, 203–4

safety
    and babysitters, 128, 130
    bathroom, 130
    and car seats, 125–27
    and holidays, 132
    kitchen, 131
    and poisoning, 129–30
    and strangers, 131
    and toys, 127
    and walkers, 131
    water, 132
Santa Claus, 254–55, 258–59
self-discipline. *See* discipline, self
self-esteem, children's
    and approval, 213
    and chores, 224–25
    and communicating unconditional
        love, 212–19
    and communication between
        parent and child, 217

and dangers of comparing siblings, 221

and discipline, 220

and encouragement, 222–23

and favoritism, 214–15

and feelings of self-worth, 227–28

and forgiveness, 223–24

and humor, 224

and the importance of words, 212–13, 215–16

and independence, 224

and insults, 216

and nonverbal communication, 214

and parental apologies, 216

and parental involvement in children's activities, 225

and physical affection, 213

and playmates, 226

and praise, 223

and sense of competence, 219–25

and separation anxiety, 213–14

and shy children, 226

and sibling jealousy, 225

and social acceptance, 225–28

and teaching children how to select friends, 226–27

and television, 224

self-esteem, new mother's

isolation and, 37–40

money issues and, 36–37

personal appearance and, 35–36

separation anxiety, 213–14

sharing, 183–84, 192

shoes, 134–35

sibling relationship

and children's self-esteem, 225

and jealousy, 201–3

sleep, 16–19

sleeping

naptime, 119

through the night, 117–18, 119–20

social acceptance

and feelings of self-worth, 227–28

and playmates, 226

and shy children, 226

and teaching children how to select friends, 226–27

solid food. *See also* food

and administering vitamins, 104–5

and breast-feeding, 98

commercial baby, 106

and feeding technique, 104–6

finger, 108–9

homemade, 106–8

introducing, 103–6

spanking, 169–70, 177

spirituality. *See also* church; devotions; prayer

and baby blues, 30–31

and children's questions, 157–60

and children's self-esteem, 218

and parental devotions, 150–52

and parental quiet time, 150–52

and parents, 149–52

and television, 163–64

and training children, 148–49, 162

and young infants, 147–48

stalling, 198–99

strangers and safety, 131

sugar, avoiding, 111

swimming pool safety, 132

swings, infant, 137

and colic, 115

table manners, 204

tangible memories, 265–74

tantrums, 195–97

teamwork
  and common commitment, 74
  and common effort, 69–74
  and common goals, 69
  and discipline, 171–72
teeth brushing, 125
teething, 124–25
television, 163–64
  addiction, 204–6
  and teaching, 224
Thanksgiving, 264
thriving families, characteristics of,
    49–50
time
  devotional, 150–52
  family, 244–47
  and husbands and wives, 62–69
  quality
    after-school, 238
    with children, 137–46
    between husband and wife, 62–
      69
    and working mothers, 244–47
  quiet, parental, 150–52
time-out, 191
Tooth Fairy, 259
toys. See also playtime
  choosing, 127
  and chores, 200–201
  and Christmas, 254–57
  for older infants, 139–41
  organizing, 123–24
  and playpens, 138–39
  for toddlers, 141–43
  for young infants, 137–39
traditions, 251–53
  and birthdays, 264–65
  and Christmas, 253–59

  and Easter, 259–63
  and Halloween, 263
  and Thanksgiving, 264
  and Valentine's Day, 263–64

vacations, 252
Valentine's Day, 263–64
vitamins, administering, 104–5

walkers, 131
weight gain, baby's, 95
words, importance of, 212–13, 215–16
working mothers. See also mothers
  and cooking, 243–44
  and day care, 237
  and family time, 244–47
  and full-time jobs, 238–42
  and home-based business, 229–36
  and household help, 247
  and housework, 244
  and husband's involvement in
    child care, 241–42
  and part-time jobs, 236–38
  and sick children, 243
  typical day, 242–44

yelling and discipline, 179–80

We want to hear from you. Please send your comments about this
book to us in care of the address below. Thank you.

ZondervanPublishingHouse
Grand Rapids, Michigan 49530
http://www.zondervan.com